COCOA IN POST-CONFLICT LIBERIA

The Role of Institutions for the Development of Inclusive Agricultural Markets

Gun Eriksson Skoog

THE NORDIC AFRICA INSTITUTE

UPPSALA 2016

INDEXING TERMS:

Liberia
Cocoa
Agricultural markets
Inclusive markets
Market structure
Institutional change
Supply chain
Farmers
Smallholders
Cooperatives
Farmers' associations
Farmer participation

Cocoa in Post-Conflict Liberia: The Role of Institutions for the
Development of Inclusive Agricultural Markets

ISBN 978-91-7106-783-8
© 2016 The author and The Nordic Africa Institute
Cover photo: Saclepea, Nimba County, Eastern Liberia, May 2015.
A community garden for cocoa and other crops, where an NGO is
helping women smallholders to improve their farming. Photo by
author Gun Eriksson Skoog from one of her field trips.

Layout: Henrik Alfredsson, The Nordic Africa Institute
Print on demand: Lightning Source UK Ltd.

The opinions expressed in this volume are those of the author and
do not necessarily reflect the views of the Nordic Africa Institute.

Abstract

This research seeks to increase understanding of the role of institutions for the development of inclusive agricultural markets in Sub-Saharan Africa by exploring recent trends in the post-war Liberian cocoa market. Case study research was undertaken in Monrovia and three counties in late 2013. It was based on combined sources of data, notably primary data derived from interviews with various cocoa market actors and external observers. The research examines changes in the market structure and their implications for beneficial market participation by smallholder farmers; identifies major institutional changes; and offers an explanation of how they may have influenced the inclusiveness of the cocoa market. It suggests that structural changes in the market have increased the participation of smallholders, and on increasingly beneficial terms: farm gate prices have increased several-fold as has the smallholders' share of world market price. Access to markets, inputs and services, not least credit, has increased, along with the farmers' freedom of choice. Farmers have responded to improved incentives and opportunities by processing higher quality cocoa and by investing in and expanding their farms.

It is suggested that a series of institutional changes have contributed to this process. These include formal changes in the institutional environment of the market and in the institutional arrangements for interaction within the market itself, as well as new 'rules of the game' that have evolved with the entry of new market actors. Four major causal mechanisms have contributed to making the cocoa market more inclusive: value addition through increased cocoa quality; increased coordination of transactions and reduced transaction costs through farmers' organisations and integrated value chains; strengthened bargaining power of smallholder farmers through increased competition and farmers' organisations; private provision of services and inputs through integrated value chains. The research makes a theoretical contribution by suggesting what institutions matter for inclusive agricultural markets and why, and by outlining the vital function such institutions may perform. These findings have implications for policy and practice applicable to Liberian cocoa, and possibly for Sub-Saharan agricultural markets more generally.

Gun Eriksson Skoog
Senior Researcher
The Nordic Africa Institute

Kakata, Margibi County, Liberia 2010. A delegation from the Swedish Embassy in Monrovia in a meeting with smallholder farmers participating in an FAO project, financed by Sida, the Swedish International Development Cooperation Agency. Sitting in the middle, Gun Eriksson Skoog, author of this book and senior researcher at the Nordic Africa Institute.

Contents

List of Tables and Figures

Tables

Figures

Appendix Tables

Appendix Figures

"Why do some countries develop and prosper, while others fail and remain poor?

1. Introduction

1.1 The Problem

Why do some countries develop and prosper, while others fail and remain poor? Why do the populations of many countries remain in poverty, in spite of high rates of economic growth? Acemoglu and Robinson argue that sustainable growth and prosperity requires economic and political institutions that are inclusive – that allow not only the elite, but a broad cross-section of society to participate in economic and political activity.[1] Hence, economic growth needs to be inclusive to be sustainable, and to be underpinned by institutions that promote such inclusiveness. Liberia, with its pre-war history of notoriously extractive economic and political institutions, illustrates how dire the consequences of non-inclusive development can be.[2] While there was high growth in enclave sectors benefiting the elite, it was paralleled by deep poverty for the majority of the population.[3] This in turn fuelled social tensions that erupted in a coup d'état in 1980 and armed conflict between 1989 and 2003. Non-inclusive growth is a problem in much of contemporary Sub-Saharan Africa (SSA). The continent has high rates of growth, but without including and benefiting large parts of the population.[4] SSA growth occurs without economic transformation or widespread poverty reduction, and inclusive growth is now high on the official agenda of African leaders.[5] However, as Booth and Therkildsen note, successful cases are few and more research is needed to learn from them.[6]

The problem of non-inclusive development may be most severe for agriculture, the sector in which a majority of the SSA population still depends for its livelihood.[7] Failure to develop smallholder farming has been a problem for decades, but globalisation offers new opportunities to increase the productivity and competitiveness of smallholders and link them to international markets through global value chains. However, such inclusion is not always beneficial for smallholders. Much depends on the conditions of inclusion, the specific institutional arrangements and power relationships within global value chains or production networks.[8] Competitive markets are one form

---

1   Acemoglu and Robinson (2012)
2   Liebenow (1987) is a classical reference on the Liberian political-economy, with a focus on political institutions, and its consequences, whereas economic institutions were briefly reviewed by Eriksson Skoog (2009).
3   Clower et al. (1966)
4   van der Veen (2004), UNECA (2013)
5   African Union (2014)
6   Booth and Therkildsen (2012)
7   UNECA (2013: 64)
8   As noted, for instance, by Ponte (2008), Gereffi et al. (2005) and Henderson et al. (2002).

of institutional arrangement, but as Dorward and others[9] argue, they do not always promote the beneficial inclusion of smallholders where markets are poorly developed, as is often the case in SSA. The development of agricultural markets depends on the broader institutional context in which they are embedded.[10] Non-inclusive development of agricultural markets in SSA needs further attention in order to assess its determinants. Institutions clearly matter, but knowledge about which institutions, at what levels, and how and why they contribute to the beneficial participation of smallholder farmers and thus inclusive agricultural markets remains scarce. To understand these factors, one needs to study the institutional context of specific agricultural markets.[11]

This research aims to increase understanding of the role of institutions – or behavioural rules for social interaction – in the development of inclusive agricultural markets, in which participation is beneficial for smallholder farmers. The overall research question – *What is the role of institutions in the development of inclusive agricultural markets?* – is explored by studying on-going processes of development in the post-conflict Liberian cocoa market. Liberia is an example of an SSA country with a long history of non-inclusive development, especially within agricultural markets, and has experienced the implications of this not only for poverty but also for conflict. Now, however, there has been a possible break with the past in the post-war period, notably in the cocoa market. Empirical research questions for the Liberian case are specified below.

1.2   The Case of Liberia

Liberia has a unique history, most notably in the fact that it was never a formal colony, but has been independent since its founding in 1847. In recent years, it has been racked by protracted and violent internal conflict. However, in terms of its economic structure and growth, it is a dual economy, a pattern common to SSA: the economy has experienced relatively high growth in enclave sectors such as rubber and iron ore, and slow growth and low levels of economic activity in the rest of the economy, where there is deep and widespread poverty. This pattern was pronounced historically and before the war, and has largely persisted after the war. Thus, Liberia may be a particularly illuminating case of non-inclusive growth and markets. At the same time, there have been recent indications of inclusive development in certain agricultural markets, suggesting that the Liberian case offers unique opportunities to study ongoing change towards more inclusive markets and the role of institutions in the process.

A root cause of poverty and conflict in Liberia in past decades appears to be the deep social divisions within the country, with a vast gap between a small economic and political elite and the majority of people living in poverty. The social divide was reflected in a dual economic structure, in which an enclave economy based on raw-material

---

9   Dorward et al. (2005)

10   For instance within the so-called making-markets-work-for-the-poor (M4P) approach (see e.g., Springfield Centre 2008).

11   Dorward et al. (2005; 2009)

extraction and exportation existed in parallel with, but with limited linkages to, a poorly developed domestic economy.[12] In agriculture, mainly foreign privately-owned plantations exporting tree crops coexisted with, but largely in isolation from, a domestically oriented sector made up of subsistence and smallholder farmers and petty traders and characterised by poorly developed and fragmented markets for food and cash crops. This dual structure was underpinned by a system of formal and informal economic institutions,[13] and linked to a long-established system of political patronage, which favoured the economic and political elite.[14] This system created growth without development,[15] deep and widespread poverty and stark inequalities which fuelled the social tensions that resulted in a coup d'état in 1980, followed by armed conflict during most of the 1989-2003 period.

While the dual economic structure and many of the economic and political institutions appear to have remained basically intact in post-conflict Liberia,[16] the civil war may yet represent a critical juncture[17] by creating opportunities for certain shifts towards more inclusive development. Some institutions were destroyed during the war and others changed. Government policies to promote more inclusive economic growth in post-conflict Liberia have been initiated, reflected in the Agenda for Transition 2012-2017 and Liberia RISING 2030.[18] This is evident not least in agriculture, on which the majority of the population depends, and in which international donors such as Sida and USAID are active. Of particular interest is the Liberian cocoa market.

1.3 The Liberian Cocoa Market

Cocoa is a tree crop, a so-called cash crop produced for export only. In Liberia it is traditionally grown by smallholder farmers for the market, but the market has been poorly developed since before the war, with unfavourable conditions and profitability for the farmers. However, in recent years the cocoa market has been undergoing change and is reported to be engaging smallholders.[19] Moreover, cocoa is assessed to be a smallholder crop with significant export and pro-poor growth potential.[20] The Liberian cocoa market may be becoming more inclusive, with increasingly beneficial smallholder participation, and therefore may represent a rare agricultural-market case study.

---

12 Clower et al. (1966); Radelet (2007); Eriksson Skoog (2009); del Castillo (2012)
13 Eriksson Skoog (2009)
14 Liebenow (1987)
15 Clower et al. (1966)
16 Eriksson Skoog (2009); del Castillo (2012)
17 Cf. Acemoglu and Robinson (2012)
18 Republic of Liberia (2013a and b) – the Government of Liberia's medium-term economic growth and development strategy for 2012-2017 and its longer-term national strategy and vision to become a middle-income country by 2030
19 Interviews with Key Informants, March 2013
20 Republic of Liberia (2007a and 2012); GRM International (2010); Adam Smith International (2013)

In the wake of the 2003 Accra peace accord, growing international demand and prices and market deregulation, the Liberian cocoa market appears to be dynamic and growing, as reflected in increased exports.[21] While still limited in size, it seems to be rapidly changing when compared to the preceding decades of stagnation and the early postwar years. However, if the problems of the past are not to be repeated, the market needs to become more inclusive by offering better conditions and benefits for smallholder participation. This is the aim of government strategies for the cocoa sector,[22] but a fundamental question is how inclusive these developments are in reality.

The picture remains unclear. On one hand, there are reports of new private buyers offering farmers various services, considerable smallholder participation in the market and donor support to farmers and their organisations. This may well indicate that inclusive development is under way in the Liberian cocoa market, as external observers suggest.[23] In combination with growing exports, smallholder benefits may increase as well. One the other hand, Liberia has a history of non-inclusive economic growth that may repeat itself. It has been suggested that large cocoa exporters, while providing badly needed inputs to smallholder farmers and their organisations, are taking advantage of the farmers' weak position and dependency.[24] If there are few buyers with stronger market power, the farmers' bargaining position may be weak, and they can expect lower prices for cocoa than they would in more competitive circumstances. If the buyer is also the sole input provider, farmers may face unnecessarily high input prices, and thus be disadvantaged, with their profit margins being squeezed from two sides. Institutional change by way of market deregulation may then simply have replaced the state monopsony on buying cocoa through the Liberia Produce Marketing Company (LPMC) parastatal with a private monopsony, to the detriment of smallholder farmers.

The inclusive nature of recent changes in the Liberian cocoa market merits further investigation from a development perspective, particularly the role of institutions and the way they change in this process. For a more inclusive cocoa market to be sustainable, institutions – the rules of the game – must change. Unless they are fundamentally altered, the problems of the past may be reproduced and poverty reduction and peace put at risk again.[25] How institutions contribute to inclusive agricultural markets is thus a vital policy concern for Liberia. It is also highly relevant from a Swedish development-policy perspective, given growing public and private Swedish engagement in Liberia in recent years. Sweden is now one of the largest international actors in Liberia.

---

21   Central Bank of Liberia (2003-2013)
22   Ministry of Agriculture (2012a); Republic of Liberia (2014)
23   Interviews with Key Informants, March 2013
24   Interviews with Key Informants, March 2013
25   As noted by del Castillo (2012) and Eriksson Skoog (2009).

1.4   Research Purpose and Question

This research analyses cocoa-market inclusiveness and institutions in post-conflict Liberia. Its purpose is two-fold. First, understanding developments in the Liberian cocoa market by exploring two inter-related empirical questions: *Have developments in the post-war Liberian cocoa market made it more inclusive, in terms of increasing the beneficial participation of smallholder farmers?* Second: *What is the role of institutions in these possibly inclusive developments?* These questions will be explored by examining recent developments in the cocoa market to understand what is actually happening and why. First, changes in the structure of the cocoa market will be examined along with their implications for beneficial participation by smallholder farmers. Thereafter, relevant institutional changes are identified and a causal explanation of their influence on the inclusive nature of the cocoa market is offered.

By answering the empirical research questions, and promoting understanding of the Liberian cocoa market, this research serves a second purpose, namely helping to answer the general research question specified earlier: *What is the role of institutions in the development of inclusive agricultural markets?* This research thus aims to make an empirical and a theoretical contribution. In doing so, it builds upon and contributes to a broad research field in various strands of literature.

1.5   Review of the Research Field

There is no research on the institutions and inclusiveness of agricultural markets in Liberia for this research to build upon. Independent *economic research on Liberia*, historical as well as contemporary, is notably thin. The best known research on the Liberian economy dates back to the 1960s.[26] It reveals the dual economic structure and huge inequalities in economic development between different segments of Liberian society. More recent studies have been conducted by consultants for policy purposes, and support both the survival of duality in the post-war period and the need for inclusive growth.[27] Explicit research on economic institutions is lacking, apart from an initial review by Eriksson Skoog,[28] and there is little research on agricultural development and markets. A limited number of descriptive, sector-specific studies exist – including on the cocoa sector – which provide background information and will be used to assess change over time.[29] English, for example, found that in 2006/07, smallholder cocoa farmers received limited price signals, due, for example, to institutional constraints, and hence obtained a limited share of the world market price.[30] There are also a few studies of the cocoa market in neighbouring West African countries that offer useful

---

26   Clower et al. (1966)
27   Radelet (2007); del Castillo (2012)
28   Eriksson Skoog (2009)
29   Hughes et al. (1989); Wilcox (2007)
30   English (2008)

information, notably that of Wilcox and Abbott, who found that cocoa-farmer organisations may countervail buyers' market power.[31]

Literature to date has failed to adopt a systemic approach, whereby institutions are looked at both within the market or value chain and in their broader context, to understand their roles and influence on the inclusive development of agricultural markets. This research, therefore, relates to, builds on and contributes to several research fields that offer partially relevant perspectives on the issues. It is located in a broad social-science strand of *New Institutional Economics* (NIE). On the role of institutions in economic development and institutional change, North is central, along with others.[32] Institutions are seen as behavioural rules for social interaction, formal and informal, and distinguished from organisations. They are seen as shaping incentives for behaviour and interaction, and thus influencing economic outcomes. Ostrom has made a central contribution by developing the Institutional Analysis and Development (IAD) framework to allow for analysis of such complex multi-level systems, including inter-related institutions at different levels.[33] The recent contribution by Acemoglu and Robinson extends the analysis with the concepts of inclusive and extractive institutions.[34] Inclusive economic institutions create opportunities for new businesses and the majority of citizens to engage in economic activity on a 'level playing field', whereas extractive economic institutions are crafted by 'the politically powerful elites to extract resources from the rest of society'.[35] The authors study the development of nations, but Robinson holds that the 'concepts equally apply to differences between regions within a country'.[36] These national-level institutional concepts have yet to be applied to agricultural markets.

A literature is emerging on the *institutions of agricultural markets*, with a focus on SSA and smallholder farmers. Fafchamps, Dorward et al., Gabre-Madhin and Kirsten et al. have made central contributions,[37] not least by developing concepts and typologies for the analysis of relevant institutions. These authors see competitive markets as one of several institutional arrangements for the exchange of goods and services, with hierarchies and gift-exchange networks as alternative solutions to the coordination problem.[38] As mentioned, Dorward et al. argue that competitive markets do not always work for the beneficial inclusion of smallholders where such markets are poorly developed. Policy should not focus on improving the working of competitive markets. Other coordination mechanisms may work better in a SSA context with thin markets, where competitive markets cannot be expected to develop due to high risks and transaction costs. In export crop markets, large private processors may have incentives to

31 Wilcox and Abbott (2006)
32 North (1990); e.g., Davis and North (1971)
33 Ostrom (2005)
34 Acemoglu and Robinson (2012)
35 Acemoglu (2012)
36 Robinson (n.d.)
37 Fafchamps (2004); Dorward et al. (2005; 2009), Gabre-Madhin (2006; 2009); Kirsten et al. (2009)
38 Dorward et al. (2005; 2009); Gabre-Madhin (2006; 2009)

make coordinated investments in e.g., inputs and credit to smallholder farmers.[39] The current research contributes to this strand of thinking by adding an empirical example of the role and impact of SSA agricultural market institutions on smallholder benefits, including the possible role of competition versus coordinating functions.

Dorward et al. also propose reviving the distinction first made by Davis and North between the institutional environment and institutional (or contractual) arrangements.[40] They argue that in poorly developed economies, contractual arrangements may be easier to change and are likely to yield more tangible benefits for defined groups. The constituency of stakeholders thus formed may push for change, which may eventually alter the institutional environment. Their notion of institutional change from below suggests that change in SSA agriculture may be easier at the sector level than at the national.[41] Gabre-Madhin urges that market development be viewed as 'an integrated whole' in order to understand the 'complexity and diversity of institutional arrangements for facilitating market exchange'.[42] This research helps to fill these gaps and uses the typologies for market-level institutions developed in the literature.

There is a growing and related body of research on *global value/commodity chains* (GVC/GCC) and *production networks* (GPN), focusing on intra-chain/network relationships, notably power and governance.[43] Henderson et al. have developed a framework for analysing the context in which value chains are embedded, the GPN , but with economic and institutional concepts not entirely consistent with those used here.[44] A central and more relevant reference is Gereffi et al., who offer a typology of governance structures that reflects varying coordination and power asymmetry within a global value chain.[45] I use this typology to help characterise the structures of and relationships within the value chains studied in Liberia, as these institutions may influence smallholder benefit. There are several empirical studies on the implications of smallholder participation in specific global GVC/GPN, such as fruits and vegetables.[46] The literature recognises the role of competition in power and income distribution within the GVC. 'Essentially, the primary returns accrue to those parties who are able to protect themselves from competition. This ability to insulate activities can be encapsulated by the concept of *rent*, which arises from the possession of scarce attributes and involves *barriers to entry*'.[47] The current research pays explicit attention to the role of market power.

A systemic perspective is, in fact, being increasingly adopted within international development cooperation, and is codified in the *Making-Markets-Work-for-the-Poor*

---

39 Dorward et al. (2005; 2009)
40 Dorward et al. (2005); Davis and North (1971)
41 Cf. Booth and Therkildsen (2012)
42 Gabre-Madhin (2009:34, 39)
43 Early references are Gereffi and Korzeniewicz (1994) and Kaplinsky (2000).
44 Henderson et al. (2002)
45 Gereffi et al. (2005)
46 E.g., Evers et al. (2014)
47 Kaplinsky and Morris (2001: 25); emphasis in the original

(M4P) approach founded on experience-based knowledge.[48] Markets or value chains are seen as being embedded in larger market systems, where core transactions between market actors are underpinned by a range of supporting/service functions and governed by institutions. This market-system framework has partly inspired this research.

1.6   Contribution of the Research

This research makes two major contributions, one empirical and the other theoretical. First, by contributing unique data, it adds important empirical knowledge for understanding the post-war Liberian cocoa market and its recent developments, in particular its inclusiveness and the role of institutions in this process. This research adds to the scarce academic research on agricultural and economic developments in Liberia, and offers research-based knowledge on a highly policy-relevant issue.

In this research, I combine inputs from different strands of literatures into an integrated, multi-level, systemic analysis of how different institutions can contribute to the development of an inclusive agricultural market. The research thereby complements the existing literature. I also claim to make a theoretical contribution by more particularly identifying changes in specific institutions at different levels and suggesting causal mechanisms through which these institutional changes, in different constellations, can contribute to a more inclusive agricultural market. I thereby suggest certain functions that institutions perform in enabling inclusive development – 'inclusive' institutions of the agricultural market, in the terminology of Acemoglu and Robinson. This research thus makes inputs into a theory of the role of institutions in the development of inclusive agricultural markets.

In addition, the research has implications for the policy and practice of promoting development of inclusive agricultural markets in Liberia and potentially in other SSA countries.

1.7   Outline of the Research Report

In order to examine the inclusive nature of recent cocoa-market developments in Liberia and the role of institutions in this process, the research report continues with *two introductory chapters.* Chapter 2 presents the theory and data used and overall research method, and Chapter 3 examines the background and significance of the cocoa market.

Three empirical chapters follow, describing and analysing changes in the structure of the cocoa market and their implications for smallholder farmers, as well as major institutional changes relevant to these developments. Chapter 4 identifies major changes in the structure of the cocoa market by examining central market actors in the

---

48   Springfield Centre (2008)

cocoa value chain, their roles and relationships, and the implications of the changes for competition, market and bargaining power of market actors, in particular smallholder farmers. The inclusiveness of these developments, in terms of smallholder participation in and benefits from the cocoa market, is analysed in Chapter 5. I do this by reviewing farm-gate prices and access to services, as well as the farmers' response to altered incentives and opportunities and, to the extent possible, their returns from cocoa-market participation. On the basis of the findings, the chapter concludes that the post-war cocoa market in Liberia has become more inclusive. In Chapter 6, I identify the major institutional changes that have taken place and have, I suggest, contributed to making the Liberian cocoa market more inclusive, largely derived from the preceding analysis.

Subsequently, the different institutional explanations are tied together into a more coherent institutional causal explanation in Chapter 7. The analysis there synthesises the findings of this research on the role institutions have played in creating a more inclusive Liberian cocoa market. I suggest four central causal mechanisms whereby institutional changes have influenced smallholders' beneficial participation in the cocoa market, and discuss implications for theory. Chapter 8 concludes and discusses implications for policy and practice.

"

My initial focus is
on understanding the
nature and change of
the core value chain.

2   Theory, Methods and Data

This research seeks to contribute to the understanding of the role of institutions in the development of inclusive agricultural markets by examining the cocoa market in post-conflict Liberia. It is an empirical case study that seeks, first, to establish whether this market has become more inclusive by including and benefiting smallholder farmers more than before, and second, to identify major institutional changes that have contributed to these developments and to suggest why. This chapter first presents the research tools I use, in terms of theoretical concepts and frameworks, and thereafter the research design, in terms of empirical method and data.

2.1   Theoretical Concepts and Frameworks

A necessary first step in this research is to review developments in the cocoa market and identify major changes that may have impacted the beneficial participation of small-holder farmers and hence the inclusive nature of the market. To this end, I use an analytical framework combined with a theoretical typology to describe and characterise potentially relevant aspects of the cocoa market and the nature of its change. This market is seen as located in a broader market system, consisting of the institutional set-up and a set of supporting functions, all of which influence the functioning of the market. Within this system, my initial focus is on understanding the nature and change of the core value chain, its structure and the relationships between the different actors in it, in order to identify the role of and implications for smallholder farmers, while at the same time, being cognisant of the broader context. The market-system framework and value-chain typology are presented in Sub-Section 2.1.1, where the market and related concepts are also defined. The inclusive nature of the cocoa market is also the dependent variable in this research, when I later seek to explain how it has been influenced by changes in institutions. In this sub-section I also discuss what I mean by an inclusive market, and what aspects of beneficial smallholder participation I focus on.

Once I have identified the major changes in the Liberia cocoa market and established whether, and in what ways, the market has become more inclusive, attention is turned to the role of the institutions involved in this process. The research sets out to identify the major institutional changes that have contributed to the more inclusive nature of the cocoa market, and to offer an explanation of how they have contributed. To identify these institutions, I combine deductive and inductive analysis, drawing on both the theoretical literature and my preceding analysis of the cocoa market. The focus is on economic institutions, except where other institutions emerge as vital in the empirical analysis. This research does not intend to map and analyse the entire institutional set up of the Liberian cocoa market, but focuses on institutions that have changed in recent years and are found to have played an important role. Institutions are the independent variables in this research, and my analysis of their role for economic outcomes relies on institutional theory, which is presented in Sub-Section 2.1.2, together with definitions and categories of institutions used, and an analytical framework that helps structure the analysis. The sub-section ends with a proposal of the kind of theoretical contribution I hope to make.

2.1.1 Markets and Their Inclusiveness

The term *market* is here used in a broad sense. It is the arena in which the exchange of goods and services – in this case cocoa – takes place, through transactions between market actors, buyers and sellers. Cocoa is typically traded for money. The market is not necessarily a competitive one, with many sellers and buyers, but can be characterised as an *oligopoly* or *monopoly*, dominated by a small number of sellers or a single one, or as an *oligopsony* or *monopsony*, dominated by a few or a single buyer. In the case of limited competition, some market actors have *market power*, and are able to influence key aspects of the transaction, such as the price. One may characterise the market as a *buyers'* or a *sellers' market*.

I also use the terms *value chain* and *market system*, which are illustrated in Figure 2.1 below. This figure depicts what an agricultural value chain embedded in a market system could look like. At the centre is the core, the value chain, which consists of the various stages of exchange a product passes through, from inputs through production and processing to end consumption, where value is (presumably) added to the product at each stage. Each stage or box in the value chain can also be seen as representing the various market actors involved in the *value addition* process, from input providers, to farmer producers, traders etc. At the nodes between each box, transactions take place between the actors, which means that each node can be seen as a sub-market in itself. For simplicity's sake, I sometimes refer to the cocoa value chain as the cocoa market.

The analytical framework in Figure 2.1 was developed for the analysis, design and implementation of programmes aimed at the development of markets that are central to the poor in ways that better serve their interests.[49] To understand markets, it is argued, one needs to see them as embedded in a larger market system and look beyond the core transactions between market actors. This is because the transactions in the core market/value chain are influenced by a range of supporting functions and governed by rules in the wider context in which the market/chain is embedded. This context determines constraints and opportunities; generates information and incentives; shapes behaviour and practices, relationships and interactions; and thus influences outcomes.[50]

---

49   Springfield Centre (2008)
50   GRM International (2010)

Figure 2.1: Analytical Framework: Example of an Agricultural Value Chain Embedded in a Market System

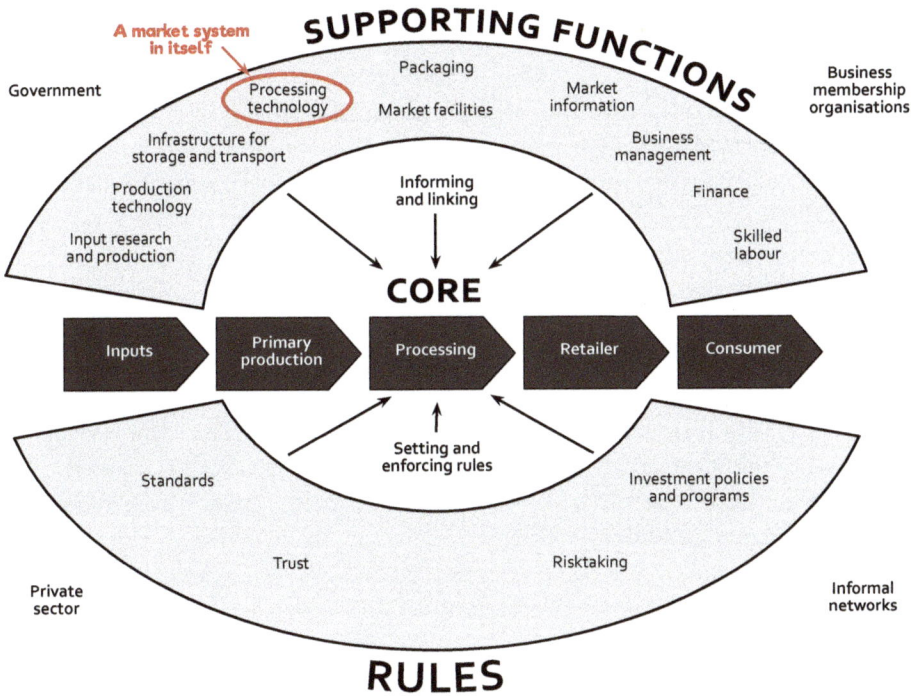

Source: Adapted from GRM International (2010: Annex 15)

Analysing the entire cocoa-market system is beyond the scope of this research, which is specifically concerned with the inclusiveness of recent developments and the role of institutions in that process. I use the analytical framework for description and orientation purposes, while focusing on the core value chain and the rules – the institutions – relevant to it. These are further discussed below. Within the core value chain, my focus is on the output market, and less so on the input market. I do, of necessity, touch upon various aspects of supporting functions as part of the wider context that shapes the conditions of market interaction. *Supporting functions* provide access to, for instance, market information and financial services, which are important for the functioning of the market. Each such function may, as shown in the figure, constitute a market system in itself, requiring its own analysis.

Markets can also be seen as one of several mechanisms for the exchange of goods and services – allocation of resources or coordination of economic activities. Other typical mechanisms are hierarchies (i.e., firms or bureaucracies) and relational or gift-exchange networks.[51] Hybrid forms also are common in practice.[52] The core value chain can thus be structured in different ways, with varying levels and numbers of inter-

---

51 Dorward et al. (2005; 2009); Gabre-Madhin (2006) – largely based on transaction-cost economics, traced not least to Williamson (1975)
52 Gabre-Madhin (2006)

acting market actors – companies and individuals exchanging goods and services with one another. In this research, we use the term *market structure* to refer to the pattern of actors in the market or value chain. In their study of GVCs, Gereffi et al. elaborate the value-chain categories.[53] They offer a typology of five so-called GVC governance structures: market, modular, relational and captive value chains, and hierarchy (a vertically integrated firm). These are determined by the complexity of the transactions, the ability to codify them and the capability of suppliers. This means that as one shifts from the market to the firm, the degree of *explicit coordination* increases and so does the *power asymmetry* within them. *Appendix Figure 2.1* illustrates the five GVC types.

In the market, price coordinates transactions, whereas in the firm, transactions are coordinated through flows of information and control. The model further implies that power asymmetry is low in the market, which suggests that Gereffi et al. rely on the assumptions that markets are competitive – in reality they often are not. Between the market and the firm, they identify three kinds of value chains. The perhaps most interesting for this case is the *captive value chain*, whereby power is exerted directly on suppliers by lead firms. This suggests a high degree of explicit coordination and power asymmetry. Coordination of this sort is the result of highly complex transactions, which are capable of being codified, but where the capability of suppliers is low. I partly use this value-chain typology to help describe and characterise the cocoa-market structure and its changes.

The *inclusiveness* of the cocoa market refers to the extent of the inclusion in the market of many small market actors, in this case smallholder farmers, and the extent to which their active participation in the market is beneficial to them. An *inclusive* cocoa market in this research thus implies active *market participation* by smallholder farmers in ways beneficial to them. Participation can take different forms. If one considers the whole cocoa value chain, the use of inputs as well as the production of cocoa is included. In Liberia no cocoa is produced for farmers' own consumption, only for the market. The use of inputs refers to participation in the input market; production is a prerequisite for participation in the output market. Cocoa supply or sales, as well as trade in cocoa (buying and selling) and value addition are indications of market participation, and investments to increase productivity or production are also considered. Investments are also signs of willingness to participate in the market. Hence, smallholder market participation can increase in a number of ways, and in varying degree. If farmers engage in more ways than hitherto, I see this as a sign of *increased participation*, in addition to any quantitative increase in particular market activity. Also, if a larger number of farmers are active in the market, this too indicates increased participation.

Benefit refers both to economic outcomes and to conditions. Beneficial *economic outcome* includes farm-gate prices – cocoa prices received by farmers (ideally) and their organisations and their marketing margin in terms of their share of world market price. Other vital economic outcomes include profit, which may be difficult to identify as smallholder farmers are not expected to separate their commercial from their family

---

53   Gereffi et al. (2005)

business, and income from cocoa market activity. Other prices and costs are, of course, relevant too, such as input prices and transaction costs. I focus on farm-gate prices, which are vital as incentives for market participation and have important implications for many other economic outcomes, and the associated marketing margins, defined as the share of the world market price, to reflect changes in the position of smallholder farmers in the cocoa value chain. A decisive indicator of *increased economic benefit* in this research is a higher increase (or smaller decline) in the farm-gate price of cocoa than in its world market price, and hence a larger marketing margin. Beneficial *conditions* include freedom of choice, access to markets, inputs and supporting functions, all of which refer to opportunities to engage in the cocoa market and respond to price incentives.[54] Improvement is these conditions is essentially qualitative. I explore a number of economic and other benefits, depending on what the analysis of the cocoa market suggests, and what the nature and availability of data allow.

In this research, the dependent variable is the *inclusive* character of the market, as defined above. However, I do not seek to establish the extent to which the market is inclusive, but whether it has become more inclusive in the post-war period. I would consider this to have been achieved if smallholder participation has become more beneficial to them and if smallholder participation has also increased. The greater the kinds and amounts of benefits, and the more the kinds of and 'volumes' of participation, the more inclusive the market becomes. Hence, both increased benefit and participation is needed for the market to become more inclusive.

2.1.2 Institutions and Their Roles

Institutions are central in this research – they are the independent variables. The overall *theoretical perspective* is institutional, located in the broad social-science strand of NIE represented by North, Ostrom, Acemoglu and Robinson and others.[55] In keeping with this perspective, I combine theoretical inputs into a multi-level analysis of how institutions contribute to inclusive agricultural-market development. This sub-section first discusses institutional concepts, then institutional theory and an analytical framework that inspired this work and finally, the theoretical contribution I hope to make.

Institutions are defined as behavioural rules of social interaction,[56] and are distinguished from organisations, which are seen as actors.[57] Institutions are sometimes also referred to as the *rules of the game*, and I use rules, rules of the game and institutions interchangeably. Together with other contextual factors, institutions define the actors' operational context, thus helping to shape the incentives actors encounter and the resulting patterns of interaction and outcomes, e.g., in terms of economic performance. Institutions guide human behaviour in recurrent situations of interaction, and

---

54   Cf. Ianchovichina and Lundstrom (2009) in relation to inclusive growth.
55   Represented by e.g., North (1990), Ostrom (2005) and Acemoglu and Robinson (2012).
56   Cf. Eriksson Skoog (2000: 36-37)
57   North (1990)

thereby perform a coordinating role. Institutions are also distinguished from structures, such as the market structure (discussed above), which is a pattern that may result as a behavioural consequence of a given set of institutions.

Institutions are of different kinds. I use the following categories. *Economic institutions* guide economic activity – investment, production, value addition, trade. etc. The economic rules relevant to markets, suggested by Gabre-Madhin, include formal and informal contracts, trading practices and codes of conduct, formal commercial laws and market regulations, and institutional arrangements such as vertically or horizontally integrated supply chains.[58] The NIE perspective is explicitly contextual, with economic institutions seen as embedded in political and socio-cultural institutions. *Political institutions* guide political activity, such as the distribution of political power and decision making, and may also influence economic institutions.[59] Institutions may be *formal*, i.e., documented, or *informal*, undocumented,[60] and formal rules may be adhered to and actually applied in practice, or may remain nominal. Hence, the extent to which institutional rules are applied, adhered to or enforced and thus effectively valid in practice is important.[61] In Liberia, where enforcement of formal rules tends to be weak, informal rules often apply instead. *Socio-cultural rules* can be expected to play an important role, linked to patron-client relationships – or 'Big Man' networks[62] – in the form of political patronage, networks or relational exchanges and corruption.

Institutions can be analysed at different levels. *Rules* in the analytical framework above (Figure 2.1) suggest that institutions are part of the core value chain context, but Gabre-Madhin notes that institutions can be seen as the links in the chain of market interactions,[63] thus guiding transactions at different nodes in a value chain. In this research, I distinguish between economic institutions at two levels. The first is the *institutional environment* of the market, i.e., the broader system in which the market or value chain is embedded, such as business regulations, and property/land rights, and which shapes general conditions for actors in the cocoa market. Then there are the *institutional arrangements* for interaction within the core market/value chain itself and its different sub-markets, e.g., various coordination mechanisms and contractual relations, which guide interactions between specific constellations of market actors. The distinction between institutional arrangements and environment, developed by Davis and North,[64] is useful. Dorward et al.[65] argue that institutional arrangements are easier to change and may, if they accumulate, eventually change the institutional envi-

---

58 Gabre-Madhin (2009: 11)
59 As increasingly recognised, and specifically emphasised and studied by Acemoglu and Robinson (2012).
60 Following North (1990)
61 Cf. Ostrom (2005) who refers to *rules in use*, i.e. rules that actors actually adhere to and their enforcement mechanisms, regardless of whether they are considered formal or informal.
62 Utas (2012)
63 Gabre-Madhin (2009: 11)
64 Davis and North (1971)
65 Dorward et al. (2009)

ronment.[66] I explore the role of institutional change at both levels and the relationship between them.

Institutional change may also have different characteristics and origins. Some such change is the result of plan and conscious design and thus *intentional* and often formalised through documentation. Certainly, some intentional institutional change, such as government reform measures, may be purely nominal: not implemented or enforced by public officials or the judicial system and/or not adhered to by market actors. If formal rules have only changed 'on paper', but led to no change in behavioural practices and patterns of interaction, I do not consider effective institutional change to have taken place. Other institutional change may emerge more spontaneously as an unintended outcome of market actors' repeated interactions in recurrent situations, sparked by, for example, a partly altered context. Yet, such change, referred to as *organic* institutional change, may remain only implicitly recognised and informal.[67]

The literature offers a *general theory* and an analytical framework for studying how institutions influence economic outcomes, and these are used to help structure the overall and, in particular, causal analysis. NIE, strongly influenced by North's theory on the role of institutions in economic performance,[68] is now a broad and varied field, with certain common basic ideas. Its essence is that by shaping incentives, institutions influence human behaviour and interactions and outcomes in terms economic performance. As behavioural rules, institutions guide human action and interaction by imposing constraints or providing options. They promote and facilitate certain types of behaviour and discourage others by affecting their relative costs and benefits, and thus influence the incentive structure facing individuals. The incentives thus created, together with others, determine the economic activities of individuals and influence economic performance via the resulting resource allocation. Rule-following may be rational for individuals, but the institutional set-up is not necessarily conducive to economic development and prosperity, or – in this case – inclusive markets.[69]

This general theory is made explicit in the Institutional Analysis and Development (IAD) analytical framework for studying the role of institutions developed by Ostrom and her colleagues.[70] The framework, which has inspired this research, is illustrated in Figure 2.2 below, and is used in this research as a general guiding tool to structure my analysis in two ways.

---

66 Cf. Booth and Therkildsen (2012) who argue that change in the economics and politics of SSA agriculture may be easier at sector than at national level.
67 This paragraph follows Eriksson Skoog (2000: 37, 50-51), based on Schotter (1986) and Menger (1963), Book 3, Chapters 1-2.
68 Notably North (1990)
69 Description drawing on Eriksson Skoog (2000: 49), largely following North (1990)
70 See, for example, Ostrom (2005), Ostrom et al. (2002) and Polski and Ostrom (1999).

Figure 2.2: The Institutional Analysis and Development (IAD) Framework[71]

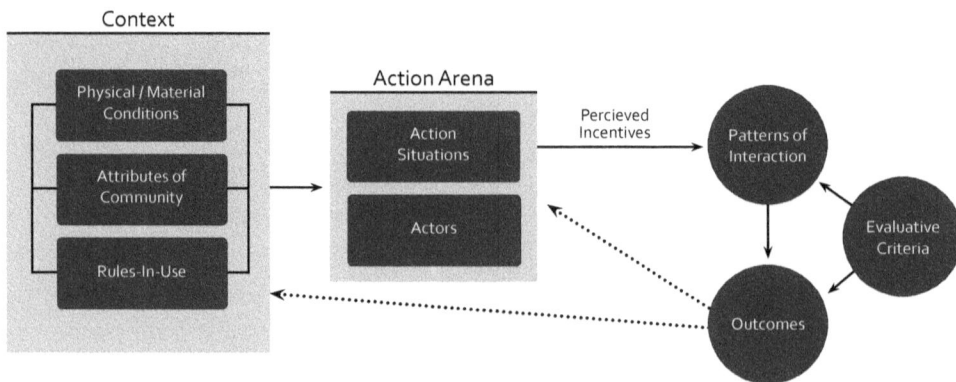

First, it helps frame the sequential and causal logic of the analysis. The research starts by examining the market structure – the patterns of interaction in the framework – and the resulting outcomes – or more specifically, changes in these – in terms of beneficial smallholder participation. Thereafter, I move backwards in the framework to identify the underlying institutional changes that have contributed to these developments. Those institutional changes are essentially derived from the preceding empirical analysis, although they are partly suggested in the various literatures discussed earlier.

Second, by making explicit a general theory on the role of institutions in economic outcomes, the IAD framework provides overall guidance in my explanation of how specific institutional changes may have causally contributed to observed changes in the inclusiveness of the Liberian cocoa market by influencing incentives for behaviour, with results for patterns of interaction and economic outcomes. My ambition is not complete analysis of the entire Liberian cocoa market (cf., the IAD framework), nor even the entire institutional set-up of that market. Rather, I focus on major changes that have occurred in recent years in the cocoa market relevant to beneficial participation by smallholders, and on contributory institutional changes.

The institutional literature thus helps to explain how institutions matter in general, but does not suggest which institutions are important for the inclusive development of agricultural markets and why, although certain useful insights are offered. This is where the current research seeks to make a theoretical contribution. My ambition is to 1) identify several institutions that may contribute to inclusive agricultural markets, 2) identify central causal mechanisms which may help to explain how institutions contribute to the outcome, and 3) suggest how several institutions, possibly at different levels, may serve to jointly contribute through these mechanisms.

The *causal analysis* seeks to explain how changes in specific institutions have influenced incentives, behaviour and interactions in the cocoa market, in ways that have identified repercussions for beneficial smallholder participation. I also intend to explore how several institutions may influence incentives, constraints and opportunities facing

---

71   Adapted from Ostrom et al. (2002: 23)

market actors in a similar direction, thus jointly contributing to a *causal mechanism* of possible importance for the inclusive outcome. A causal mechanism can, according to Beach and Brun Pedersen, be 'a theory of a system of interlocking parts that transmit causal forces from X to Y'.[72] I adopt a less stringent definition, by replacing the 'interlocking parts' with reinforcing parts. The causal analysis is thus inspired by – but does not strictly apply – process tracing[73] as a method to both identify institutional changes of importance, by tracing them backwards from the inclusive nature of the market, and to trace the causal mechanism that links 'cause' to 'outcome'. In addition to promoting understanding of the post-war Liberian cocoa market, this research thereby hopes to contribute to a theory and broader understanding of what institutions matter, and in what ways, for the development of inclusive agricultural markets.

2.2   Empirical Method and Data

This research is an empirical case study which generates much of its own data. This sub-section presents its design, the methods employed and the data used.

2.2.1   Research Design

Liberia is a country case of an SSA economy with a dual economy, long experience of growth without development, with serious poverty – as well as conflict – implications, but with a post-war situation serving as a possible critical juncture for change, as discussed earlier. The post-war Liberian cocoa market is an example of an agricultural market with both an export and pro-poor growth potential,[74] as well as indications of possible development towards more inclusiveness, benefiting smallholder farmer participation, as also discussed. Another, related, major reason for selecting the cocoa market is that is a typical smallholder sector, with most of the output produced by smallholder farmers.[75]

This research addresses broad issues and seeks to capture multiple developments and complex causal relationships in an under-studied and data-poor market and country. It seeks to gain an overall picture of developments in the Liberian post-war cocoa market, their causes and consequences, and has had to start very much 'from scratch'. To tackle this task, the overall *empirical research method* linking data to the research questions and findings is the case-study method, inspired by the approaches of George and Bennett as well as Yin.[76] It is particularly well-suited to complex empirical analysis,

---

72 Beach and Brun Pedersen (2013)

73 In particular by Beach and Brun Pedersen (2013), but also e.g., Bennett and Checkel (2012)

74 Cocoa and rubber are considered to be the two major tree/export crops in Liberia with the highest pro-poor growth (GRM International 2010, Adam Smith International 2013) and export potential (Republic of Liberia 2012). Rubber is not a primarily a smallholder crop, however, but a typical plantation crop, even though smaller farmers also grow rubber.

75 E.g., Republic of Liberia (2014: 10)

76 Inspired by George and Bennett (2005) and Yin (2014)

because of its 'ability to deal with a full variety of evidence'.[77] This allows adaptation to the data-poor environment and facilitates triangulation in the study of causal processes in a complex environment.[78] Hence, this research uses and combines multiple sources of data: primary data generated through interviews with different market actors and external observers, but also available secondary data. These are triangulated to corroborate and qualify findings.

The *unit of analysis* is the entire cocoa market in Liberia. To study it, I use a mix of data collected at two major levels: aggregated data from secondary and primary sources and local-level data generated by different cocoa-market sites. Since aggregated data is scarce, I have sought to capture the diversity of the market and conditions within it by collecting primary data from selected cocoa-market districts with varying characteristics. The aim of the selection is to obtain a picture of developments of the market as a whole, offering a broad reflection of experiences, observations and perceptions in the absence of a representative sample. Districts are thus selected to maximise variation in the cocoa market, and possibly inclusive development and institutional conditions.

Hence, in addition to aggregated data relevant to the entire market, local-level data reveal information about identified parts of the market, which may indicate relationships and changes in the market as a whole. If similar changes can be observed in different localities regardless of the level or intensity of market activity, this may be an indication of the general nature of the change. The time period studied is post-war, 2003–October/November 2013, when most data were collected. The research is concerned with capturing overall changes in the Liberian cocoa market, including implications for smallholder farmers and institutions of potential relevance, over time during this time period.

Given the extreme scarcity of cocoa-market data, including recent historical data, it is not possible to consistently study change between two specific points in time, ideally 2003 and 2013. Therefore, this research studies a *continuous process of change* over time during this period. Limited baseline data do exist and are used, together with a combination of secondary sources and interviews to capture this process of change, partly as perceived by interviewees. In reality, most data collected lend themselves to capturing changes during the latter half of the post-war period.

2.2.2   Data and Data Collection

The nature and sources of data, and means of collecting them, are presented here. First a few words on the conditions for empirical research, in particular for conducting field research, in Liberia.

Conditions for Empirical Research

This research is a rare empirical analysis of developments in agricultural markets in

---

77   Yin (2014: 12)
78   George and Bennett (2005)

Liberia and contributes to the scarce literature on the Liberian economy. There is no research on the institutions and inclusiveness of agricultural markets in Liberia that this research can build on. Independent economic research on Liberia, historical as well as contemporary, is conspicuously rare. The most prominent academic research on the Liberian economy dates back to the 1960s.[79] It reveals the dual economic structure and vast inequalities in economic development between different segments of Liberian society. Most recent studies have been conducted by consultants for policy purposes. Radelet and del Castillo are exceptions and confirm the persistence of duality into the post-war period and the need for inclusive growth.[80] Research on economic institutions is absent, apart from an initial review by Eriksson Skoog,[81] and there is little on agricultural development and markets. A limited number of descriptive, sector-specific studies exist, including on the cocoa sector. These offer scarce but important background information and are used here partly as points of reference.

There is a corresponding absence of basic statistics on agriculture and its development in post-conflict Liberia. The severity of this constraint was confirmed and a central primary observation during this research. There are virtually no statistics on the cocoa sector and its performance at an overall national/sector level, e.g., in terms of numbers of cocoa farmers, volume of cocoa produced and land used for cocoa production – let alone on the cocoa market. Quantitative data are notoriously scarce. What is available beyond estimates are data on officially recorded exports and officially registered exporters, which I make use of.

This lack of data on the cocoa market sets the stage for, and has important implications for, this research. It means that data collection has to begin more or less 'from scratch', imposes limitations on what data can be collected and how, and thereby makes this empirical research exploratory in its search for data and the methods employed. As indicated above, limited access to baseline data also makes it impossible to consistently study change from a specific point in time, and limits us to the study of a continuous process of change up to late 2013.

In addition, this is the first time the researcher has conducted field research in rural Liberia, which also contributes to its exploratory nature. Initial interactions with Liberian local communities, cooperatives and smallholder farmers as a researcher requires contacts and learning how to gain confidence so as to access vital information. The researcher has partly had to rely on other individuals and organisations for introductions to local communities, cooperatives and farmers, and to some extent to identify interviewees.

Another vital circumstance that has determined conditions and methods of data collection is the severe logistical constraints in Liberia. Not only are roads in rural Liberia poor, if not appalling, – at times even impassable during the rainy season – but there is also no system of public transport. There is no route network for buses and

79   Clower et al. (1966)
80   Radelet (2007); del Castillo (2012)
81   Eriksson Skoog (2009)

local transport by sedan or motorbike taxi is risky due to the poor conditions of roads and vehicles and for personal safety reasons. To make this research feasible at all, I had to rely on safe transport to rural areas offered by individuals and organisations already known to me. This imposed limitations on the geographical areas and communities I was able to visit, and the time I could spend there, as I have sometimes had to conduct research when transport was available. It also meant that on occasion I had to seize the opportunity to conduct ad hoc interviews.

The conditions for field research in rural Liberia have had consequences for the availability and nature of the data collected and the methods employed to do so. In particular, the constraints limited my ability to collect data as consistently as I desired, and to collect it from interviewees, particularly farmers and other market actors, as broadly as desired, with regard to geographical coverage and variation in the characteristics and context of interviewees.

Primary Data Collection

My observations on market developments, implications for smallholders and institutional changes are primarily based on a large number of interviews, including individual and group interviews. There were two major types or sources of interviews: a) semi-structured interviews with *market actors* at all nodes of the cocoa value chain, including input providers, smallholder farmers, cooperatives, middlemen and large buyers-cum-exporters; and b) in-depth interviews with *key informants*, including external observers within the public sector and the donor/NGO community with considerable insight into and an overview of the whole or parts of the cocoa market at national and local levels. The interviews were conducted in six districts in Lofa and Nimba, the two largest cocoa-producing counties, the less-developed but emerging Gbarpolu County and in the capital Monrovia. They primarily concerned cocoa-market developments at the national level and in these localities. The combined quantitative and qualitative primary data were generated during field research in October and November 2013. It has been reviewed, sometimes compiled and presented in tables in the text or the Appendix, and analysed in relation to the different questions examined in each chapter, together with relevant secondary data indicated by the sources.

Liberian English is the official language of Liberia but not all citizens have a good mastery of it, particularly in rural areas. It is sometimes difficult for foreign English speakers to understand, or be understood by Liberians, especially those with limited education. For this reason, a research assistant-cum-translator was used during interviews in rural areas. Written notes from the interviews were taken by the researcher, and her understanding was corroborated through comparison with the notes and understanding of the research assistant. The latter helped with translations between English and Liberian English as needed. In Foya district of Lofa County, the assistant interpreted to/from the local vernacular. In Kolahun District in Lofa, where some interviewees had no knowledge of Liberian English, a translator from the local community was chosen by the interviewee to translate from the local vernacular into English/Liberian English. Informed consent was obtained from all interviewees, whose anonymity was promised. Interviews were carefully conducted to ensure respect for local customs and conventions of courtesy, e.g., by first approaching village elders and community leaders and seeking permission, and by being sensitive to the situation and needs of interviewees, some of whom had to take time off from farming.

The *market actors* interviewed reflect a broad spectrum in varying contexts and with a variety of experiences, to capture possible variations in developments and underlying factors as well as patterns of change cutting across these variations. I selected interviewees in two of the three major cocoa-producing counties, Nimba and Lofa, which both have a long tradition of cocoa trade, as well as in Gbarpolu County, which has a less-developed but emerging cocoa market. In Lofa, I had interviews with market actors in three districts, including Kolahun and Foya, with considerable cocoa tradition, and Quardo Gboni with less of that. Due to logistical and time constraints, I made fewer interviews in Nimba and even fewer in Gbarpolu. In the selection of farmer interviewees, I explicitly sought younger male as well as female farmers, to complement the seeming predominance of older male farmers (although age is not explicitly reflected in my interviews). Similarly, I explicitly sought what I refer to as independent farmers, to complement the many members of farmers' organisations, who were more easily identified. I consciously identified farmers' organisations (and their members) that were relatively successful in cocoa marketing as well as those were relatively less so. I selected farmers with experience of selling cocoa to different types of buyers. The diversity of the market actors interviewed (in particular farmers) notwithstanding, they do not constitute a representative sample of a certain population. Hence, the observations made on the basis of the information they offer can only be said to represent these particular respondents. A total of 38 individual interviews and five group interviews were conducted with market actors. Some of these actors perform several roles in the value chain, for example, a large input provider is also a cocoa buyer-cum-exporter. Some smallholder farmers also serve as local buying agents, and one farmer is also a plantation employee, etc.

I undertook six interviews with individuals associated with large buyers-cum-exporters (three from LAADCO, one from LMI, two from Wienco), at national and local level. Buying agents (middlemen) proved difficult to identify. I interviewed five of them: three of the individual farmers interviewed also serve as local buying agents; an informal interview with one middle buyer in Foya town, Lofa; and in one of the group interviews with key informants, one former buying agent participated and contributed. I interviewed two individuals from a cocoa plantation (LCC).

I had 29 individual interviews with farmers, but in two of these interviews (with two persons each) the individuals were exclusively interviewed as leaders of farmers' organisations, which leaves us with 27 interviews with individuals as farmers, a few of whom also have leadership positions in a farmers' organisation. Most farmers are members of farmers' organisations (cooperatives or associations) or more informal farmers' groups, but two had actively left a farmers' organisation. Another seven farmers are not members of any group and are referred to as independent. Of the farmers interviewed, seven are women. Individual interviews were complemented by five group interviews with farmers in five farmers' organisations, members as well as leaders. There were at least 8-18 farmers in each group, including women, totalling almost 70 farmer members and leaders. Many, but far from all, individually interviewed farmers were also present in group interviews, giving rise to some overlap. In addition, I had brief informal interviews with two representatives of farmers' organisations. Altogether some 80 farmers participated in my interviews.

Eight individual interviews with different kinds of input providers were conducted: one individual interview with two persons from a specialised local seedling producer; two interviews with a seedling producer, also serving as a cocoa plantation; three individual interviews with a provider of seeds/seedlings, mainly serving as a large cocoa buyer; two individual interviews with a large provider of fertilisers and other chemicals (pesticides, fungicides, etc.), also serving as a cocoa buyer.

Due to the aforementioned conditions for field research, the largest number of and most systematic individual interviews with smallholder farmers were conducted in Lofa, based on the researchers' initial experience in Nimba, whereas interviews in Gbarpolu were conducted under severe time constraints.

The interviews with market actors are complemented with data from interviews with *key informants*, selected for their in-depth knowledge and overview as well as their potential perspectives on developments over time at national and district level. Fifteen individual interviews with key informants were conducted. Eight key informants are from the public sector, representing various central government bodies at policy and regulatory level (3 MoA, 2 LPMC, 2 CDA, 1 NIC), including one person who works with a donor-funded programme (STCRSP). Together with one interviewee from an international donor (World Bank) and six interviewees from an international NGO (ACDI-VOCA), a total of eight key informants work on implementation of donor-funded projects in the cocoa sector. Of these key informants, 10 are active at apex/national level and five at county/district level. In addition, one group interview was conducted with key informants from an NGO implementing a comprehensive cocoa programme, including people at national level and six cocoa-producing counties, including Lofa, Nimba and Gbarpolu. In addition, I had five informal interviews with key informants: one from the government/public sector, three from the NGO sector and one independent observer. Altogether, I interviewed some 25 key informants, nine from the public sector and the rest mostly working with cocoa-market actors 'on the ground'.

Complementary primary data were provided through four conversations with groups of mixed participants. Each group included some key informants and three of them also included some market actors. In addition, data from certain interviews conducted in February-March 2013 are used, as relevant.

Secondary Sources

As noted above, secondary data, especially research and quantitative data/statistics, on the issues studied here are scarce. A few studies of the cocoa market do exist, and provide some useful information. The reviews of cocoa and coffee marketing by Hughes et al. in the late 1980s, before the war, provide some background information.[82] A certain number of studies have been conducted by consultants for policy purposes or development project and programme planning. Some are useful, others less so, partly in not being thorough enough. The only study based on thorough empirical research of the cocoa sector is a survey of cocoa farmers in 2006 and 2007 by Wilcox,[83] in relation to and funded by the IITA (International Institute of Tropical Agriculture) project. This survey aims to serve as a base-line for future research and was used as input e.g., into the Liberian government's 'Comprehensive Assessment of the Agriculture Sector' of 2007.[84] It has given rise to a few publications, e.g., by English,[85] who studies determinants of Liberian farm-gate cocoa prices. Data from these sources from 2006-2007 are used as baseline data, partly for comparison with some of my primary data from 2013. A useful source of information is the major donor-funded cocoa project to date, the USDA-funded LIFE project implemented by ACDI-VOCA since 2008, which has produced a number of documents e.g., on institutional reforms of the cocoa market. A limited number of additional documents and statistics have been collected from secondary sources.

---

82 Hughes et al. (1989)
83 Wilcox (2007)
84 Republic of Liberia (2007a)
85 English (2008)

Liberia's history as a dual economy has meant that political priority has been given to the enclave sector.

3   The Liberian Cocoa Market
   – Background and Significance

This chapter sets the stage for the analysis of post-war developments in the Liberian co-coa market, by addressing its recent history, relative importance and overall structure.

3.1   Recent History of Liberian Cocoa Market

Liberia's history as a dual economy has meant that political priority has been given to the enclave sector, dominated by rubber plantations and large farms, whereas smallhol-der farming has been largely neglected or discriminated against. Smallholder farming is focused on food production, essentially for subsistence, but also on certain cash-crops. Historically, as pointed out by one of my key informants, cocoa and coffee were the major sources of income in rural Liberian communities.[86] Liberian cocoa is mainly grown by smallholder farmers, on farms of 1-3 hectares.[87]

Cocoa is a tree crop and is grown in the rain forest. The trees bear cocoa pods, which contain the cocoa beans. These are fermented and dried to produce quality co-coa, but there is also a market for raw, or wet, cocoa. The productive lifespan of a cocoa tree is 25-30 years, and traditional varieties bear fruit after about six years. However, new high-yielding varieties are entering Liberia. So far mainly adopted by large far-mers, they bear fruit much earlier, some only 18 months after planting the seedlings.[88] The harvest season is traditionally between October and March, but with the new varieties there is also a good mid-season in June, and some harvest all year round.[89] Cocoa farming is labour intensive, as the farm requires under-brushing three times a year, canopy cutting, pruning of older trees, removal of black pods, etc.

Historically, the Liberian trade in cocoa was controlled by the Liberian Produce Marketing Corporation (LPMC), a state-owned company (parastatal enterprise) with extensive regulatory powers over internal and external trade and a market actor it-self.[90] Prior to the war, cocoa was marketed through a chain that included cooperati-ves, sub-licensed and licensed buying agents and the LPMC, which appears to have had exclusive rights to export into the international market.[91] The LPMC's monop-sony power to buy cocoa in the country today as well as in the past is claimed by staff

---

86   According to Key Informant 3, rural communities were traditionally based on food farming of mainly upland rice, and forest gardening (of cocoa, coffee and other forest products), which generated the extra rural farmer income.
87   Republic of Liberia (2014: 10)
88   Individual Interviewee 23
89   Key Informant 2
90   Republic of Liberia (1961) – the legal act establishing the LPMC
91   Hughes et al. (1989)

from both the LPMC and the Ministry of Agriculture, [92] although this power is not explicitly stated in its establishing act.[93] In practice, by virtue of its size and parastatal status,[94] it may have been perceived to have these powers, and assumed them even by the use of force.[95] At the same time, private, even unlicensed, traders were reportedly already prevalent before the war,[96] so the picture is somewhat unclear. LPMC also performed regulatory functions, such as to 'set standards' for cocoa and 'fix prices'.[97] Prices for cocoa were determined at different levels of the supply chain, but in reality, 'the majority of small farmers are receiving substantially less than the official price for their produce'.[98] LPMC was notorious for its inefficiency, corruption and malpractices, was highly indebted and famers received but minute returns for their cocoa. Already in 1989, the cocoa sector was at 'a point of crisis'.[99] Then the war came.

By the early 1990s, LPMC's financial situation had so deteriorated that it could no longer perform its central task, trade in cocoa, and in reality it withdrew from the Liberian cocoa trade. Thus the market was informally deregulated, and the void was filled by private traders.[100] As noted by English, '[t]he conflict in Liberia partially liberalized the cocoa market', but given the inability to collect information during the conflict, 'Liberia lacks reliable information with which to judge the effects of this de facto liberalization'.[101] According to Gerdes, the cocoa trade during the first war (1989-1996) 'appears to have been largely controlled by the NPFL rather than any other faction, and much in the tradition of African marketing boards, Taylor bought the whole production in his territory at a price he fixed himself'.[102] Moreover, during the Liberian wars, many farmers abandoned their farms, and according to official figures, cocoa production was 'almost totally destroyed'.[103]

The Liberian cocoa market emerging out of the war was monopolistic, with the leading exporter handling around 80 per cent of total exports,[104] possessing strong

---

92 Key Informants 6 and 15; Ministry of Agriculture (2012a); Hughes et al. (1989)

93 Republic of Liberia (1961)

94 A curiosity is that when the LPMC was established, it was only half-owned by the Liberian government. The other half of its shares was owned by a private company based in Denmark, the East Asiatic Company Ltd. (Republic of Liberia 1962 – the LMPC articles of incorporation). In the mid-1970s, the Government of Liberia bought all the shares and the LPMC became a fully state-owned enterprise. (Key Informant 15)

95 Hughes et al. (1989: 24) report that during the 1987/88 marketing season, 'LPMC overcame the farmers' reluctance to sell at half-price by bringing soldiers with them on the buying campaign, telling the farmers or village warehouse managers that LPMC was the only authorized purchaser, and, when resistance was offered, confiscating the cocoa'.

96 Hughes et al. (1989: 15-17, 24)

97 Republic of Liberia (1961: 441)

98 Hughes et al. (1989: 23); cf. Footnote 40

99 Hughes et al. (1989: 59)

100 Key Informant 15

101 English (2008: 4)

102 Gerdes (2013: 96-97)

103 Gerdes (2013: 96); the Liberian wars: 1989-1996 and 1999-2003

104 Ministry of Commerce and Industry (2009: 46)

market power. Limited competition at different levels of the domestic value chain was to the detriment of farmers. According to a study by the Ministry of Commerce and Industry, 'monopsonistic forces are at work, and traders are extracting too large a margin, either at farm gate or in district towns, and paying a low price'.[105] Another observer noted that '[s]ince the end of civil war in 2003, Liberian cocoa production has stagnated'.[106] As late as 2007, an agricultural review found that markets for Liberian cocoa persisted in an 'underdeveloped and chaotic state'.[107] It seems reasonable to conclude that incentives for farmers to participate in the cocoa market, and opportunities for them to do so profitably and to benefit, were weak several years after the end of the war, not least given the institutional set-up of the cocoa-market system.

Eventually, things began to change. Cocoa prices on the international market were increasing rapidly (by 132 per cent between late 2005 and late 2009).[108] Prices have fluctuated since, but continued to increase, due to growing international demand for cocoa, not least in the Chinese market, and production declines in major cocoa-producing countries, such as Côte d'Ivoire, where conflict resumed in 2010.[109] In parallel, donor-funded projects were initiated to increase the capacity of smallholder cocoa farmers and help them self-organise in associations and cooperatives to strengthen their position in the cocoa market and benefit from actively participating in it. The LIFE project, funded by USDA, implemented by ACDI-VOCA and initiated is early 2008, is one such example and the perhaps most influential project in the cocoa sector.[110] A year later, several steps towards deregulation of the domestic Liberian cocoa market were decided by the President's Office, most of which began to be implemented in 2010.[111] Some of these institutional reforms have had important implications for the Liberian cocoa market, its structure and inclusiveness. These are specifically discussed in Chapters 6 and 7.

3.2   Significance of the Post-War Cocoa Market

That the cocoa market has remained important for smallholder farmers after the war, all the more so in recent years, is beyond any doubt. However, given the lack of quantitative data and reliable statistics, demonstrating the scale with certainty is difficult. It is generally agreed there are a large number of cocoa farmers in Liberia. A 2006-2007 review of the tree-crop sector holds that it is 'likely that a greater number of Liberians participate, formally and informally, in the entire tree crop sector, providing income

---

105 Ministry of Commerce and Industry (2009: 128)
106 English (2008: 5)
107 Republic of Liberia (2007a, Volume 2.1: 114)
108 See Table 5.1 below.
109 Personal communication with key informant March 2013
110 ACDI/VOCA (2013) describes major activities and achievements.
111 ACDI/VOCA (2010) offers a summary.

opportunities to thousands in the rural areas of Liberia'.[112] It refers to FAO/MOA estimates from 2001 of almost 40,000 cocoa-producing households, about a quarter of an estimated total of 151,940 agricultural households in Liberia (excluding Lofa County).[113] The number of farmers engaged in cocoa marketing by mid-2012 is estimated at 30,000-40,000 in a comprehensive donor-consultancy report, but the source is not stated.[114] A key informant with insight into and an overview of the cocoa market estimates that there are about 30,000 cocoa farmers in Liberia,[115] which may be as good an estimate as any, being eventually repeated in a 2014 government publication.[116] To access the most recent official information I asked a centrally placed official at the Ministry of Agriculture, who confirmed both the approximate number and the uncertainty of specific numbers:[117]

> As to the total number of cocoa farmers, we have no idea. We have a document from 2010-11, but we have not finalised it. It is not detailed and there may be double counting of farmers, since both owners and users may refer to one and the same farm. I would prefer to count the number of farms, and am not so eager to use these figures/this report, which is not official. According to the unofficial document, a survey of cocoa sector found a total number of about 35,330 cocoa households in 2011, of which 29,007 male (headed) and 6,260 female (headed) households … And the number of cocoa farms was estimated to 38,680.

In a country with a population of some 4 million people this is a significant group, in particular as one farmer may contribute to the livelihoods of several family members. Since cocoa farming is labour intensive, it also generates employment and income beyond the farming household itself. According to the 2014 government document mentioned earlier, '[t]he cocoa sector accounts for as much as 12.6 per cent of total employment in the agricultural sector'.[118]

Whereas rubber has been and remains by far the most important export crop in Liberia, cocoa is not an insignificant export crop. Cocoa is sometimes referred to as the second most important export crop, for instance in 2004,[119] when it accounted for 3.4 per cent of Liberia's total official export earnings as shown in Table 3.1 below. The table gives official figures on total cocoa production and exports based on the annual reports of the Central Bank of Liberia. These figures are uncertain for several reasons,[120] but I have chosen to report them as a complete time series from a single source. Hence any

---

112 Republic of Liberia (2007a: 77)
113 Republic of Liberia (2007a: 77-78)
114 GRM International (2012, Annex 3: 15)
115 Key Informant 1
116 Republic of Liberia (2014: 10)
117 My notes from interview with Key Informant 4
118 Republic of Liberia (2014: 10)
119 Republic of Liberia (2007a, Volume 2.1: 77)
120 The uncertainty stems partly from the fact that several figures for the early post-war years differ from those given by other official sources, for instance, government and IMF figures reported by Ministry of Commerce and Industry (2009: 4) and Republic of Liberia (2007a, Volume 2.1: 77).

errors in the data may be systematic, wherefore the figures may reflect actual trends over time, even if the specific figures do not reflect the actual numbers.

Table 3.1: Official Cocoa Bean Production and Exports

Year	Production (metric tons)	Annual Change (%)	Exports (million USD)	Share of Total Exports (%)
2013	8.337	3.2	9.9	1.8
2012	8.082	-69.7	6.6	1.5
2011	26.692	275.0	14.3	3.9
2010	7.117	40.2	5.0	2.3
2009	5.075	54.5	3.6	2.4
2008	3.285	54.5	3.4*	1.4
2007	2.126	92.9	2.2*	1.1
2006	1.107	-49.5	0.3*	0.2
2005	2.192	95.7	0.3*	0.2
2004	1.120	0.0	3.4*	3.3
2003	1.120	-27.3	0.9*	0.8

Source: Central Bank of Liberia (2003, 2006, 2007, 2009, 2011 and 2013)
Notes: Some figures are reported as provisional or revised, not indicated here.
* Cocoa and coffee together

Table 3.1 suggests that official Liberian cocoa exports have increased during the post-war period from 0.9 to 9.9 million USD. This trend has been consistent since 2006 – except 2011, a special case – and particularly after 2009. According to these data, the value of cocoa exports has increased eleven-fold between 2003 and 2013, but part of the increase reflects price increases in the international market. I only have official statistics on volumes of cocoa exported over the last three years provided by the LMPC – 20,242 metric tons in 2011, 7,531 in 2012, and 9,838 metric tons in 2013[121] – and cannot confirm a corresponding ten-year increase in terms of cocoa volume.

Official export figures are reportedly based on data from LPMC (on export clearance and stamps on cocoa bags), the customs service and the Ministry of Commerce and Industry (MoCI) (on export permits), but all cleared or permitted cocoa may not be exported.[122] Hence, actual exports may be lower. However, according to a key informant, people tend to under-report exports and, therefore, MoCI export data are not accurate.[123] Thus, actual exports may be higher. On average, however, there is reason to expect official data to under-state actual cocoa exports, because of the prevalence of informal exports, in particular to neighbouring countries in border areas, which may at times be substantial. Informal exports are by their very nature difficult to quantify.

---

121 LPMC (2012a, 2013a and 2014)
122 Key Informant 4
123 Key Informant 2

A key informant estimates informal exports of Liberian cocoa through Guinea and Sierra Leone at 7,000-8,000 metric tons per year.[124] A senior official at the Ministry of Agriculture estimates annual cocoa exports in 2012 and 2013 at 19,000-20,000 metric tons,[125] which would suggest that some 40 per cent of total exports (37-42 per cent) are informally exported. The official further notes that not all cocoa exported from Liberia is produced in the country, but some of it is informally imported from neighbouring countries across the porous borders and then re-exported.[126] The large amount of cocoa exported in 2011, and its dramatic increase in volume terms (cf. Table 3.1 above), is explained by several interviewees as reflecting the resumed conflict in Côte d'Ivoire, as a result of which large amounts of Ivorian cocoa were channelled to Liberia as informal imports – or even stolen from Ivoirians, according to some[127] – eventually to be re-exported as Liberian cocoa.[128]

Although some cocoa exported from Liberia is re-exported imports, Table 3.1 also suggests that production of Liberian cocoa has increased in the post-war period. The official figures show an increase from some 3 to 8 metric tons between 2008 and 2013, with an extreme leap to 26 metric tons in 2011. This growth is claimed to reflect 'the continuous rise in the rehabilitation of smallholder farms'.[129] However, the record production of 2011 at least partly reflects informal cocoa imports from Côte d'Ivoire, key informants suggest.[130] Again, data on the amounts of cocoa produced in Liberia are uncertain and perceptions about recent developments in cocoa production differ, as these contrasting quotations by two key interviewees reveal:

> Total production – contrary to what is often believed – has not increased much or at all during the last 6 years, because much cocoa has been stolen from plantations in Ivory Coast during the war there ... Perhaps some 25,000 tonnes in total over the years. So the recorded increases in exports have not been matched by increases in production, but reflected informal imports from Ivory Coast ... Or, only this year production may increase a little, but exports are not expected to, since informal imports from Ivory Coast are declining.[131]

> LPMC often contends that there is little cocoa produced in Liberia itself, and most exported from Liberia is actually from Côte d'Ivoire. However, this does not square with the facts. There was quite a bit of poor quality Ivoirian cocoa coming across the border into Liberia during the 2011-12 season because of the civil war and blocking of cocoa exports in Côte d'Ivoire at that time, but before and since

---

124 Key Informant 1; A similar figure (7,000 metric tons) is reported from the Liberia Cocoa Certification Workshop in 2012, but the source of the figure remains unknown (ACDI/VOCA 2012b: 2).
125 Key Informant 4
126 Key Informant 4
127 Key Informant 2
128 Key Informants 1 and 2
129 Central Bank of Liberia (2011: 14)
130 Key Informants 1 and 2
131 My notes from Key Informant 2

higher transaction costs in Liberia and differences in the type and quality of cocoa (i.e., exporters indicate that the Ivoirian cocoa that came through Liberia is of inferior quality to that procured from Liberian coops/associations and they can readily tell the difference) illustrate that most cocoa exported from Monrovia is indeed cocoa produced within the borders of Liberia.[132]

Developments in cocoa production remain uncertain and contested, and for this reason it is difficult to estimate its contribution to total output and economic growth in Liberia. That it plays a role in the inclusiveness of economic growth is suggested, but its quantitative contribution remains uncertain. The share of cocoa and coffee together in GDP was estimated at around 1 per cent before the war (1987-1989), even less (0 per cent or not measurable) in the immediate post-war period (2003-2005),[133] while cocoa alone contributed 0.3 per cent of real GDP in 2006 and 2007, but was not measurable in 2008.[134] Later estimates are not available.

In spite of its domestic significance, Liberian cocoa accounts for but a fraction of the international market. Côte d'Ivoire and Ghana are the two major cocoa-producing countries in the world, and West Africa accounted for 60 per cent of the world's 5 million tonnes of cocoa bean production in the 2011/12 crop year.[135] Liberia's estimated cocoa production, as set out in Table 3.1 above or even according to a somewhat higher FAO estimate, amounts to less than 1 per cent of world production.[136]

3.3 The Liberian Cocoa Value Chain

Before I explore developments in the Liberian cocoa market in terms of its structure, inclusiveness and institutions, let me briefly explain my aim. It is not to study the entire cocoa-market system, but the core cocoa value chain, including market actors at different levels, their major roles in the chain, and the relationships and interactions between them. One can distinguish four major levels of market actors in the Liberian cocoa value chain: input providers, producers, traders and exporters. Between each of these actors transactions take place, hence each transaction node is a sub-market in itself and will be discussed. In addition, the value chain extends beyond Liberia's borders into neighbouring countries and the international market, but this aspect is only marginally considered here. Liberian cocoa is only exported as basically processed – fermented and dried – cocoa beans. No further processing takes place in Liberia.

The main *producers* of cocoa in Liberia are smallholder farmers, who often manage a farm of only one or a few hectares. Cocoa is also produced by larger farmers and the recently established Liberia Cocoa Corporation (LCC) private plantation in Quardo

---

132 My notes from Key Informant 1
133 Republic of Liberia (2007a: 9), based on WB, UNDP and IMF sources
134 Central Bank of Liberia (2008: 31)
135 According to FAOSTAT, the world production in 2012 was 5,003,211 tons, including West African production of 2,986,948 tonnes (Grow, 2015: 7).
136 FAO estimates Liberia's cocoa production to 12 000 tonnes in 2012 (Grow 2015: 9-10).

Gboni District in Lofa County. As mentioned, there are informal imports into Liberia of cocoa produced in neighbouring countries, notably Côte d'Ivoire. In addition to growing and harvesting cocoa, some smallholder farmers process the cocoa by fermenting and drying it to increase its quality, but this practice was not commonly pursued in the early post-war years. Smallholder farmers may access inputs, notably cocoa seeds/seedlings – even fertiliser and pesticides, insecticides and fungicides – from *input providers*. As will be explained, markets for these inputs have largely been lacking in post-war Liberia, while important changes have taken place in recent years. Farmers may also produce their own seedlings from cocoa seeds derived from their existing trees.

Buyers of cocoa from smallholder farmers are of various kinds, and exploring changes among these *domestic cocoa traders* in Liberia forms an important part of this analysis. My impression is that before major changes began in the post-war period, farmers used to sell their cocoa to private buying agents operating in the counties. Buying agents – often referred to as middle buyers – may be officially licensed or operate informally, be independent or work for large buyers/exporters. The agents collect the cocoa and may transport it to Monrovia, but this may also be done by larger buying companies. Whereas before the war, there were farmers' cooperatives which also served as cocoa traders, in the early post-war years many cooperatives appear to have remained dormant in the cocoa trade. Buying agents sell cocoa to *exporters*, either larger private buyers-cum-exporters selling the cocoa into the international market, or to smaller buyers from neighbouring countries, notably Guinea or Sierra Leone, who carry the cocoa across the borders. Buying agents and smallholder farmers may also export directly and informally by taking their cocoa across the borders themselves. Cocoa processing, if not done by smallholders, can be done by any of the domestic traders, if at all. As will be explained, there have been major changes in the role and structure of domestic traders and buyers-cum-exporters in recent years.

Apart from farmers' organisations such as associations and cooperatives, which are collectively owned, most market actors are private enterprises or entrepreneurs, although smallholder farmers may not see themselves as businesspeople, and may mix their business and private household finances. In the past, LPMC directly served as a state-owned market actor. Although not a general characteristic of the post-war period, public actors and several donor-funded projects implemented through NGOs may perform certain market functions and thus intervene directly in the cocoa market. They are more likely, however, to have influenced the market by performing regulatory, policy and/or supporting functions. In these circumstances, they are regarded as part of the broader market system in which the cocoa value chain is embedded.

This brief review of the Liberian cocoa market suggests that incentives and opportunities for smallholder farmers to benefit from cocoa-market participation were meagre when Liberia was coming out of war, despite the importance of the cocoa market as a source of income for many Liberian smallholder farmers. It also shows growing official exports and production in the post-war period, particularly in recent years, although data are admittedly uncertain, and indicates that several changes have been taking place in terms of government measures, donor projects and new market actors. These changes are examined below, as well as their implications for the inclusiveness of the market and underlying institutional change.

The number of cocoa buyers has increased and there are strong indications that this has led to increased competition for cocoa produced by small-holder farmers.

4   Changing Market Structure and Market Power

The initial task of this research is to examine and characterise major changes in the market structure of the core Liberian cocoa value chain that may have implications for market inclusiveness. I do so by studying change in the roles of and relationships among central market actors, with a particular focus on market power from the perspective of smallholder farmers. Analysis of the data collected reveals three major emerging patterns in market structure and market power. They are discussed in the three ensuing sections. The first section reviews the number of cocoa buyers and competition among them at national and local level. Section 4.2 examines the entry of a new kind of buyer and their implications for the structure of the cocoa market, for competition and for market power. The third section considers the re-entry of cooperatives as market actors and the role they play in structural change. Section 4.4 summarises the findings, and draws conclusions about what they mean for the market position and bargaining power of smallholder farmers.

4.1   More Cocoa Buyers and Increased Competition

First, the number of cocoa buyers has increased – both middlemen and large buyers at national and local level – and there are strong indications that this has led to increased competition among buyers for cocoa produced by smallholder farmers. This section examines this emerging trend and the supporting data by focusing on cocoa buyers and their market power at different levels of the value chain. The first sub-section examines how the number of cocoa buyers and the competition between them has changed at the national level, including among cocoa exporters, who are also large domestic buyers of cocoa. It looks at official figures on cocoa exporters and calculates their market shares and market-concentration ratios. In particular, it relies on interviews with market actors and external observers. Sub-Section 4.1.2 seeks to establish changes to the number of buyers and to competition at the local level in the districts and counties studied. The analysis relies heavily on interviews with market actors at different levels in the cocoa value chain and key informants, and includes comparisons with data on earlier post-war conditions.

4.1.1   Buyers and Competition at National Level

Let us first consider the cocoa exporters, some of whom are leading firms in the Liberian cocoa value chain, and largely influence conditions within it. One major change that has taken place is the increase in the number of companies buying cocoa in Liberia and exporting it to the international market through Monrovia Freeport. Public time-series data are not available, but Table 4.1 below seek to establish the number of officially recognised exporters by drawing on several sources.

Table 4.1: Number of Officially Recognised Liberian Cocoa Exporters 2005-2014

Cocoa-Season/Year	Number of Liberian Cocoa Exporters
2013/2014	28[1]
2012/2013	21[2]
2011/2012	19[3]
2010/2011	
2009/2010	
2009	A few
2008/2009	
2007/2008	3[4]
2006/2007	1[4] or 5[5]
2005/2006	
2005	5

Sources and Notes: 2011/12-2013/14: LPMC (2011; 2012c; 2013d): [1] 'Registered' exporters by July 2013; [2] 'Declared local' exporters; [3] 'Local' exporters. 2009: GRM International (2010: 19). 2006/07-2007/08: [4] English (2008: 70-71, 77) referring to Gockowski and Wilcox (2008); [5] Wilcox (2007: 114). 2005: English (2008: 32).

These national-level exporters obviously also buy cocoa in Liberia, and hence are buyers-cum-exporters – both terms are used interchangeably below. Table 1 shows that officially recognised buyers-cum-exporters have increased considerably in number, from a handful between 2005 and 2009 to 20 or more in the last few years. A marked shift appears to have taken place between 2009 and 2011, when a large number of exporters apparently entered the market. This increase suggests that in the same period, exporters experienced growing competition in buying and exporting cocoa. However, not all registered exporters actually export cocoa.[137] For example, whereas there were on average 20 registered cocoa exporters in 2012, only 11 of these actually exported cocoa through Monrovia that year, as revealed by Table 4.2 below (Column 1). This still represents a substantial increase in the number of exporters from earlier post-war years, with implications for competition.

However, the extent to which more buyers-cum-exporters actually increase competition in the market is also related to their relative strength in terms of market share and position. Table 4.2, which also draws on data from various sources, shows market shares – by volume of cocoa exported – and concentration ratios among Liberian cocoa exporters in the post-war period. Column 1 shows that the number of firms actually exporting cocoa in the last few years was roughly half of those officially registered as exporters. In particular, it shows in several ways that a limited number of firms have dominated the cocoa export market throughout most of the post-war period, and hence that market concentration has been considerable, albeit with certain variations and a marked recent change. The market share of the largest exporter has generally ranged between 61 and 90 per cent, although with a clear decline in more recent post-

---

137 Key Informant 6 notes that some licensed cocoa buyers-cum-exporters are inactive.

war years, and a sharp decline of 39 per cent in 2013 (Column 2). When the limited number of market actors during the earlier period is taken into account, the degree of market concentration would seem to have declined between the two periods, with a possible downward shift around 2010, and a sharp decline in 2013.

Table 4.2: Market Shares and Concentration among Liberian Cocoa Exporters

Cocoa Season /Year	(1) # Firms Exporting	(2) Export Share of Largest	(3) # Firms >10% Export Share	(4) Export Share of 3 Largest	(5) Conentration Ratio CR$_4$[6]	(6) Concentration Ratio HHI[7]
2013[1]*	11	39%	4	73%	83%	0.24
2012[1]	11	62%	3	91%	94%	0.43
2011/2012[2]		75%				
2011[1]	14	61%	2	84%	89%	0.40
2010/2011[2]		67%				
2009/2010						
2009[3]		88%				
2008						
– 2007[4]		80%				
2003-2005[5]		90%				

Sources and Notes: [1] LPMC (2014, 2013a and 2012a), shares of volume (tons) exported; [2] Individual Interviewee 1, estimated share of volume (tons) exported; [3] GRM International (2010: 119); [4] Ministry of Commerce and Industry (2009: 46); [5] Key Informant 6; [6] The Concentration Ratio Index, CR$_4$ gives the market share of the four largest exporters. (Wikipedia); [7] The Herfindahl-Hirschman Index, HHI, calculated as the sum of squares of market shares of all market actors, ranges between 0.1 and 1.0 (Wikipedia); * The 2013 market shares estimated by large exporters themselves are, in some instances (Individual Interviewees 1 and 36) substantially lower than those of the LPMC reported here, but not verified by documented data, which is why they are disregarded here.

The more detailed data available for the last three years on all registered cocoa exporters and their official cocoa exports enable us to calculate concentration ratios, and thus implicitly market power, in the export market for Liberian cocoa. The sharp decline in market share of the largest exporter in 2013 is also evident in the market share of the three largest exporters, which declined from 84 to 73 per cent between 2011 and 2013 (Column 4). A more common measure of market concentration is the Concentration Ratio Index (CR$_4$), which measures the market share of the four largest exporters. This also dropped, from 89 to 83 per cent (Column 5). A CR$_4$ above 80 per cent shows high concentrations in the market, and suggests oligopoly power among the largest exporters, although a decline approaching medium concentration levels (below 80 per cent) is observed in 2013.[138]

---

138 On degrees of concentration according to the CR$_4$, see e.g., Wikipedia.

At the same time, the number of exporters accounting for 10 per cent or more of the total exports grew from two to four (Column 3). This may not seem to be much of a change, but its implications are important. What matters for competition is not necessarily the number of market actors, but how market power is distributed among them. A measure of market concentration that takes this into account, and better represents actual market power, is the Herfindahl-Hirschman Index (HHI). Column 6 in Table 4.2 shows that the concentration ratio in the cocoa export market remained very high in 2011 and 2012, with an HHI of 0.40-0.43, where anything above 0.25 reflects high concentration of dominant players in the market.[139]. In 2013, however, the HHI dropped sharply (indeed almost halved) to 0.24, to a level of moderate concentration. These data strongly suggest that during the last three years there has been a shift from high market concentration, dominance by a limited number of firms with strong market power, and hence limited competition in the export market, towards more moderate levels of concentration with higher levels of competition. A qualification is required, however. If Liberia Marketing International (LMI), the largest exporter, and LAADCO, a smaller exporter but a large domestic buyer that used to export through its mother company LMI, are counted as one exporter, the figures for 2013 in Table 4.2 change. Then there are 10 exporters; LMI and LAADCO have a combined 45 per cent market share; the share of the three largest becomes 79 per cent; of the four largest (CR_4) 89 per cent; and the HHI concentration ratio becomes 0.29 in 2013. This is still a high rate, suggesting certain market domination, but considerably lower than in the two preceding years. Hence, the dominant cocoa exporter is definitely facing competition from other exporters, which are also claiming large market shares, and its position is not as dominant as it used to be.

The changes proposed by the data presented here – that competition increased among Liberian cocoa exporters between 2009 and 2011, from 'a near perfect monopsony',[140] but that considerable market power remained until 2013 – are supported by large market actors interviewed, including buyers-cum-exporters,[141] and key national-level informants in the public sector and among NGOs.[142] One informant reported that as competition grew, the dominant exporter in the early post-war years eventually disappeared from the market, as it could not compete with the new entrants.[143] Another had found the cocoa market 'seriously distorted' before 2008, dominated up to 60 per cent by one exporter during the last few years, but possibly less so in 2013 due to new entrants.[144] According to the staff of one major exporter, the degree of competition in the Liberian market is definitely higher than in the past, with more buyers competing for the cocoa produced, and the change has been marked since 2009-2010.[145]

---

139 On degrees of concentration according to the HHI, see e.g., Wikipedia.
140 GRM International (2010), Annex 16, p. 119
141 Individual Interviewees 1, 2, 3, 35 and 36
142 Key Informants 1, 2, 3, 4 and 6
143 Key Informant 6
144 Key Informant 4
145 Individual Interviewee 1

My observations also suggest that the export market is volatile, in the sense that some exporters remain the same over the years, while others drop out of the market and new ones enter. In 2013, for example, four entirely new exporters (at least by the name, and in addition to LAADCO), entered the market, while five old ones from 2012 disappeared.[146] One possible reason some new market entrants don't remain in business is that they adopt a short-term perspective, hoping to make fast profit but not willing or able to make longer-term investments. This is yet another indication of increased competition in the export market, as expressed by one exporter:[147]

> There were Lebanese exporters, Mandingo exporters, and there were some local exporters but they disappeared. They don't have the financial means and they are not serious, they are only in it for short-term business. Most of the exporters have disappeared. …The Lebanese do no productive investments. …There are a handful of large exporters. Some are not serious… and cannot survive. There are many competitors… The degree of competition has increased much since 3-4 years ago, and new buyers/exporters are coming all the time, but many don't survive.

The picture of the Liberian cocoa-export market is complicated by the circumstance that not only large registered concerns are involved in exporting. Certain farmers' organisations have been able to export cocoa themselves. At least six farmers' cooperatives and associations have sold cocoa directly to a buyer in the international market – a US-based cocoa-trading company, Transmar Commodity Group – and such exports are reported to have taken place at least in 2011 and 2012.[148] This means that Liberia-based exporters have in recent years faced competition for Liberian cocoa also from at least one US-based firm. The exports to Transmar appear to have somehow involved LMI and/or LAADCO,[149] but it is unclear in what way and how the exports were recorded.

Perhaps more significant are the unregistered – informal – exports of Liberian cocoa to neighbouring countries. Informal exporters may be Liberian traders, or traders from neighbouring countries who buy cocoa in Liberia and carry it across the porous national borders:[150]

> These informal exports are largely due to cross-border itinerant traders who are willing to buy cocoa wet at good prices, take it back across the border and ferment and dry it there and the easier/cheaper transportation across the border into Sierra Leone and Guinea from some high production areas in Lofa and Nimba than to Monrovia.

As shown in Sub-Section 3.2 above, informal cocoa exports may account for 40 per cent of total exports. Other interviewees acknowledge the practice or consider it to be

---

146 LPMC (2013a and 2014)
147 My notes from Individual Interviewee 36
148 ACDI/VOCA (2013); Key Informants 6, 7 and 12; Group Meetings 6 and 7
149 As suggested e.g., by Key Informants 6 and 12 and Group Interview 7, but denied by Individual Interviewee 34, who mentions another company channelling the exports.
150 Key Informant 1

'a lot'.[151] More recently, the 2014 government strategy for cocoa exports estimates that about half the cocoa produced in the country is exported to neighbouring countries, predominantly informally,[152] but it is unclear what this estimate is based on. Various estimates of national-level informal exports are too uncertain for drawing conclusions about changes in the number of informal exporters and competition among them. The total number of exporters is larger and the competition for Liberian cocoa for export is higher than reflected by figures on officially recognised exporters.

The lack of data makes it impossible to establish whether any particular change over time has taken place in the number of informal exporters and competition from them at an overall national level. What is most immediately experienced by smallholder farmers is the number of buyers and competition between them at the local level, to which I now turn.

4.1.2   Buyers and Competition at Local Level

Several – perhaps most – of the large cocoa exporters are major buyers not only in Monrovia, but throughout the country where cocoa is produced. Hence the increased number of exporters-cum-buyers is reflected in increased competition among them as buyers in the domestic market. And some registered exporters that are not actually exporting may operate mainly as large buyers of cocoa, further adding to competition for cocoa within the country. This means that competition ought to have increased at the local level as well, as confirmed by a major buyer. 'The degree of competition is high. This year it is more intense. Buyers don't sit and wait in Monrovia'.[153] Many large buyers buy cocoa from independent agents or have their own agents – referred to as middle buyers – in the counties, while at least one of the majors buys mainly from co-operatives and another directly from farmers.[154] They compete for cocoa in the counties and districts with each other and with informal exporters.

That there are several – even many – buyers and there is competition for cocoa at the local level is reported by a majority of interviewees, market actors as well as external observers. Of the 38 market actors individually interviewed, all but eight spoke of several or a large number of cocoa buyers.[155] Most of the eight unable to provide information on this are farmers who have not, for various reasons, yet been very active in the cocoa market. The number of buyers and the competition appears to vary, for example between counties, as indicated by one of the large buyers, who reportedly sets the price paid for cocoa in relation to the degrees of competition in different counties.[156] My impression is that there are more buyers and there is greater competition in

---

151 Key Informant 3; Individual Interviewee 35 (quotation from my notes)
152 The document states that the majority of cocoa are thus exported, and underpins this by referring to 4,000-5,000 tons exported out of 9,000 tons produced (Republic of Liberia 2014: 10), which I interpret to represent half of the production.
153 My notes from Individual Interviewee 35
154 Individual Interviewees 1-2, 4 and 34-36
155 All but Individual Interviewees 5, 7-10, 20-21 and 24
156 Individual Interviewee 1

Lofa and Nimba, with a long tradition of producing cocoa, than in Gbarpolu, where only one or two large buyers were reported, in addition to middle buyers.[157] According to one market actor, 'There is huge competition for cocoa now in Nimba'.[158] There is competition in Gbarpolu too, where the number of buyers is reported to 'be floating around all over'.[159] According to a group of key informants with an overview of market developments in several counties, Gbarpolu, River Gee and Grand Gedeh Counties have less developed cocoa markets with fewer buyers and less competition than Lofa, Bong and Nimba.[160] The situation may also vary within counties, although further analysis is necessary to confirm this.

Change over time in terms of number of buyers and competition for cocoa is reported by many interviewees. At least 17 of the individual market actors interviewed, mostly farmers, as well as participants in at least four group interviews, including three cooperatives and one key informant group, perceive the number of buyers and/or competition for cocoa at the local level to have increased or increased a lot in recent years.[161] As reported by one market actor:[162]

> The degree of competition for cocoa from buyers in Nimba – and in Saclepea – started to grow in 2009, but has since then increased steadily every year, and there are now many buying agents and exporters.

Yet another source is a cocoa trader in Foya, Lofa County, who states that 'the degree of competition for cocoa in the market has increased very much in the last years'.[163]

However, not all interviewees were able to comment on change over time. Several farmers interviewed had just started to grow cocoa, and had either not produced cocoa and entered the market yet, or have only a short history of cocoa marketing.[164] This circumstance emerged clearly in a group interview with one of the cooperatives in Saclepea District in Nimba County, where many farmers had recently commenced or returned to cocoa farming – several after first having destroyed their cocoa trees after the war in order to plant rubber trees, only to replace them with cocoa trees[165] – a picture further supported by other interviewees.[166] In addition, some large buyers and other market actors had only recently entered the market and found it difficult to give a clear picture of change over time.[167] In addition two individual interviewees, both in Lofa, expressed the contrary view. One farmer, close to the border areas, reports that

---

157 Key Informant 14; Group Interview 9
158 Individual Interviewee 4
159 My notes from Individual Interviewee 37
160 Group Interview 3
161 Individual Interviewees 1, 4, 12-13, 17-19, 22, 25-29, 34-36 and 38; Group Interviews 3, 5-7 and 9
162 My notes from Individual Interviewee 22
163 Informal Conversations 4
164 For example Individual Interviewees 5, 7 and 24
165 Group Interview 5
166 Informal Conversation 3; Key Informant 7
167 Individual Interviewees 2-3, 23 and 35

there are many buyers – particularly from Sierra Leone and Guinea, less so from Liberia – but that there is nothing new in this, and that competition has remained more or less the same since 2006.[168] According to another farmer in an adjacent district, 'we notice no competition from buyers for our cocoa, no increase in the last few years, no change',[169] but this farmer refers to the lack of large buyers-cum-exporters while recognising the existence of several middle buyers.

That the role of informal exporters was strongest along the borders, and can be significant in certain local markets, is suggested by the magnitude of informal exports reported by my interviewees. In Lofa, which borders both Sierra Leone and Guinea, a key informant estimates the volume of informal exports to Sierra Leone to be in the range of 25-30 per cent,[170] and one farmer cooperative estimates that Guinea receives 30 per cent of the region's production.[171] A cooperative in another Lofa district estimates farmers to be side-selling about 70 per cent of their produce to Guinea and Sierra Leone, most likely in the form of informal exports,[172] and a key informant acknowledges the practice.[173] My interviews also suggest considerable flexibility and responsiveness in the cross-border trade (including exports) to variations and changes in relative costs and prices on the different sides of the borders.[174] However, my data do not reveal any particular change over time in the number of informal exporters at local level and in competition for cocoa among them.

These caveats notwithstanding, the overall impression is that the number of buyers and competition for cocoa has increased at the local levels of Liberia studied. This picture becomes even clearer when one looks deeper into the structure of the cocoa buyers (see the subsequent sub-section), but also when one compares the current situation with the past.

First, there are the buying agents or middle buyers, who used to dominate the local cocoa markets in the past. Recall from Chapter 3 the study by the Ministry of Commerce and Industry that reported traders with monopsony power at farm-gate level or in district towns.[175] The local monopsony – sole buying power – middle buyers used to have is further recognised by a senior official in the Ministry of Agriculture, another national-level public official and other key informants.[176] It is not entirely clear how these monopsonies were granted and upheld, but it was reported that regional monopsonies were granted to licensed buying agents by LPMC[177] formally – or informally by individual LPMC officials. The latter is suggested by a key informant who relates how a private buyer 'bought cocoa in the name of the LPMC after the war, up to 2008 or so',

---

168 Individual Interviewee 15
169 My notes from Individual Interviewee 33
170 Individual Interviewee 11
171 Group Interview 7
172 Individual Interviewee 25
173 Key Informants 13
174 Key Informants 3 and 11
175 Ministry of Commerce and Industry (2009: 128)
176 Key Informants 3 and 6; Group Interview 3
177 Key Informant 6

and that 'all LPMC staff worked for him'.[178] This regional and/or local buying-agent monopsony now seems to be largely broken, as suggested above, and further suggested by the interviewees. The regional monopsonies for licensed buying agents are said to have been entirely abolished in 2010,[179] which is reported to have increased competition.[180] Hence, as key informants note, 'mid-level buyers face competition' in several counties now,[181] and 'the reality is that there are many middle buyers'.[182] Indeed, most market actors individually interviewed, 25 of 38, informed us of the prevalence of buying agents/middle buyers. Sixteen market actors now encounter several middle buyers in the cocoa market, [183] and nine report many such buyers.[184] Nine market actors explicitly noted a growing number of middle buyers, and some remarked on correspondingly growing competition.[185]

Despite the overall picture of more middle buyers and growing competition among them at the local level, there may still be some buying agents enjoying a local monopsony and thus market power. This was revealed by two key informants,[186] and implies that even if competitive pressure may have increased overall and in most locations, this may be a process that develops gradually and with variations, just as there may be pockets of market power remaining.

4.2   New Kind of Buyers and Integrated Value Chains

A second major pattern observed in the market structure of the cocoa value chain is *the emergence of new kinds of buyer-cum-exporter.* Large companies are investing in lasting relationships with cocoa farmers and cooperatives. This has important implications for the nature of the cocoa market, which is *changing from a pure spot market towards integrated value chains.* The following section examines the entry of these new buyers, how they differ from others, what they mean for relationships and interactions between market actors, the structure of the cocoa market as well as competition and market power within it. The first sub-section describes the cocoa-market structure of the past and the interaction between smallholder farmers and buyers. It then presents the new kinds of buyer and shows how they account for an important part of the increased competition in the Liberian cocoa market. Sub-Section 4.2.2 describes the business models of the new buyers and explains how they give rise to integrated value chains, interactions within them, and help to change the structure of the cocoa market. Sub-Section 4.2.3 analyses what this means for competition and market power in the

---

178 My notes from Key Informant 2
179 Key Informant 6
180 Personal communication with key informant, 12 March 2013, Monrovia
181 My notes from Group Interview 3
182 My notes from Key Informant 13
183 Individual Interviewees 1-4, 6, 11, 13-14, 16, 23, 25, 30-31, 33 and 36-37
184 Individual Interviewees 12, 15, 17, 19, 22, 28, 34-35 and 38
185 Individual Interviewees 12-13, 16-17, 19, 22, 25, 28 and 38
186 Key Informants 2 and 3

cocoa market, which changes and takes partly new forms. The integrated value chains supply inputs and other services, which has implications also for input markets, the development of which is briefly reviewed in a subsequent sub-section.

4.2.1   From Spot Market to Lasting Relationships

Before the new buyers emerged, the domestic cocoa market in post-war Liberia was largely a spot market, the nature of which is first described in this section. In the spot market, the commonest practice of buying agents/middle buyers – also referred to as itinerant buyers[187] – was apparently to shop around for cocoa in villages, buy the cocoa from farmers at the farm gate, often in smaller volumes, and pay cash on the spot. Most often, each transaction is an isolated event, completed there and then. Middle buyers are reported not to care about quality and quality grading of cocoa, but are known to mix different grades of cocoa, and hence to pay farmers a low price,[188] since the mixed cocoa counts as low quality. Some middle buyers are even reported to buy wet cocoa from farmers[189] – which is entirely unprocessed and thus fetches a very low price – and then to process it themselves, in order to capture the added value.[190] Middle buyers and large buyers-cum-exporters are believed to almost exclusively engage in trading cocoa[191] – buying, selling and/or exporting – even if some may ferment and dry it to get better paid. This traditional mode of trading cocoa reflects a short-term perspective, whereby buyers at different levels seek to realise profits within the current crop season.[192] The transaction and buyer-farmer interaction is mostly instantaneous, although the relationship may be longer, reflecting repeated on-the-spot transactions, due to farmer indebtedness.

Significant elements of the spot market remain,[193] particularly in the interactions between cocoa farmers and middle buyers, and possibly in the interactions between buying agents and larger buyers. The continuing importance of itinerant buyers is reflected in the large and increasing number of middle buyers reported earlier, and is illustrated by one village in Kolahun District in Lofa County, where several actors report comprehensive spot market interactions .[194] Several actors, for instance in the government, want to get rid of the middlemen, who are seen as exploiting farmers.[195] One key informant refers to 'middlemen who give them nothing and make all the pro-fit',[196] and according to a farmer, 'buying agents press the price down and pocket the

187 E.g., by Key Informant 1
188 Key Informants 1 and 6; Group Interview 5
189 Key Informants 1 and 14; Individual Interviewees 31-32, and 35
190 Key Informant 1; Individual Interviewees 35
191 Individual Interviewee 35
192 Individual Interviewee 2
193 Key Informant 3
194 Individual Interviewees 15- 16; Group Interview 7; to some extent Individual Interviewees 11 and 13-14
195 Key Informants 3 and 6
196 Key Informant 1

difference. I produce grade A but get no compensation'.[197] However, it is important to note that even if farmers are paid low prices when selling cocoa to middle buyers, they do get cash in hand, an important consideration for smallholders, particularly when they are short of cash, such as after the rainy season before the harvest begins in earnest.

A simplified structure of the cocoa spot market is represented by Figure 4.1 below, where the thick arrows reflect the one-way flow of cocoa from smallholder farmers to various buying agents, implying a counter-flow in the form of cash payment. The figure shows that buying agents may be of different kinds, and farmers may have a choice where there are several and there is competition between them, as for instance Farmer 3, or no choice, if there is only one middle buyer with monopsony power, such as Farmer 2 in the figure.

Figure 4.1: Structure of the Cocoa Spot Market for Smallholders

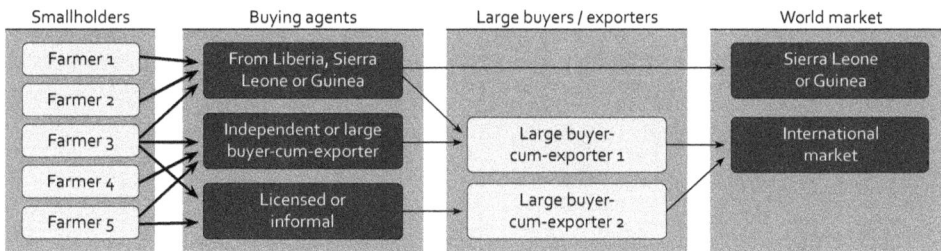

An important change in the cocoa market in recent years has been the entry of an entirely new type of large buyer-cum-exporter, who operates and buys cocoa nationally and locally in the counties and competes with the old types of buyers, but in partly new ways. In contrast to the traditional cocoa buyers, the new large companies adopt a longer-term perspective by investing in the development of lasting relationships with farmers, either directly or through farmers' organisations such as cooperatives. While a growing number of companies have entered the market as buyers and exporters, presumably in response to increasing world market prices and potential profits, the new investors act strategically, either in order to secure a supply of cocoa – in larger quantities, of higher quality and hence for greater returns – over longer periods of time, or to secure long-term demand for their products in terms in inputs for cocoa production. They all promote farmers' processing of high-quality cocoa, thus adding value to the product, and pay relatively high prices.

Two large companies in particular have established themselves in the Liberian cocoa market since a few years back and seek to build longer-term relations with farmers or cooperatives: the Liberia Agriculture and Assets Development Company (LAADCO) and Wienco. They seek to formalise and secure agreements with farmers and their organisations through formal contracts of varying lengths – from one crop season up to 30 years or more. In addition to the core cocoa transactions, contracts include va-

---

197 Individual Interviewee 15

rious combinations of exchange between the companies and the farmers/organisations, notably for different kinds of services and inputs to farmers. While their core business differs – LAADCO is primarily a cocoa buyer-cum-exporter and Wienco is primarily an input importer-cum-supplier – both see business opportunities in complementing their core functions with supporting functions that help develop smallholder cocoa production and marketing (cf., Figure 2.1 above.). Both offer services (e.g., extension, training, pre-finance and supply of consumer goods) and inputs (notably seedlings and fertiliser, pesticides, etc.) to farmers and their organisations, largely on credit (which is another service) in order to increase productivity and the quality of cocoa and buy the cocoa produced at an agreed and attractive price that rewards quality. The contracts and supporting functions are detailed in Section 5.2.

The new companies reflect a fundamental break with the past in several respects, not least because they represent commercial investments in the productive capacity of the farmers – a rare means to add value, generate new resources and move beyond the mere extraction of existing primary resources. From the perspective of the future growth potential of the Liberian cocoa market and the beneficial participation of smallholder farmers, this represents a significant qualitative change.

The establishment of these two companies as important market actors and their contribution to much of the increased competition for cocoa in the Liberian market is strongly reflected in the interviews. According to one key informant, 'Wienco and LAADCO are the two major buyers of cocoa in Liberia'.[198] LAADCO was established in 2011 as a 'pure' development company by the largest cocoa exporter LMI[199] – some actors refer to LAADCO and LMI as one and the same company, even some of its own staff.[200] It is a registered Liberian company but with foreign financial support,[201] and has established itself as a strong market actor in several counties, with various kinds of contractual agreement, including very long ones (25-30 years or so). LAADCO is reported to operate in at least four of the six cocoa producing counties: Lofa, Bong, Nimba and Gbarpolu, while its mother company LMI buys cocoa in River Gee and Grand Gedeh.[202] Whereas competition is considered by key informants to have increased among middle buyers in Bong County, for instance, the exporters are reported to be the major competitors, and 'LAADCO is the biggest one'.[203] LAADCO is reportedly the largest buyer in Lofa, and perceives its position to be strong both there and in Nimba, but less so in Bong.[204] Of the six cooperatives I visited in Lofa, Nimba and Gbarpolu, five had negotiated or were negotiating contracts with LAADCO. According to one source, LAADCO has agreements with seven farmers' associations/

---

198 My notes from Key Informant 2
199 Individual Interviewees 1 and 36
200 Individual Interviewee 4
201 Individual Interviewee 1
202 Group Meeting 3
203 My notes from Group Meeting 3
204 Key Informant 13; Individual Interviewee 1

cooperatives in Lofa.[205] These findings are supported by the LPMC figures on cocoa exports reflected in Table 4.2 above, which show that during 2011, 2012 and 2013, LMI/LAADCO was the largest cocoa buyer-cum-exporter in Liberia.[206]

Wienco, the other company, is Ghanaian and established itself in Liberia in 2011.[207] It operates in the three main cocoa counties, Lofa, Bong and Nimba, where it contracts with farmers individually and helps them organise in smaller groups.[208] At the time of the interviews, Wienco was reported to be working with 1,400 farmers; in Lofa alone it was collaborating with 38 groups, each comprising 8-12 persons.[209] I talked to five farmers who were members of Wienco farmers' groups in two villages in Kolahun District in Lofa County. According to two interviewees, Wienco is one of the large buyers competing for cocoa in Nimba and perhaps LAADCO's major competitor in the country overall.[210] According to official (LPMC) data, Wienco was the ninth largest cocoa exporter in 2012 and the seventh largest in 2013.[211]

4.2.2 Integrated Value Chains and Increased Complexity

The establishment of these companies, selling combinations of inputs and services to smallholder farmers while also buying their cocoa on the basis of contractual agreements, means that interactions between companies and farmers and their organisations are manifold, and their relationships complex. The commercial interactions integrate a number of services and products – such as credit, fertiliser and seedlings – that in principle could be sold and bought on the market, except that such markets serving smallholders have been largely lacking in Liberia up to now. This has led to the emergence of integrated value chains in the Liberian cocoa market – or perhaps more correctly, more or less integrated value chains, as they need not be fully integrated. In Liberia, two major business models for lasting relationships with integrated functions – integrated value chains – have developed, forming around the two companies discussed above.

The first is the cocoa *buyer-cum-exporter driven – output-driven* – integrated value chain of LAADCO, illustrated by Figure 4.2 below. The figure shows that LAADCO buys cocoa from farmers' cooperatives or associations, which in turn buy from member farmers, or independent farmers who choose to sell to them. Cooperatives and associations buy directly from the farmers or through their own designated buying agents in surrounding villages. LAADCO establishes contractual agreements with cooperatives and associations, and hence only deals with farmers indirectly. It provides inputs and services to cooperatives and associations, which in turn forward them

---

205 Individual Interviewees 34
206 LPMC (2014, 2013a and 2012a)
207 Individual Interviewees 2 and 35
208 Individual Interviewee 2
209 Individual Interviewees 2 and 35
210 Individual Interviewees 4 and 36
211 LPMC (2014 and 2013a) If LAADCO and LMI are counted as one and the same exporter, Wienco was the 6th largest cocoa exporter in 2013.

to member farmers, as represented by the thick dotted arrows from the right to the left in the figure.

Figure 4.2: Output-Driven Integrated Cocoa Value Chain of LAADCO

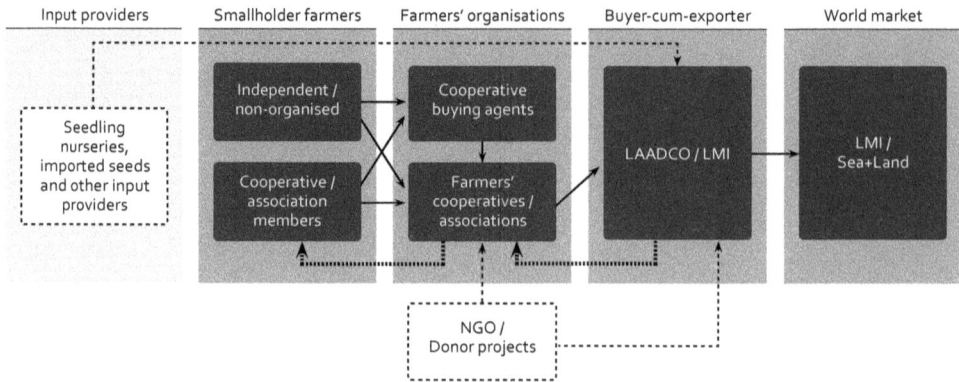

The prices LAADCO pays, the inputs and services it offers, the conditions and length of contracts vary, depending on specific circumstances.[212] Prices paid for cocoa are relatively high. This company operates in the cocoa market in two different positions, firstly, as private market actor on purely commercial grounds in several counties, and secondly, as a buyer-cum-implementer of part of a government-owned and IFAD-funded programme promoting smallholder farming and marketing in Lofa, the STCRSP. It thus has different positions in different local markets, but also dual positions in one and the same market. When LAADCO plays a role in the STCRSP, contracts tend to be shorter (1-5 years) compared to 6 month-25 year contracts – or more – when it plays a purely commercial role. The longest contracts are reported to be in Nimba. The inputs and services provided are diverse and vary to some extent, but include cocoa seedlings, transportation equipment for cocoa collection, pre-finance to cooperatives for purchase of cocoa from farmers and in-kind loans for rice, cement and other basic consumer goods. Contracts within the STCRSP programme appear to be standardised, whereas the purely commercial contracts are negotiated on a case by case basis. The thin dotted arrows show that LAADCO may source e.g., seeds and seedlings abroad as well as locally, and that donor-funded programmes may be involved in the interaction between LAADCO and farmers' organisations and farmers.

The second business model is that of Wienco, an *importer-cum-supplier driven – input-driven –* integrated value chain, illustrated by Figure 4.3 below. Wienco is essentially a large importer and supplier of fertiliser and chemicals such as pesticides, fungicides and herbicides for different agricultural crops, which it sells to various agricultural companies in Liberia.[213] The company's approach to selling such inputs

---

212 This paragraph is based on the following sources: Individual Interviewees 1, 4 and 34; Key
    Informant 13; Group Interview 3.
213 This paragraph is based on the following sources: Individual Interviewees 2 and 35; Key Infor-

to smallholder cocoa farmers draws on its experience in Ghana. It sells fertiliser and chemicals on credit to farmers to help increase cocoa tree and farm productivity, and then offers to buy the cocoa at a good and stable price. It buys only high quality cocoa. However, as indicated by the thin arrow in the figure, farmers are free to sell their cocoa to any buyer. The debt for the chemicals is repaid by deduction when farmers deliver and sell their cocoa. Wienco's strategy is to offer a secure market with an attractive price for cocoa, thus creating smallholder demand for the inputs. Wienco interacts and con-tracts directly with individual farmers – its contracts are one year/seasonal. It organises and trains farmers in smaller self-help groups at village level, to facilitate their learning from each other and for joint farm labour. They prefer to form their own farmers' groups rather than to work with existing farmers' organisations, which they believe to be spoilt by the NGOs and used to getting free inputs.

Figure 4.3: Input-Driven Integrated Cocoa Value Chain of Wienco

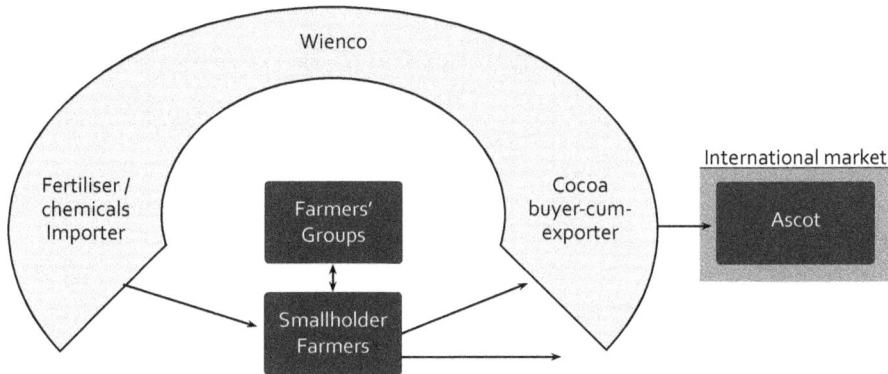

A third business model and integrated value chain may be in the making, based on *out-grower* schemes of the Liberia Cocoa Corporation (LCC).[214] LCC is a large cocoa plantation that was established in Quardo Gboni District in Lofa County in 2011, and is seeking concession status. It is in the process of expanding its cocoa farm, planning to export cocoa directly and has its own seedling nursery, where it produces improved high and quick-yielding varieties. The seedlings are used for the expansion of its own farm, and are offered for sale as part of an out-grower scheme to smallholder farmers in surrounding villages. LCC will buy the cocoa they produce, offers services and inputs on credit, which farmers can repay in cocoa once the trees start to yield. The LCC has no formal contracts yet, but will have memorandums of understanding. At the time of the interviews, the out-grower scheme was only in its second year and farmers' cocoa production had not yet begun.

The development of integrated value chains since 2011 has had important implica-tions for the characteristics and structure of the cocoa market. It is no longer a typical

---

mant 2
214 The sources of this paragraph are Individual Interviewees 3 and 23-24.

spot market – although elements of spot market remain, particularly in the interaction between smallholder farmers and middle buyers. The observation of one of the farmers interviewed pinpoints the recent developments:[215]

> When it comes to the number of buyers, before there used to be few big buyers, but many small buyers/middlemen. The number is increasing. Now... there has been a change from few large and many small. Now there are big buyers such as LAADCO, The Farmers' Union in Foya... and many other.

The structure of the Liberian cocoa market has become more diversified – and more complex – combining components of both spot market and several integrated value chains. The complexity of the overall structure of the Liberian cocoa value chain by late 2013 is illustrated in Appendix Figure 4.1, which maps the market actors at different levels, their major roles in the chain and the connections between them –without claiming to be complete, since I focus on actors and relationships of relevance to smallholder farmers.

A more stylised picture of the structure of the Liberia cocoa market is presented in Figure 4.4 below. This illustrates the different cocoa suppliers (farmers and/or co-operatives) and buyers (middle buyers and/or buyers/exporters), as well as the relative simplicity versus complexity of interactions in the different models: the spot market, the output-driven versus the input-driven integrated value chain and the out-grower scheme.

The integrated value chains are part of the cocoa market, but are not markets in themselves. Neither are they fully integrated hierarchies, such as firms. They are a kind of hybrid mechanism for coordinating buyer-seller interactions.[216] With their contracts and combinations of exchanges, they imply new relationships and interactions between farmers and buyers, with greater emphasis on ongoing partnerships, with mutual rights and obligations, which extend into the future. The very introduction of a contract, which commits the parties to trade with each other, amounts to stepping out of the market into a relational form of interaction for a period of time, during which competition is limited. Hence integrated value chains reflect new forms of *collaboration and coordination* between market actors at *different nodes* in the value chain. They also have implications for *competition* between actors within *the same node*, more particularly between different cocoa buyers. Integrated value chains have not only increased competition in the cocoa market, but competition also takes on partly new forms – and possibly market power too.

---

215 My notes from Individual Interviewee 19
216 Cf. Gabre-Madhin (2009)

Figure 4.4: The Diversified Liberian Cocoa Market – A Stylised Version

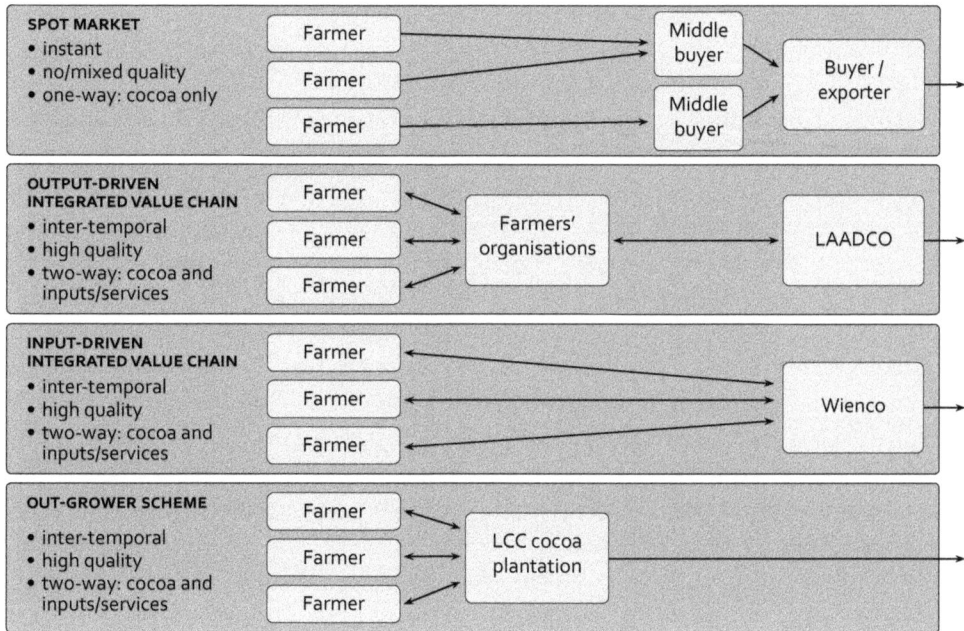

4.2.3 New Forms of Competition – and Market Power

New Forms of Competition

With not only a growing number of middle buyers and buyers-cum-exporters competing for cocoa, but also a new kind of buyer, buyers face different and partly new competitors and have to compete in partly new ways. For *middle buyers*, the competitive situation has changed compared to the past. In addition to increased competition from each other on the spot market, they now have to compete with large buyers in integrated value chains. This means that whereas some middle buyers could more or less unilaterally set the price paid to farmers, they now compete with each other largely on the basis of the price they offer farmers. What is more, they have to compete with new buyers who offer whole packages of services – and considerably higher prices. This may seem to place middle buyers in an untenable situation, but they are reported to pay prices at par with the large buyers: agents of other large buyers are reported to pay the same price as LAADCO in Nimba.[217] Besides, middle buyers have a competitive advantage. They usually pay farmers cash on the spot – which, in particular, farmers' organisations, who bulk and store farmer's cocoa until a large buyer comes to collect it, find more difficult to do. Selling to middle buyers may thus be attractive to farmers, in spite of the lower rates, particularly when farmers are in acute need of cash, as is common after the rainy season, before harvest time, when school fees often have to be paid.

---

217 Individual Interviewee 4

Farmers selling their cocoa through cooperatives to LAADCO may have to wait for payment. This competitive disadvantage explains why LAADCO offers pre-payment to cooperatives – to enable them to pay farmers cash for at least part of their harvest on delivery. Hence, the *new buyers* have to actively compete with middle buyers for small-holders' cocoa, and offering inputs and services to increase productivity and quality as well as paying higher prices is not always enough. Money to cooperatives up-front is in fact a central component of LAADCO's strategy in dealing with increased competition from other buyers. Its marketing strategy is to build a relationship with farmers through their cooperatives, to buttress their commitment to sell to the company.[218]

However, farmers' *side-selling* is reportedly prevalent and problematic for Wienco and LAADCO, as several interviewees confirm.[219] One of them noted that 'the loyalty of farmers is a challenge, particularly as there is a difference between incentives for farmers in the short versus the long run. In the long run they will benefit from sticking to us, but in the short run they may need cash'. Another reports that competition from middle buyers is so intense that farmers and cooperatives sell more to other buyers and the company has 'to counter this competition, which we do by introducing traceability and a warehouse system, with careful records where we can see who is committed, and then motivating them by compensating them – rewarding loyalty'. Yet another interviewee finds the situation frustrating. 'We make the investment and somebody else may reap the benefits – through side-selling'. Apart from reflecting competition between the spot market and integrated value chains, farmers' side selling shows that integrated value chains are more or less but not fully integrated. Contract enforcement is difficult, if not impossible, as another market actor explicitly noted.[220] Side-selling is also a problem for farmer's organisations, and can be significant, accounting for about 70 per cent of the produce, one actor suggested.[221] Side-selling also means that value chains cannot be characterised as fully captured, in the terminology of Gereffi et al. (cf. Chapter 2).[222] Buyers – lead firms – try to exert power over cooperatives and/or farmers to enforce contracts, but only partly succeed. Side-selling is thus a strong indication that new buyers face competition from middle buyers at local level.

In addition, integrated value chains – which, for simplicity, I continue to call them – compete with *each other*, at least in the counties and districts where several of them are present. That competition takes place between LMI/LAADCO, Wienco and LCC, and has sometimes been fierce, is explicitly reported by several interviewees.[223] These buyers compete with their different business models – different packages of prices, services, conditions and contracts – to have farmers and/or their organisations sign up to their specific model for a certain period.

---

218 Individual Interviewee – number to remain confidential
219 Individual Interviewees 1-2, 4, 34-36, including quotations of my notes
220 Individual Interviewee 1
221 Individual Interviewees 25 and 33
222 Gereffi et al. (2005)
223 Key Informants 1-2; Individual Interviewee 3

The implications of the emergence of integrated value chains for competition and market power in the Liberian cocoa market are complex. While there are strong indications they have contributed to increased competition, in partly new forms, there are also signs that new forms of market power may be emerging.

New Forms of Market Power

While farmers' side selling shows that the new buyers face competition from middle buyers during the contract period, the fact that there is a contractual agreement somehow constrains side selling. Once farmers and their organisations have signed a contract, they are committed to a certain supplier for as long as the contract runs. With their unique combinations of services and transaction, different integrated value chains constitute their own network of relational exchange, where competition is at least partly limited and buyers have at least certain market power. This is implicitly acknowledged by an interviewee from one of the two large companies when asked about the degree of competition: 'it is difficult to say... we have our own suppliers'.[224]

After contract completion, or before new or renewed contractual agreement, competition from other integrated value chains may again be stronger. However, if cocoa suppliers have limited alternatives when seeking a long-term contractual partner, competition between integrated value chains is limited and buyers may enjoy certain market power. Indeed, in spite of increased and new forms of competition, there are also signs that new forms of local market power may be emerging, related in part to the emergence of integrated value chains.

First, not all three integrated value chains operate in all counties, thereby limiting the competition between them correspondingly. At the time of my interviews, LAADCO had a presence in all six cocoa counties, except River Gee and Grand Gedeh, where its mother company LMI was buying cocoa, possibly in collaboration and on similar conditions; Wienco was engaged in Lofa, Bong and Nimba, and LCC in Lofa.[225] All of them are present in Lofa, suggesting that this is where competition among them is strongest, but on the other hand, not all are present in all districts of Lofa.

As already shown, LMI retains a strong position in the export market, and there are indications its development company LAADCO may be gaining a similar position in parts of the domestic market. That LAADCO is a large, even the largest, buyer in some counties was reported by several interviewees, but this does not necessarily imply local monopsony. I have shown that LAADCO faces competition from middle buyers and some other large ones in certain local markets, but in some localities LAADCO seems to be the only realistic alternative, if farmers' and their organisations want access to services and inputs, good prices for high quality cocoa and – in particular – prefinance for cocoa purchases. In fact, three of the farmers' organisations I was in contact with said they have no alternative large buyers.[226] One such organisation reported that

224 Individual Interviewee, to remain anonymous
225 Individual Interviewees 2 and 3, Group Meeting 3
226 Group Interviews 7 and 9; Individual Interviewee 25

there were other buyers-cum-exporters around, but in reality they were no alternative because the organisation was indebted to LAADCO. 'To be frank: we have no alternative exporter to challenge them… The reason is the lack of funds… which makes us dependent'.[227] The lack of other buyers offering similar credit services gives LAADCO a competitive advantage and gives them certain local market power. A possible reason for the limited competition is that development of the domestic market has only recently been initiated and other large buyers have yet to establish themselves in all counties, particularly the remote ones.

Secondly, large buyers-cum-exporters of cocoa are also claimed to exercise market power and try to establish a monopsonistic buying position in the market. LAADCO has been accused of wanting to be 'the only player in the market, the dominant monopolist', not only by other market actors, but also by external observers.[228] This is to some extent acknowledged by one LAADCO interviewee, who nonetheless argues that 'we are not really controlling the market yet'.[229]

Third, an important reason LAADCO may have certain local market power is that it has been granted explicit monopsonistic power in certain localities by the government of Liberia and IFAD. As an implementer of the STCRSP programme in three of seven districts in Lofa, collaborating with one farmers' organisation in each district, it has the exclusive right to buy all the cocoa produced and sold by the three farmers' organisations who participate in the programme for five years, in return for the services and funding it contributes to the programme. Moreover, it reportedly provides prefinance, inputs and services to all seven farmers' organisations and actually buys cocoa from all of them.[230] Beyond doubt, this is preferential treatment for LAADCO at the expense of other actual or potential buyers, which distorts and limits competition and grants market power. Moreover, key informants argue that LAADCO was unfairly granted the contract to co-implement the STCRSP by the Ministry of Agriculture, as there was no bidding, the award process was not transparent and other potential bidders were refused.[231] Hence, the government and the donor may have granted local monopsony power to one private cocoa buyer in certain local markets.

What this implies for the emergence of new local market power in other parts of the domestic cocoa market remains unclear, but LAADCO has been accused of using 'its large market share and donor funding to monopolize the market and limit options for producers'.[232] What in particular have been called into question are the long-term contracts, of 25 years or more, it sometimes signs with farmers' organisations when it performs its purely commercial role, and the allegedly poor terms of these contracts.[233] If contracts are long-term and binding, the temporal market power of buyers may be

227 My notes from Group Interview 7
228 Individual Interviewee 3; Key Informant 1
229 My notes from Individual Interviewee – number to remain confidential
230 Individual Interviewee 1; Key Informant 13
231 Key Informants 1-2, key informant interview March 2013
232 Key Informant 1
233 Key Informants 1-2

stronger than if contracts are short-term. But if contracts cannot be effectively en-forced due to farmers' side-selling, LAADCO's market buying power is diluted. And, as will be shown in Section 5.1 below, LAADCO is reported to pay the highest price for cocoa, compared to Wienco, middle buyers and cooperatives. Whether long-term contracts are beneficial or not to smallholder farmers depends on their content and conditions, and it is beyond the scope of this research to scrutinise their detailed ap-plication in practice.

I am unable to draw any conclusions about LAADCO's ability to exercise monop-sony power through its long-term contracts on the basis of the data available to me. There is a risk, however, that initially beneficial conditions for farmers may be weak-ened over time if the market power of the buyer-cum-input-provider is strengthened. Hence, long-term contracts may become problematic if farmers are locked into an integrated value chain on conditions that are difficult to get out of if there is little competition between value chains and there are few marketing alternatives available to farmers, and if input markets remain under-developed or monopolistic. Under such circumstances, farmers and their organisations may become dependent on a single integrated value chain. There is a risk of such a development if competition is not maintained in the output market.

4.2.4 Moderate Change in Poorly Developed Input Markets

An additional observation of this study is that input markets for smallholder farmers remain seriously underdeveloped. Markets for inputs, notably improved seeds and seedlings, fertiliser and chemicals, and various services, notably credit, are virtually non-existent or are barely emerging. Still, certain changes have occurred in recent years. Inputs of particular importance for smallholder cocoa farmers are improved varieties of cocoa seeds and seedlings. They are the major input in the core cocoa value chain and vital to cocoa market development in Liberia in terms of increased productivity, output and returns. Fertiliser and chemicals are also an important input in one of the integrated value chains, and a potentially important input for smallholder farmer more gene-rally, for similar reasons. Credit, which is not an input, is a supporting function in the broader context of the core value chain (cf., Figure 2.1 above). As implied in the discussion above, it is a vital, perhaps decisive, supporting function for cocoa market development, in particular for smallholder farmers as discussed later. It is beyond the scope of this research to study the credit market. Other significant support functions include extension services and market information, neither of which is examined here. However, the government of Liberia notes a lack of extension system on how to use cocoa inputs.[234] Such services are, however, at least partly provided by the integrated value chains, and by cooperatives, as will be discussed later. Market information will also be touched upon in subsequent sections. Here I briefly review the development of cocoa input markets and discuss the role and impact of integrated value chains.

---

234 Republic of Liberia (2014)

Fertiliser and Chemicals

As regards fertiliser and chemicals for pest and fungus control, these have not been much used by Liberian smallholder cocoa farmers. My impression is that when Wienco established itself in 2011, it was the first and only supplier of these inputs to smallholders. There is still no market for such inputs, at least not for smallholder farmers, but they are sold by Wienco under near perfectly monopolistic conditions in the locations where it is operating, as an integrated service. In other locations or for non-integrated smallholders, there appears to be no supply of fertiliser or chemicals whatever. This means that Wienco can be expected to apply monopoly pricing, i.e., to charge prices that are higher than they would be under competitive pressure. Indeed, LCC appears to provide this kind of input to its own out-grower farmers, and to procure its inputs as part of a broader collaboration with Wienco,[235] but this does not change the Wienco monopoly. Given the old stock of Liberian cocoa trees with poor productivity and serious black pod fungus infestation, which destroys the cocoa and further reduces productivity – both confirmed by many of the individual farmers interviewed[236] – Wienco's supply of fertiliser and chemicals represents an important input for smallholder farmers. However, a market for these inputs, involving several providers any farmer can buy from, does not appear to be in the making.

Seeds and Seedlings

Several changes in the market for improved cocoa seeds and seedlings have been observed in recent years. During the war and early post-war period, seeds and other farm inputs were provided by NGOs through donor-funded projects as grant aid – 'handouts'.[237] Persistent handouts to smallholder farmers may have contributed to preventing the emergence of sustainable private-sector provision and a market for seeds and seedlings in Liberia. A *change* can be observed in the behaviour of some donor-funded NGOs, in terms of their desisting from providing handouts. NGOs have partly shifted from direct involvement as market actors themselves towards a more facilitating role aimed at the more sustainable provision of seeds and seedlings. The LIFE project in particular,[238] but possibly also the STCRSP,[239] can be considered as working in this direction. Note, however, that even if some NGOs have restricted handouts in recent years, key informants report that the practice continues and constitutes a major problem.[240] It may thus still hinder the development of a seed and seedling market. Nonetheless, some NGOs work actively to facilitate the emergence of self-sustaining private nurseries that operate on a commercial basis.[241]

Hence, the establishment of a limited number of private domestic cocoa-seedling

---

235 Individual Interviewees 3 and 23-24
236 Cf. the column on Yields/Productivity in Appendix Table 5.5.
237 GRM International (2010:12); Key Informant 1
238 ACDI/VOCA (2013)
239 STCRSP (2013)
240 Key Informant 1; Group Interview 3
241 ACDI/VOCA (2013)

nurseries is a *second change* that has taken place in recent years. Whereas domestically grown and improved cocoa seedlings do not appear to have been commercially supplied in the past, in 2012 and 2013 the LIFE project facilitated the establishment of seedling nurseries in several counties, to be managed by three private companies, in order to help create a private seedling value chain. The large private LCC plantation, established in 2011, is also producing seedlings at three large nurseries – improved varieties with quicker returns after planting and high yields.[242] Apart from being used on the plantation, they have been provided to cooperatives and farmers on credit over the last two years,[243] but probably few smallholders, other than those in the LCC out-grower scheme, can afford them, as noted by one cocoa smallholder farmer.[244] The *third change* is thus that large companies, notably LAACDO and LCC, provide seeds and/or seedlings as integrated services to farmers in their respective integrated value chains.

All these changes appear to have helped *increase the supply* of improved cocoa seeds and seedlings in recent years. One private nursery reportedly produced 300,000 seedlings in both 2012 and 2013, and LCC 400,000 seedlings in each of its three nurseries, apparently twice a year.[245] In addition to selling to individual farmers, the private nursery sells large amounts to ACDI-VOCA, which sells them to smallholder farmers through the cooperatives they work with at a subsidised price.[246] ACDI-VOCA reports that it has '[f]acilitated and ensured the replanting of up to one million seedlings on smallholder cocoa plantations' through the LIFE project.[247] Additional seedlings have been distributed by LAADCO through the STCRSP, although their quality has been questioned,[248] and through its commercial relations, as well as by other projects.[249]

Most of the improved cocoa seeds and seedlings appear to have been provided either as a) integrated services by LAADCO or LCC, or b) sold to farmers by a few private nurseries through cooperatives and NGOs. In both cases, the inputs are provided at a subsidised rate and/or on credit. Those provided by LAADCO in its commercial role are reportedly free of charge, but conditioned on farmers' past performance and compulsory sale of future cocoa to LAADCO.[250] Since farmers tend to be short of cash, LAADCO can be seen to have a comparative advantage *vis-á-vis* private nurseries, and hence certain market power in the supply of these inputs. The same applies to LCC, in its more limited area of operation. However, the LIFE project, for instance, provides a market outlet for private nurseries by facilitating their selling seedlings to farmers, and by subsidising the price paid by farmers, which gives an advantage to the nurseries

---

242 ACDI/VOCA (2013); Key Informants 1-2; Individual Interviewees 3 and 23 – referring to both the LIFE project and the LCC
243 I.e., up to late 2013 (Individual Interviewee 3)
244 Individual Interviewee 38
245 Individual Interviewees 22-23
246 Individual Interviewee 22
247 ACDI/VOCA (2013)
248 Individual Interviewee 3
249 Key Informant 1
250 Individual Interviewee, to remain anonymous

in their competition with LAADCO and LCC. (Thus an NGO like ACDI-VOCA is to a certain extent still actively involved in the seedling market by influencing prices.)

However, while there appears to be smallholder demand for improved seeds and seedlings provided by projects or as integrated services, *demand for seedlings* outside these channels is reportedly limited. One private nursery reports how difficult it is to sell improved cocoa seeds and seedlings directly to individual farmers, which may be partly due to the higher unsubsidised price, but which appears to have more to do with farmers' lack of cash and credit.[251] This means that the nursery struggles to be profitable. I suggest that *lack of access to credit* by smallholder farmers prevents effective market demand and hence the development of a market for improved seeds and seedlings – or at least retards such a process. Nonetheless, the new private nurseries may constitute the embryo of such an emerging market.[252]

It is difficult to get clear picture of this 'market'. Indeed, there is currently no integrated national market nor effective local markets for improved cocoa seeds and seedlings, although such markets may be about to develop as a result of recent changes. Emerging private nurseries could form the basis of a future domestic seed/seedling market, but in the absence of farmer credit demand may remain limited. The suppliers are few, and there is limited competition among them,[253] although one probably cannot talk of market power since there is such limited demand. In the absence of a market, improved seeds and seedlings are provided as integrated services, for which there is a demand among smallholder farmers since they are provided on credit. The providers within the integrated value chains obviously have strong market power – possibly a monopoly – in selling to farmers and cooperatives, and thus an opportunity to charge monopoly prices. However, in the absence of a functioning market there is no realistic alternative, and they perform an important function for smallholder farmers. Besides, donor-funded projects facilitate farmers' access to seedlings from a few private providers at subsidised prices, which ought to at least partly neutralise that market power. The remaining role of NGOs and donor-funded projects in subsidising prices for farmers, as well as the dual role of LAADCO as both commercial market actor and donor-project implementer, further clouds the picture.

4.3   Re-entrance of Farmers' Organisation as Market Actors

A third pattern emerging in the structure of the cocoa market, with implications for market power, is the *re-entry of farmers' organisations as market actors* in the cocoa market. This section presents the primary and secondary data that together generate this pattern and discusses what this has implied for the structure of the cocoa market and market power within it. The first sub-section reviews the revitalisation of farmers' organisations – old and new ones – and cocoa farmers' increased engage-

---

251 Individual Interviewee 22
252 ACDI/VOCA (n.d.); Key Informant 1
253 According to one seedling provider, there is no competition at all (Individual Interviewee 22).

ment with them, while the second sub-section reports on the organisations' increased market participation through bulking and selling cocoa. These new actors contribute to structural change in the cocoa market and, as discussed in Sub-Section 4.3.3, to changing power relationships among market actors, in particular between buyers and sellers. I explain how farmers' organisations help to countervail some of buyers' market power, strengthening the position of smallholder farmers, and present supporting data. Sub-Section 4.3.4 argues, however, that farmers' benefit depends to the extent that their organisations act in their interest, and shows that this may not always be the case.

4.3.1   Revitalisation of Cooperatives and Farmers Increasingly Organised

While cooperatives used to play an important role in the pre-war cocoa market, they dwindled during the war,[254] many were abandoned,[255] and many that remained were dormant long after the war. A major change in recent years is the revitalisation of farmers' groups, associations and cooperatives. Many cooperatives established in the 1980s have been restarted,[256] farmers' associations have graduated as cooperatives and new cooperatives have been established.[257] In 2001, the total number of registered cooperatives was 224, of which 116 were dormant and 108 active.[258] By late 2013 there were 313 (or 319 – figures differ) reactivated and new cooperatives registered by the Cooperative Development Agency, while 50 more were awaiting registration,[259] an increase of 139 cooperatives.

'There is a lot of change going on in the cooperatives', according to a key informant,[260] partly as a result of the growing number of donors working with and supporting farmers' organisations. According to one interviewee, cocoa farms were better established before the war than farms for vegetables and oil palm, which 'means that it is easier now to organise cocoa farmers' than farmers of these other cash crops.[261] So far, LIFE is perhaps the most influential project promoting smallholder cocoa production and marketing. Operating in six counties, training and capacity building of farmers' organisations is a central priority.[262] From February 2008 to July 2013, the project

---

254 Key Informant 8

255 Key Informant 13

256 Wilcox (n.d.a)

257 Cooperatives are formally registered and certified by the public Cooperative Development Agency (CDA), are legal entities, and required to apply certain measures and rules, such as a democratic organisational structure. Associations are a looser form of farmers' organisation, free to set their own rules, and sometimes form the pre-stage of becoming a cooperative. (Key Informants 7 and 8)

258 This is a reported decline from 408 during the 1980-1990 period, of which 325 in agriculture. (Key Informants 7 and 8) It remains unclear exactly what dormant, inactive and active means.

259 Key Informant Interviews 7 and 8

260 My notes from Key Informant 7

261 My notes from Informal Interviewee 2

262 LIFE is the Liberia Livelihood Improvement for Farming Enterprises Project, funded by the US Department of Agriculture (USDA) and implemented by ACDI/VOCA, still on-going in its third phase. See e.g., ACDI/VOCA (2013) for a brief overview.

reports having '[s]trengthened five pre-existing cocoa cooperatives, representing 1,070 members, in Bong and Lofa Counties', and to having '[f]acilitated the formation of 32 new farmer organizations, representing about 8,000 cocoa farmers, in Bong, Nimba[,] Lofa, Grand Gedeh, River Gee and Gbarpolu counties'.[263] Not all these groupings are formalised, but by November 2012, 25 listed cooperatives and associations linked to the LIFE project were, accounting for 5,458 'general' members, of whom 3,938 were 'core' members holding shares in the organisation.[264] By mid-2013, there was estimated 10,000 farmers in LIFE-supported organisations, and another few thousand cocoa farmers incorporated into some type of farmers' cooperative, association or group.[265] This suggests that in less than two years the number of farmers in LIFE-supported organisations had almost doubled. Second, it suggests that about one-third or more of the estimated 30,000 cocoa farmers (cf. Section 3.2 above) are organised.

The major changes in the cooperative sector appear to have taken place in the last few years, possibly related to the comprehensive LIFE project, initiated in 2008 and subsequently expanded, as well as other donor projects. Another large project in the smallholder-cocoa (and coffee) sector, initiated in 2011, is the joint government of Liberia and IFAD STCRSP project,[266] which works with seven cooperatives (old and new) in Lofa County, and aims to reach 15,000 farmers, of whom 80 per cent produce cocoa.[267] Both LIFE and STCRSP are focused on developing the cocoa value chains to the benefit of smallholder farmers by, for example, strengthening their organisations' linkages to large buyers and the international market.[268]

4.3.2 Increased Market Engagement – Bulking and Selling in Volume

The revitalisation and growing number of cocoa farmers' organisations is reflected in their engagement in the cocoa market by buying cocoa from farmers, and bulking and selling it on their behalf. The recent nature of this engagement is suggested, first of all, by the limited role these organisations played in the early post-war years. A comprehensive survey of cocoa farmers in the main cocoa-producing counties (Lofa, Bong and Nimba) reveals that during the 2006/07 season, farmer organisations were rarely involved in cocoa transactions. 'Only five of the market transactions captured in the survey [of 794 respondents in 40 villages: comment added] were brokered by a farmer group,

---

263 ACDI/VOCA (2013)
264 ACDI/VOCA (2012a)
265 Key Informant 1
266 STCRSP (Smallholder Tree Crop Revitalization Support Project) is a Government of Liberia (GoL) project, implemented by IFAD (International Fund for Agricultural Development) – and by LAADCO, which thus assumes a dual role as market actor and implementing agency in Lofa County, as reported earlier. IFAD is the main funder, an important financial contribution is given by LAADCO and a smaller one by GoL. (IFAD 2011; STCRSP 2013)
267 Key Informant 13
268 For general information about the projects, see ACDI/VOCA (2013), IFAD (2011) and their web-pages

only 7 respondents belonged to a farmer organization …'.[269] By the following year an increased presence of farmer groups in cocoa-market transactions has been suggested, with an estimated one-sixth of cocoa produced being channelled through cooperatives.[270] Secondary data thus suggest that sometime around 2007, farmers' organisations became more active in the cocoa market again, but also that this trend has not been uniform or simultaneous everywhere. This is illustrated by the evaluation of another project, STCP,[271] which found that during the 2010/11 cocoa season none of the six farmer organisations supported provided marketing services to their farmers, who sold their cocoa individually and did not engage in group selling.[272]

My interviews support the view that the growth and restoration of farmers' organisations as cocoa-trading market actors has been a major change in recent years, but also that developments have varied. A group of key informants with deep knowledge of the cocoa market offered certain overview.[273] Nimba County is reported to have the highest proportion of farmers organised in cooperatives, all of which are eager to expand. 'Nimba is extreme in cocoa', as cocoa production and trade continued during the war, at least to an extent. This contrasts with Gbarpolu – 'the least developed in cocoa' – where 'nobody was buying cocoa after the war' and farms were abandoned. In 2011, the LIFE project entered and encouraged farmers to set up and rehabilitate farmers' associations. In Bong also cocoa farmers are increasingly engaged, and in Lofa 'a lot has been done on the cooperatives'. In River Gee, improvements in the organisation of cooperatives and their 'selling cocoa together as cooperatives' is reported. The large buyer in this county reportedly started buying cocoa from cooperatives in 2012, when they were established. Similarly, farmers' associations recently established in Grand Gedeh sell cocoa to a large buyer there.

I visited six cooperatives/associations in Nimba, Lofa and Gbarpolu – in the following I sometimes refer to farmers' organisations as cooperatives, regardless of their formal status, for simplicity. Information from group interviews with member farmers, some of whom are also cooperative leaders, and other staff, and individual interviews with a few leaders-cum-farmers, illustrate recent developments, market activity, and certain issues related to performing these functions. They also show that conditions between cooperatives vary, even within counties.

The first cooperative visited in Lofa is new, established in 2008. It has 507 members, of whom 98 are shareholders, and all are cocoa farmers. 'We bulk and sell together', cocoa sales have increased from 105 metric tonnes in 2012/13 to an estimated 150 metric tonnes in 2013/14.[274] This cooperative is reported by a key informant

---

269 English (2008: 59)
270 English (2008: 70) and Wilcox (n.d.a)
271 STCP, the Sustainable Tree Crops Program, was an essentially US-based programme for West and Central African smallholder tree-crop development, with several funding and implementing organisations, initiated in Liberia in 2005. (USAID 2011: 1)
272 USAID (2011: 2, 14 and 23-24)
273 Group Interview 3 is the source of the entire remainder of this paragraph; quotations are from my notes from the interview.
274 Group Interview 7; quotations from my notes

to produce the largest amount of cocoa in Lofa.[275] It has a five-year contract with LAADCO, which provides cash in advance to enable the cooperative to pay farmers on delivery of cocoa. It claims that farmers are committed to selling to the cooperative, but nonetheless suspects that some farmers – even villages – produce much more than they deliver.[276] Cooperative two in Lofa is also new, established in 2009 and certified in 2013. During this period, its number of members has increased from 72 to 250. 'We decided to sit in a group, to go together to get a better price, to bulk'. They 'bulk together and sell directly to town', but don't have a contract with an exporter, which they regret. A big problem is that the cooperative does not have enough cash to pay for cocoa to all farmers, who thus side sell to middlemen in order to get cash on the spot.[277] The third Lofa cooperative was established in the 1970s. It remained dormant during the war, reactivated itself in 2004, became dormant again, and was eventually reactivated in August 2013. It had an agreement to sell three metric tons of cocoa to LAADCO in 2013, and got pre-financing to be able to pay farmers on delivery. In spite of this, this cooperative also finds it difficult to get farmers to sell to it – only an estimated 30 per cent of farmers' marketed cocoa reaches the cooperative – because of its limited ability to provide pre-finance.[278]

These experiences underscore the shortage of cash facing many market actors in the cocoa value chain, not least smallholder farmers, and the advantage buyers with access to working capital and the ability to pay on the spot have in the competition for smallholders' cocoa. Cooperatives with contracts with large buyers that pre-finance are thus likely to find it easier to obtain cocoa from farmers, even if they too may face limitations. Hence the strength of cooperatives as market actors may be related to their ability to forge links with such buyers.

A related issue is illustrated by a cooperative in Nimba. 'The positive changes started with ACDI-VOCA in 2008'. Before that, the cooperative used to sell 500-600 kg, but after training and farm rehabilitation, it made its 'first shipment' – presumably to Monrovia – of 3,423 kg in 2008, and it sales have climbed almost six fold since then, to 11,560 kg in 2011 and 20,000 kg 2013. A major change reported is the introduction of a bulking system.[279] A warehouse-receipt system has been established in cooperatives supported by the LIFE project, which considerably facilitates cooperatives' aggregating and storing cocoa in the cooperative's warehouse for farmers until it is sold in bulk to buyers. As explained by a key informant, farmers get a warehouse receipt they can cash in when the cocoa is sold. This increases the security of the farmers, who in the past had no proof of having delivered cocoa.[280] Thus, the cash-constrained cooperative can bulk cocoa without having to pay the farmer before the cocoa is sold to the buyer, and thus offers an alternative payment mechanism. It also suggests that some farmers can

275 Key Informant 12
276 Group Interview 7; Informal Interview with management
277 Group Interview 8; Individual Interviewee 33 (quotations from my notes)
278 Individual Interviewee 25
279 My notes from Group Interview 6
280 Key Informant 11

make do without cash on delivery, provided they have proof of their future claim on the cooperative.

The second cooperative visited in Nimba also pools cocoa in its warehouse and reports that 'we sell in bulk'. Several farmers explain how their involvement in cocoa as well as the cooperative arose: 'With the help of ACDI-VOCA and the cooperative, we now go back into cocoa... But we just started'. 'I decided to join the cooperative and they increased my interest in cocoa, and I got help from ACDI-VOCA'. 'When ACDI-VOCA came, I went back into cocoa'.[281] The farmers' association in Gbarpolu was established in 2011. Before the LIFE project started there, most cocoa farms were abandoned. Now farmers sell cocoa and 'get something out of it'.[282] In late 2013, I was informed that LIFE works with three active cooperatives in Gbarpolu, and that two more are in the process of being established.[283]

The frequent references to the LIFE project and its implementing organisation ACDI-VOCA reflects the fact most of the cooperatives I talked to receive support from them. It is possible that the role of the project in cooperatives and with farmers is overstated by interviewees, and there is no independent documentation of its achievements, although a senior Ministry of Agriculture official notes that 'where projects are implemented the situation is changing for the better'.[284] The early post-war neglect of smallholders' cocoa-market participation, the early entrance of the LIFE project in 2008, its persistence, broad outreach and market-based approach,[285] suggest that the project has played a significant role in facilitating market participation by cocoa farmers and their cooperatives. Senior LIFE staff report that the 32 supported farmer organisations became stronger and improved cocoa production, processing, quality and marketing during the 2008-2013 period. Farmers' organisations not receiving support, by contrast, face greater difficulties in developing their marketing functions, as 'reports from exporters indicate that many of these are unable to bulk their cocoa because of organisational and monetary issues'.[286] An informal interviewee confirms the picture by noting that in Nimba County, cocoa cooperatives and associations beyond those supported by the LIFE project are 'not strong'.[287]

A final indication of the increasing engagement in the cocoa market by farmers' organisations is the fact that six of them were, for the first time ever, involved in direct export of cocoa to a US-based cocoa buyer, Transmar Commodity Group.[288] These direct exports took place in 2011 and 2012, as reported by several interviewees, including farmers,[289] and three of the cooperatives I interviewed exported to Transmar once or several times.[290]

281 My notes form Group Interview 5
282 My notes from Group Meeting 9
283 Key Informant 14
284 My notes form Key Informant 3
285 ACDI/VOCA (2013)
286 My notes from interview with a Key Informant, to remain anonymous here
287 My notes from Informal Interviewee 3
288 ACDI/VOCA (2013)
289 For example Key Informants 7 and 11-12; Individual Interviewees 18-19, 21-22 and 34
290 Group Interviews 6-7; Individual Interviewee 33

4.3.3   Reducing Transaction Costs and Countervailing Market Power

The entry of farmers' organisations has helped change the structure of the cocoa market and its increased diversification and complexity, as illustrated by Appendix Figure 4.1 on the overall cocoa value chain in Liberia. Cooperatives add an organisational level on the supply side of the cocoa market. As shown by the more stylised picture of the cocoa market in Figure 4.4 above, some cooperatives also form part of one of the emergent integrated value chains.

Farmers' organisations perform a number of functions for both buyers and sellers of cocoa. Cooperatives now offer an alternative, or complementary, marketing channel for farmers, who previously had access to middle buyers only. They simultaneously offer an alternative or complementary supply channel for large buyers-cum-exporters, and are preferred by some of them – but not others. With farmers increasingly organised in cooperatives and bulking/selling together in larger volumes, it ought to be easier, cheaper and more attractive for large buyers to invest in lasting relationships with cocoa producers by channelling inputs and services through cooperatives. Hence, the re-emergence of cooperatives is likely to have facilitated the development of integrated value chains in the Liberian cocoa market, although only one buying company (LAADCO) appears to have chosen this model. As reported earlier, another (Wienco) consciously avoids cooperatives and deals directly with farmers and forms its own farmer groups, and a third (LCC) also relies on direct contacts and contracts with farmers.

The cooperatives' market entry may have important implications for market power within the cocoa value chain, particularly in their role as cocoa sellers, hence on the cocoa supply side. By buying cocoa produced by many smallholders in surrounding communities and remote villages, which are known to the cooperative, and collecting, aggregating and storing it, cooperatives perform a coordinating function. They thereby reduce transactions costs that buyers otherwise would incur, associated with, for instance, searching for cocoa in many locations, negotiating prices and other conditions, striking deals with a large number of individual farmers and making sure the deals are honoured.[291] For buyers, buying large volumes of cocoa from cooperatives is thus beneficial. Besides, cooperatives offer an avenue to reach smallholders for the provision of various inputs and services, again in a coordinated and transaction-cost saving way. There are hence economies of scale in buying cocoa from cooperatives. This cost saving is a kind of efficiency gain, that can benefit farmers in terms of higher cocoa prices if the cooperatives manage to negotiate a good deal with the buyers, and if they let the farmers share in the gain.

Benefits to farmers from selling through cooperatives can also accrue for another reason. For buyers wanting large volumes of cocoa in a certain geographical area, a

---

291 Transaction costs are costs incurred in making an economic transaction, and are often divided into three broad categories: search and information costs; bargaining and decision costs; and policing and enforcement costs (Dahlman 1979). Coase (1937) and Williamson (1975; 1979) are among the classical references of the broad strand of transaction-cost economics. See, for example, http://en.wikipedia.org/wiki/Transaction_cost.

cooperative may be the only – or one of a few – large cocoa supplier. This leaves the buyer of large volumes with few if any alternatives, which gives the cooperative certain market power as a supplier, countervailing some of the buyers' market power. As noted by Wilcox and Abbott, '[m]arketing cooperatives, in particular, are an institutional construct… that may help relatively numerous farmers overcome the possible market power of more concentrated downstream agents'.[292] Cooperatives can use this counter-vailing power to negotiate higher prices for the cocoa sold, but also cheaper prices for inputs bought. Wilcox and Abbot, who explored whether cocoa farmers' organisations could countervail buyer market power in the 2004 cocoa market in Cameroon, found that marketing cocoa via farmers' groups certainly appears to countervail buyer market power, and that farmers received higher prices for cocoa, but that the results are sensi-tive and depend on the functioning of cooperatives.[293]

Hence, the re-emergence of cooperatives as large sellers of cocoa may have strengthened the bargaining position of smallholder cocoa farmers for at least two major and interrelated reasons: economies of scale and countervailing market power. Economies of scale determine how much efficiency gain there is to be shared in the value chain, and the relative bargaining strength of actors within the chain determines the distribution of the gain. I am not able to distinguish the effects. More important here is that there is a perception among informed observers and market actors that cooperatives contribute and have contributed to strengthening farmers' bargaining po-sition *vis-à-vis* buyers, first of all in relation to middle buyers.[294] Referring to farmers, an NGO officer explains:[295]

> We first help them to organise, because there is not much you can do when you are an individual farmer and also poor… Farmers selling to agents and buyers are not educated and lack access to information. Now that they form themselves into associations to bulk produce, this leads to strengthening of their bargaining power.

According to a senior Ministry of Agriculture official, the government works with co-operatives and associations, which are considered to 'strengthen [smallholder farmers'] bargaining power and reduce dependency of buying agents', aiming to 'minimise', 'bypass' and 'get rid' of middlemen in the cocoa value chain.[296] During the group interview with one cooperative, two different inputs explain what the cooperative has meant to them:[297]

> It has meant that farmers put themselves together to do things together – it is beneficial. They sell in bulk and get a better price.

---

292 Wilcox and Abbott (2006: 5)
293 Wilcox and Abbott (2006: 2)
294 Notably Key Informants 3-4; Informal interviewee 2; Individual Interviewees 17-19; Group Interviews 3, 6, 8 and 10
295 Notes from Informal Interviewee 2
296 My notes from Key Informant 3
297 My notes from Group Meeting 8

> It has meant a price change. Before we used to sell to middle buyers at a local price and in small quantities. Perhaps we only met them in the street and sold directly to them. With the cooperative we stand strong on the price – our bargaining power has increased. Now middle buyers cannot just come and give any price.

The suggestion here is that the stronger bargaining position has translated into higher prices for farmers, which is in line with the Cameroonian experience reported earlier and further explored in Section 5.1 below. I also find that several actors refer to cooperatives' 'bulking' as a major reason farmers' bargaining power has become stronger, and as discussed bulking is facilitated by the provision of pre-finance as well as by the warehouse-receipt system. The role of pre-financing, from new buyers' to cooperatives, in increasing the bargaining power of farmers is also highlighted in one of the group interviews.[298]

The strengthened bargaining power of farmers organised in cooperatives is, secondly, reflected in their relationships and behavioural interactions with large buyers, as indicated in contractual negotiations. I learnt that farmers in one cooperative have turned to LAADCO to cancel a 30-year contract and shorten its term, and that another cooperative refused to sign a 30-year contract.[299] Dissatisfaction with very long-term contracts is reported by two sources to have made the buyer modify conditions, resulting in shorter contract periods.[300] 'Now they have 6-7 month contracts in Bong, or one year contracts, and also in Nimba'.[301] As expressed in one group interview, farmers have 'gained a stronger bargaining power with LAADCO, and that if they are not satisfied they simply say that they will go to another buyer'.[302] In another group interview, cooperative members said that 'we negotiate tougher with LAADCO every season and get stronger every time, because we have the goods they want'.[303]

Whereas my data suggest that cooperatives have helped strengthen farmers' market power over time, this does not mean that cooperatives always have strong bargaining power in relation to the buyer. This depends on their relative market power and bargaining strength between buyers and sellers. As reported earlier (in Sub-Section 4.2.3), one cooperative found its bargaining power weak *vis-à-vis* the buyer, because the cooperative was dependent on the buyer for cash to be able to pay farmers directly.[304] There were alternative buyers around, but not of the new kind who could provide the desired credit (and other integrated services). This case illustrates how the countervailing power of cooperatives as large cocoa suppliers may be partly limited by the relatively stronger market power of the new kind of large buyers. If there were more integrated value chains competing for contractual relationships with cooperatives, the latters' bargaining power would likely be stronger.

---

298 Group Meeting 3
299 Key Informant 10
300 Key Informant 10; Group Interview 3
301 My notes from Key Informant 10
302 My notes from Group Interview 3
303 My notes from Group Interview 6
304 Group Interview 7

4.3.4   Not Always Representing Farmers' Interest

However, the extent to which cooperatives' countervailing market power actually benefits smallholder farmers depends on the degree to which cooperatives act in the interest of farmers by using their bargaining power to achieve beneficial conditions and forwarding the proceeds to the farmers.

The Cameroon example referred to earlier shows that the extent to which cooperatives' countervailing market power does lead to price increases for farmers depends on how the cooperatives operate, how efficient and well-functioning they are, and in particular on the 'transparency of the internal governance'.[305] Although I have had no access to detailed data about price margins transferred and retained by cooperatives, changes in prices received by farmers are discussed in a subsequent chapter, and offer overall indications of benefit to farmers. Neither have I explored farmer-cooperative relationships or interactions in depth, but the data presented so far indicate favourable collaboration, which is my overall impression, given the generally beneficial outcomes reported in a subsequent chapter. Besides, virtually all the individually interviewed farmers who are cooperative members (11 of 12) expressed satisfaction with their relationships with the cooperatives.[306] Four of them explicitly stated that their cooperative speaks on behalf of the farmers and represents their interests.[307]

However, I also received information that not all cooperatives behave in ways that are appreciated by member farmers. Three farmers who used to be cooperative members have reportedly chosen to leave because of dissatisfaction with their organisation.[308] One cooperative in particular that I was in contact with was the subject of farmers' complaints. Two former members told of their experience:

> I was a founding member, but left the cooperative in 2010. This is not the cooperative that I entered. I saw nothing good from being a shareholder. There is no fairness. After a year there should be a report to the shareholders, for them to know how their interest has been served, but there was no report in 2-3 years.[309]

> I am not a member of any farmers' group, because my husband was first a member of the cooperative, but he left it because of how they treated him. They did not give him the returns on his share, his profit as a shareholder. They only divided it between themselves in the town where the cooperative headquarters are located. The cooperative promised to build dryers, but they never delivered it to our town, only to the other towns. And they never asked why my husband withdrew.[310]

Another farmer, although a happy member of the same cooperative, still offers a mixed assessment: 'The cooperative talks for our interest, but how well can they negotiate

---

305 Wilcox and Abbott (2006: 38)
306 Individual Interviewees 5-8, 10, 13-14, 17-19 and 37
307 Individual Interviewees 17-19 and 37
308 Individual Interviewees 15, 21 and 30
309 My notes from Individual Interviewee 15
310 My notes from Individual Interviewee 30, slightly edited so as not to reveal the farmer's identity

good prices for us? I don't know how well they represent our interest when they talk to the buyer'.[311] A fourth farmer, also a member, tells of how farmers are being cheated by the cooperative's own buying agents, who underpay them for their cocoa, pay them even less if they want cash, and do not reward them for producing high quality cocoa but instead mix it with other grades and pay them less. The farmer goes on to express disappointment with the treatment of members and distrust of the cooperatives leaders, and notes how difficult it is to obtain redress from the cooperative's headquarters or from village leaders, who are not viewed as representing members' interests either.[312]

These reports suggest that some cooperatives may not represent the interests of their members/owners, and not only for want of experience or competence. These are signs of possible elite capture of certain cooperatives, with cooperative leaders using their position to serve other interests, possibly their own. Liberian cooperatives have a history of being top-down organisations rather than bottom up,[313] and such practices may easily recur.

4.4 Conclusions: Smallholder Farmers' Bargaining Power Strengthened

This chapter has sought to identify major changes in the structure of, and market power within, the post-war Liberian cocoa market, by examining changes among central market actors, their roles and relationships, and the implications of this for competition and market power within the core cocoa value chain. This section summarises the findings, and draws conclusions about what they mean for the market position and bargaining power of smallholder cocoa farmers.

4.4.1 Summary

The analysis of the data collected reveals three major emergent patterns in the market structure and in market power.

First, during the post-war period, in particular during the last few years, *the number of cocoa buyers has increased* – middlemen as well as large buyers at national and local level – and there are strong indications that this has *led to increased competition among buyers* for cocoa produced by smallholder farmers. A combination of primary and secondary data indicates that the official Liberian export market for cocoa has experienced gradual change in the post-war period from near monopoly, with one firm accounting for some 80-90 per cent of exports, towards something of an oligopoly in which two-four firms dominate the market, with the share of the largest firm declining

---

311 My notes from Individual Interviewee 14, slightly edited so as not to reveal the cooperative's identity
312 Individual Interviewee 11
313 Informal Interviewee 3; Group Interview 3

gradually to around 40 per cent. The change appears to have been initiated around 2009/2010, and the degree of competition among official cocoa exporters has increased consistently, although a certain amount of market power remains. The number of exporters is larger and the competition for cocoa for export is higher, however, than is reflected by reference to officially recognised exporters, given considerable informal exports, but it is impossible to establish any particular trend over time in terms of their relative importance or competitive pressure.

Based on a large number of interviews with market actors and key informants, the research finds that the number of cocoa buyers, largely middle buyers, and competition for cocoa has also increased at the local level, at least in the districts and counties studied and possibly beyond. Many interviewees report such changes, although several market actors have not been active long enough to observe change over time. However, an overwhelming majority of market actors attest to the prevalence of many buyers and/or competition, which in light of the market power of the past lends further support to the finding. Competition has increased not only from more large exporters-cum-buyers and middle buyers, but also because new kinds of buyer have entered the market.

Hence, a second major pattern observed in the market structure of the cocoa value chain is *the emergence of new kinds of buyer-cum-exporter* in the last few years. Large companies are investing in lasting relationships with cocoa farmers, directly or through farmers' organisations. This has several important implications for the nature of the cocoa market and for competition and market power:

a) The emergence of new kinds of cocoa buyers – who make productive investments in the cocoa market by providing integrated services, inputs and credit to farmers and their organisations based on contracts of varying length – accounts for an important part of the increased competition for cocoa produced by smallholder farmers. This finding is based on a substantial number of interviews and is supported by official statistics.

b) The provision of integrated services to farmers under contract has meant that integrated value chains are emerging in the Liberian cocoa market. Thus, the Liberian cocoa market is changing from the pure spot market of the past. The structure of the Liberian cocoa market *has become more diversified – and more complex* – combining elements of both spot market and integrated value chain. There are several integrated value chains emerging, two of which are dominant. They are distinguishable by their different business models, with varying characteristics in terms of integrated functions and contractual relationships, which adds to the complexity.

c) My primary data show that with the emergence of integrated value chains, competition for cocoa has increased and assumed new forms – and become more complex too. Middle buyers compete with each other, as well as with buyers from the integrated value chains, who also compete with each other. The competition involves not only prices paid for cocoa, but also various combinations of services, inputs and credit, the conditions for these, the length of contracts and not least the modes of payment.

d) However, in spite of increased and new types of competition in the overall co-coa market, there are signs that new forms of local market power may be emerging in parallel, involving the new large buyers in the integrated value chains. The number of integrated value chains is limited in some locations, which limits competition among them. According to interviewees, one of them may have been granted local monop-sony power to buy cocoa from cooperatives as part of a joint government-donor fun-ded project, thus enjoying preferential treatment. On the other hand, farmers' side selling of cocoa to middle buyers dilutes some of this market power. *While buyers from integrated value chains do face competition from middle buyers, there is a risk of their gai-ning monopsony power if the level of competition from other integrated value chains is not maintained in the market.*

e) Market power also applies to the input-side of the cocoa value chain. An addi-tional observation is that input markets for smallholder cocoa farmers remain severely underdeveloped, with market power prevailing among the few suppliers that exist. In recent years, inputs have been increasingly provided as integrated services, but markets for improved seeds and seedlings, fertiliser and chemicals, as well as for services such as credit, are virtually non-existent or are barely emerging. A single provider of fertiliser and chemicals has monopoly power, but the market power of providers of improved seeds and seedlings appears to be somewhat countervailed by a few established private cocoa nurseries. These nurseries may also form the basis of a domestic seedling market, but I suggest that lack of credit to smallholder farmers may retard this development. Hence, there is currently no integrated national market or effective local markets for improved cocoa seeds and seedlings, although they may be about to develop. Existing input providers with strong market power may charge farmers and cooperatives mo-nopoly prices. In the absence of a functioning market there is little alternative, and the input suppliers facilitate smallholder access to inputs by providing them on credit.

A third major pattern emerging in the structure of the cocoa market during the recent post-war years is that *farmers' organisations have re-entered as market actors in the cocoa market,* which has important implications for power relationships in the market. A combination of primary and secondary data show that Liberian cocoa farmers are increasingly organised in cooperatives or associations, which have been revitalised or newly established in recent years, and that these organisations are more engaged in the cocoa market, bulking and selling cocoa in larger volumes. The process may have star-ted around 2007/2008, but gained momentum more recently with increased support from donor-funded projects and the emergence of the new kinds of buyer from 2011 onwards. The re-emergence of cooperatives as sellers of larger volumes of bulked cocoa produced by many farmers has contributed to strengthening the bargaining power of smallholder farmers in two major ways. First, by performing a coordinating func-tion, cooperatives reduce transaction costs and generate economies of scale for buyers, which can be shared with cocoa farmers and cooperatives. Second, by selling larger volumes of cocoa, cooperatives become large suppliers and gain market power on the supply side, countervailing some of the market power of buyers, which enables them to negotiate better prices and conditions for farmers (to be discussed below). Thus, the entry of cooperatives has helped diversify the structure of the cocoa market on the sellers' side.

However, the extent to which cooperatives' countervailing market power actually benefits smallholder farmers depends on the extent to which cooperatives use it in the interest of farmers. Whereas the overall picture is that cooperatives have strengthened the position of cocoa farmers, reports from farmers suggest that some cooperatives do not represent farmers' interests well. These observations indicate *a risk for 'elite capture'* of re-established and new cooperatives, which are controlled from the 'top down' as in the past rather than 'bottom up' by members-cum-owners. *If cooperatives leaders cannot be held to account by farmers, the benefits that may otherwise accrue to cocoa farmers from organising themselves may be endangered.*

4.4.2 Conclusions

The picture of recent post-war changes in the structure of the Liberian cocoa market that emerges from the analysis is one of a growing number of market actors selling and buying cocoa. This has contributed to increased competition for cocoa at national and local levels among and between small and large buyers, including new investors providing integrated services. The market power of buyers at all levels has thus been reduced compared to the past, although certain market power remains. By implication, the market position of smallholder farmers producing cocoa has been correspondingly strengthened. Simultaneously, the re-emergence of farmers' organisations as sellers of cocoa on behalf of smallholders has given them some market power on the supply side of the market and helped to countervail some of the buyers' market power, which has further strengthened farmers' bargaining power. A central conclusion is that *the structural changes in the Liberian cocoa market have contributed to strengthening the market position and bargaining power of smallholder farmers, from both the supply side, through the cooperatives, and the demand side, through increased competition.* Changes in the structure of the market have shifted power relationships within the cocoa value chain to the benefit of smallholder farmers. There are additional changes in the Liberian cocoa market that have contributed to increasing farmers' bargaining position. These are touched upon in the ensuing chapter.

Whereas the three major patterns of structural change and their implications for market power and smallholder farmers are clear, one cannot take their continuance for granted. There are remainders of market power among cocoa exporters, possibly new local market power emerging on behalf of buyers from integrated value chains, market power in poorly developed input markets and possible elite capture of farmers' organisations. If market power and elite capture are reinforced over time, favourable developments to date in the cocoa market may be jeopardised, especially smallholder bargaining power and the benefits that accrue therefrom.

The inclusiveness of these structural changes, in terms of the implications for smallholder farmers' participation in and benefit from the cocoa market is explored in Chapter 5. Has, for example, the improved market position of farmers, reflected in their stronger bargaining power, actually translated into better prices for cocoa?

5 Implications for Smallholder Participation and Benefit

The developments observed in the structure of the Liberian cocoa market have had important implications for both the incentives available to smallholder farmers and their opportunities to participate in and benefit from the cocoa market. This chapter reviews those implications, as well as farmers' responses and any observable outcomes to establish whether those changes have made the cocoa market more inclusive.

I examine this in Sub-Section 5.1 by looking at how farmers' strengthened bargaining power and other changes may be reflected in the prices farmers receive for cocoa, as well as in farmers' relative share of the world market cocoa price – their marketing margin. To the extent that farmers do receive higher prices, the price incentives to participate in the cocoa market have been strengthened, but only if their marketing margin has increased are price increases considered to reflect a more inclusive market. Second, the structural changes in the cocoa market have also affected the opportunities available to farmers to respond to improved price incentives so as to further increase their returns from cocoa farming through increased access to e.g., markets, inputs and services. These opportunities have been discussed throughout the text and are briefly reviewed in Sub-Section 5.2. I also look there at how farmers have responded to the improved incentives by using the new opportunities available to them, as reflected in farmers' investments in their cocoa farms. In combination with some of the findings reported earlier, this reflects changes in their market participation. The structural changes have also, and thirdly, had implications for the choices available to farmers, and hence opportunities for their livelihood strategies, which are briefly discussed in Sub-Section 5.3, as well as any observed farmers' response. In the subsequent sub-section I look at what farmers' behavioural responses to strengthened incentives and new opportunities may have meant for their current and future returns, in terms of the performance of their cocoa farms as well as farmers' income and other benefits. Sub-Section 5.6 concludes.

5.1 Implications for Cocoa Prices and Marketing Margins

This sub-section looks at if and how the structural changes in the Liberian cocoa market and the resulting increase in smallholder bargaining power is reflected in the prices farmers receive for cocoa, as well as in their relative share of the world market price. The influence of other factors is also considered. This rather comprehensive sub-section is structured as follows.

The first two sub-sections examine developments in the world market price of cocoa and the so-called domestic reference price for cocoa, which serve as two important reference points in examining price changes. To study changes in farm-gate cocoa prices, different steps are taken. First, Sub-Section 5.1.3 reviews changes in cocoa prices received by farmers over time, as revealed by interviewees, and discusses how price increases are perceived to be related to the structural changes and farmers' strengthened bargaining power. Sub-Section 5.1.4 then looks at farm-gate prices reported by market actors during a single cocoa season, late 2013, and then compares prices paid by different kinds of buyers for different grades of cocoa, and in relation to the reference price. To discern change over time, the quantitative price data thus generated are thereafter, in Sub-Section 5.1.5, compared with secondary historical data from the early post-war period. First, change over time in farm-gate prices in relation to the reference price is calculated and analysed. Then farm-gate prices are compared with the world market price to establish the marketing margin, which in turn is compared with historical data to calculate change in marketing margin over time. A qualification of my findings is discussed in Sub-Section 5.1.6. A final sub-sub-section discusses structural and other causes of the changes observed in prices and marketing margins.

5.1.1   Changes in Prices for Liberian Cocoa at the Border

Since Liberia is a small cocoa-producing country, it cannot influence prices in the world market, but is a price taker. The world market price for cocoa is the major determinant of the price for exported Liberian cocoa in the international market, although there are additional factors that influence the price of cocoa at the Liberian border – the price eventually to be shared between producers and traders within the Liberian cocoa value chain.

The world market cocoa prices mostly referred to are reported by the ICCO, the International Cocoa Organisation.[314] In the early Liberian post-war years, annual cocoa prices declined somewhat and bottomed out in 2005.[315] Since then cocoa prices on the world market have displayed a clear upward trend, although with considerable fluctuations, including seasonal variations. Table 5.1 below gives the ICCO world market prices at the end of each year, which reflects the cocoa mid-season, and their changes since 2005. It shows that ICCO world market cocoa prices have increased rapidly since 2005, peaking in the 2009/2010 cocoa season (12/2009 in the table), when they more than doubled. The price then dropped for two years, before rising sharply again in 2013. Over the whole December 2005-December 2013 period, around the time of my interviews, world market prices increased by 87 per cent.

---

314 'The ICCO price is a composite price for cocoa on the London (LIFFE) and New York futures markets'. (English 2008: 27)

315 Historical data on daily ICCO cocoa prices at Mongabay Commodities, 8 September 2014, www.mongabay.com/commodities/prices/cocoa.php, referring to ICCO Secretariat and World Bank

Table 5.1:   World Market Cocoa Prices and Price Changes 2005-2014

Month/Year	Cocoa Price (cents/kg)	Annual Change (%)
December 2005	150.91	
December 2006	170.72	13.1
December 2007	211.27	23.8
December 2008	239.39	13.3
December 2009	349.76	46.1
December 2010	306.00	-12.5
December 2011	219.69	-28.2
December 2012	241.03	9.7
December 2013	282.40*	17.2
Total Change (%)		87.1

Sources and Note: ICCO and World Bank, referred to by Mongabay Commodities, 8 September 2014
* As per 31 December 2013: World Bank, referred to by Ychart Indicators, www.ycharts.com/indicators/world_cocoa_price, 8 September 2014

However, it is only recently that Liberian cocoa has been able to fetch these high prices and fully benefit from the price increases. For many years, much – if not most – of the cocoa exported from the country was rated poor on the international market. Liberian exporters could only get a discounted price for their poor quality beans. During the 2006/07 cocoa season, this 'Liberian origin discount' amounted to 189 USD/ton or some 11 per cent of the world market price.[316] The following season, 2007/08, the discount was 349 USD/ton (in December) or more than 16 per cent.[317] One could argue that the poor quality of Liberian cocoa was 'institutionalised', since Liberia maintained a non-grading quality system, referred to as Fair Average Quality (FAQ), which accepted inferior quality cocoa inconsistent with international quality standards.

In recent years, the Liberian-origin discount has declined, or perhaps been eliminated for a combination of reasons. Perhaps most importantly, Liberia has for the first time adopted a cocoa quality-grading system compatible with international standards, and has begun to grade and sort cocoa according to the quality criteria adopted. The system was reportedly agreed in 2009 and developed in 2010, but sources differ on its implementation, which nonetheless appears to have gained momentum with the entrance of new buyers/investors in 2011. It is reported that the grading was initially done at the farm-gate level, but also at least partly applied at the port, meaning that only quality cocoa can be exported.[318] Second, Liberia officially joined the ICCO in 2012,[319] which contributed to reducing – or possibly eliminating – the Liberia-origin

316 English (2008: 99)
317 Wilcox (n.d.a: Table 3)
318 Key Informants 1 and 6
319 Liberia becoming an ICCO member was, in fact, a process that may have not have been finalised until the end of July 2013, when the final payment of the membership fee was to be registered, as reported at a monthly meeting of the Cocoa Sector Technical Working Group (CSTWG 2013: 1).

discount deducted by international cocoa traders. Sources differ on the size of the discount, which is reported to have declined from £100 to £75 per metric ton or to have been eliminated altogether, just by Liberia's becoming an ICCO member.[320]

These price increases have strongly increased incentives to trade and invest in Liberian cocoa for export into the international market. And as shown in the previous chapter, the number of exporters and buyers has recently increased with new buyers invested in lasting relationships in the Liberian cocoa market.

The extent to which these price signals from the world cocoa market – information about levels and changes in world-market prices – are actually transmitted to farmers depends, inter alia, on the market power of buyers along the chain.[321] The transmission of price signals in the Liberian cocoa market during the 2006/07 season was studied by English, who found that 'Liberian cocoa farmers are receiving limited price signals due to the institutional, market-level and infrastructure oriented transaction costs that constitute a sizeable gap between farm-gate and world prices'.[322] More specifically, data suggest that '…a $1 increase (decrease) in the LIFFE price translates into only a $0.146 increase (decrease) in the farm-gate price'.[323] Limited price signals up to around 2008 were also reported by one of the key informants, who relates how a large exporter with strong market power kept prices low for farmers, who 'had no other links to the international cocoa market and prices'.[324] In recent years, however, when buyers' market power has declined and farmers' bargaining power has increased, price signals are more likely to have been effectively transmitted through the value chain to farmers.

The extent to which they are is reflected in the price increases farmers actually receive as well as in changes to the farmers' marketing margin. But first I explore the so-called reference price, which serves as a point of reference in the domestic cocoa market.

5.1.2 The Reference Price

The reference price for cocoa is an indicative farm-gate price announced by the Liberian Produce Marketing Corporation (LPMC), and is intended to serve as a point of reference in negotiations of final prices between buyers and sellers in the Liberian market. The reference price was introduced in 2009,[325] and gives prices for the different

---

320 Key Informants 1 and 6
321 As shown e.g., in a study of market power in other West African cocoa markets by Wilcox and Abbott (2004). Cf. also the case of Cameroon, related earlier, where Wilcox and Abbott found that the transmission of price signal dissipated along the value chain, i.e. all the less information was reflected in the price paid for cocoa the closer to the farmer (Wilcox and Abbott 2006: 1).
322 English (2008: ii)
323 English (2008: 63)
324 Key Informant 2
325 One of our sources relates that the reference price was introduced in 2005 (Key Informant 6), but a facsimile of an LPMC circular shows that prices announced by the LPMC in the earlier post-war years took a different format. In September 2006 the LPMC announced 'official minimum prices' for FAQ and sub-grade cocoa respectively: 0.65 and 0.32 USD/kg at farm gate, and 0.80 and 0.43 USD/kg in Monrovia (LPMC 2006).

grades according to the new grading system, in which Grade 1 is the highest quality.[326] The reference price is announced quarterly in advance.[327] Only Grade 1 and 2 are officially to be exported.[328] Table 5.2 below shows the reference prices in US dollars I have been able to identify, with the corresponding values in Liberian dollars calculated by me by using the official exchange rate.

Table 5.2: Liberian Reference Prices for Cocoa at Farm Gate, in US and Liberian Dollars

Grade / Exchange Rate	2009/10 Season	2010/11 Season#	July-Sep 2012*	Oct-Dec 2012	Jan-March 2013	2012/13 Season**	April-June 2013	Oct-Dec 2013
USD/Kg	USD/kg	USD/kg	USD/kg	USD/kg	USD/kg	USD/kg	USD/kg	USD/kg
Grade 1	1.70	2.04	1.26	1.42	1.37	1.40	1.19	1.39
Grade 2	1.45	1.73	1.12	1.26	1.21	1.24	1.04	1.24
Sub-grade	1.28***	1.02	0.95	0.99	1.04	1.02	0.86	1.07
LRD/USD	70.50	71.50	74.00*	72.50	75.00	73.75	77.50	82.00
LRD/Kg	LRD/kg	LRD/kg	LRD/kg	LRD/kg	LRD/kg	LRD/kg	LRD/kg	LRD/kg
Grade 1	120	146	94	103	103	103	92	114
Grade 2	102	124	83	91	91	91	81	102
Sub-grade	90***	73	70	72	78	75	67	88

Notes: Exchange rates used: 2009/10: 70.50 LRD/USD, Oct-Dec 2012: 72.50; Jan-March 2013: 75.00; 2012/13: 73.75 LRD/USD; April-June 2013: 77.50; Oct-Dec 2013: 82.00 LRD/USD; # Effective August 12th 2010; * For July-Sep 2012, prices were explicitly given in both LRD/kg and USD/kg, which implies an exchange rate of approximately 74 LRD/USD – about 2% higher than that reported by the Central Bank of Liberia (2012), which is 72.50 LRD/USD. The reason for this discrepancy is unknown. ** Calculated as the average of the prices given for the last 2012 and first 2013 quarters – the main cocoa season. *** At this time, 'sub-grade' was still referred to as FAQ/Grade 3. Sources: LPMC (2012b and d; 2012/13; 2013b and c); 2009/10 Season: Republic of Liberia (2009); #: Prah (2010: 53); Exchange rates: Appendix Table 5.1

Changes in the Liberian reference price in US dollar (USD) terms reflect the overall trend in world market prices between 2009 and 2013 rather well, but not the increases in 2012 and 2013 in the world market prices (cf. Table 5.1 above), due in part to missing data. A comparison between the reference price in USD terms and the world market price for cocoa also shows that the Liberia reference price for Grade 1 cocoa was 49 per cent of the world market price in 2009/10, increased to 58 per cent in 2012/13

---

326 Republic of Liberia (2009)
327 The price is calculated on the basis of the ICCO monthly price index (futures prices), the CIF (cost, insurance, freights) and FOB components, and internal price factors along the domestic value chain, such as handling and transportation costs from the farm gate to the port. (Key Informant 6)
328 Key Informant 4

and then dropped to 49 per cent in late 2013.[329] Hence, the reference price suggests that farmers should get at least half of the world market price in USD terms.

When reference prices are calculated in Liberian dollar (LRD) – which is what is relevant to Liberian farmers – the picture changes. The decline between 2009 and 2013 is smaller. And whereas in 2013, the reference price remained more or less unchanged in USD terms, it actually increased in LRD terms, from 103 to 114 LRD/kg or by 11 per cent from the year before, which is still less than on the world market (17 per cent, cf. Table 5.1). This increase is entirely related to the depreciation of the LRD against the USD – a continuous process since the end of the war in 2003. The official exchange rate for USD increased from 72.50 to 82.50 LRD between the end of 2012 and 2013.[330] This depreciation has thus had a positive effect on the LRD reference price for cocoa, which has increased more in the most recent years than the reference price in USD terms.

However, the reference price is only a recommended price and does not tell us how actual farm-gate prices have changed. To this I now turn, recognising that there is no systematic information available on actual prices. By combining the primary data collected and limited secondary data, I nonetheless seek to establish a plausible scenario.

5.1.3   Reported Price Increases Over Time and Role of Structural Changes

According to my primary data, there are strong indications that Liberian farmers have received higher prices for cocoa in recent years. All ten key informants – external observers with insight and/or an overview of the market – and cocoa buyers interviewed, who commented on price developments, reported that Liberian cocoa prices have increased in recent years.[331] All ten of totally ten interviewees reported about this. In addition, of the 16 farmers and five farmers' organisations who provided information on changes in cocoa prices, 14 farmers – cooperative members and non-members alike – and three cooperatives either explicitly reported or implicitly referred to price increases in the last few years.[332] Only two farmers reported a price fall when they shifted buyers from a cooperative and Wienco to middle buyers; one cooperative also saw a price decline when changing buyer and another gave mixed signals about price changes.[333] Quite a few of the farmers have not yet sold cocoa or only sold in the current year, and hence cannot really report of price changes over time. The voices of some of the smallholder interviewees illustrate these developments:[334]

---

329 Prices for Grade 1 cocoa in Table 5.2 are compared with world market prices at the end of 1009, 2012 and 2013 in Table 5.1 above.

330 See Appendix Table 5.1.

331 Key Informants 2, 3, 4, 6 and 7; Group Interview 3; Informal interview with middle buyer; Individual Interviewees 23 and 35

332 Group Interviews 3, 6 and 8; Individual Interviewees 6, 7, 13, 14, 17, 18, 19, 20, 25, 29, 31, 32 and 37

333 Group Interviews 5 and 9; Individual Interviewees 12 and 30

334 The text from my notes is carefully edited here – only shortened and sometimes the order is reversed.

Farmer 1: The competition is increasing. More and more buyers are coming, so I think the price is going up – the price is already increasing, e.g., since last year. Before, the price used to be 55-60 LRD/kg, by the time we organised as an association [December 2009[335]]. When we did, we started to know our value as farmers – I now feel stronger. The cooperative talks on our behalf! It helps us to sell at a good price. In 2011, I sold for 105 LRD/kg. In 2012, I sold cocoa for 110 LRD/kg. 2013 I got 115 LRD for Grade 1, and 80 LRD for Grade 2.[336]

Farmer 2: I sell to no specific buyer, but to the cooperative. The prices I received were 75 LRD/kg in 2011 and 80 LRD/kg in 2012 – these two years most of the cocoa was Grade 1. In 2013, I received 110/LRD/kg for Grade 1, but this year I produced all the different grades, and for Grade 2 I got 70 LRD/kg, and for Sub-grade I got 25-30 LRD/kg. Regarding our relationship with buyers, we feel more strong as farmers now, as prices are increasing and there are more buyers – there are many compared to the past.[337]

Farmer 3: In 2011, I got 70-80 LRD/kg as the middle buyer complained about the quality, that it was not dry etc. I sold my cocoa through the cooperative in 2012 and 2013 – we bulked together. In 2012 I received 110 LRD/kg for Grade 1, which I had learnt to produce by ADCI-VOCA. The price I received in 2013 was also 110 LRD/kg for Grade 1. The number of buyers is increasing. Now the cooperative's buyers come and ask for the price, and when the cooperative shows the reference price, the middle buyers draw back. We have bargaining power.[338]

Farmer 4: Last year there was no large buyer, so I sold to a local buyer, for 40 LRD/kg – it was wet cocoa. This year I paid some debt to Wienco, for fertiliser and sprayed medicine, and then I sold the rest of my cocoa to Wienco for 100 LRD/kg.[339]

These farmers report increases in the prices they received for cocoa over the past few years, which appears to be as far back as they recall cocoa prices. The first three farmers report price increases in the range of 10, 47 and 38 per cent in two years (2011-2013), which can be compared with a 29 per cent increase in the last two years in the world market. At least the first two farmers report these increases for the highest cocoa quality (Grade 1) *on average* at par with the increase in the world market price. The fourth farmer received a price increase of 150 per cent in one year (2013), which is much above the 17 per cent increase in the world market and the 11 per cent increase in the reference price for 2013. However, this farmer also changed cocoa quality and buyer, which would help to explain the staggering changes. Moreover, the first farmer, who recalled the price in 2009 (55-60 LRD/kg), actually experienced a 92-109 per cent increase over the 2009-2013 period, while both the world market and the reference price declined during this period.

---

335 Group Interview 8
336 My notes from Individual Interviewee 18
337 My notes from Individual Interviewee 17
338 My notes from Individual Interviewee 19
339 My notes from Individual Interviewee 32

These figures are neither extreme nor uncommon in my material. They clearly show that some Liberian farmers have experienced substantial price increases in recent years, on par with or well above those on the world market and the reference prices. In combination with the cocoa-price increases reported by the majority of interviewees, individual farmers' experiences suggest that price increases may have been most marked in very recent years.

I argued above that increased competition, new large investors and the re-emergence of cooperatives have strengthened the bargaining position of farmers, and the farmers quoted above indicate that these structural changes have contributed to the higher prices they receive.[340] The findings are supported by other cocoa-market actors and external observers. Three of the four farmers (Farmers 1, 2 and 3) above explicitly state that they have stronger bargaining power or feel stronger now. They refer to more buyers and increased competition as reasons for obtaining higher prices, which is an interpretation confirmed by key informants. Whereas middle buyers used to have a monopoly in the past, 'this is now changing and, and now cocoa prices are increasing'.[341] 'There are more buyers now… The competition is in favour of farmers, who are offered better prices'.[342] Yet another observer notes that as farmers have become better connected with the world market, they have realised high prices/price increases.[343] Another three of the farmers (Farmers 1, 3 and 4) explicitly or implicitly reflect bypassing or moving away from middle buyers towards selling directly to new investors (Farmer 4) or through farmers' cooperatives/associations (Farmers 1, 2 and 3).

The role of farmers' organising in cooperatives/associations and selling to them in realising higher prices is referred to by several market actors and observers. By selling to cooperatives instead of middlemen, farmers are reported to get a higher price,[344] and several farmers refer to bulking as an explanation. According to one of them, the cooperative 'has meant that farmers put themselves together to do things together – it is beneficial. They sell in bulk and get a better price'.[345] As explained by another, 'now farmers get 90-100 LRD/kg. In the cooperative you have 1,000 kg – maybe you get 110 LRD/kg'.[346] A third farmer confirms this, but suggests yet another explanation for price increases, namely quality increases, which I discuss later. 'Major changes are that we have introduced a bulking system, and that we have been taught how to make preparations of quality cocoa. Both these have meant that we receive a better price. We attract buyers'.[347] Others refer to the countervailing power of cooperatives. Farmers 'are grouping themselves, which gives them a stronger bargaining power and leads to them receiving a higher price compared to before'.[348] To one farmer, the cooperative has

---

340 Strictly speaking, the quotations are from my notes from the interviews with the farmers.
341 My notes from Group Interview 3
342 My notes from Key Informant 4
343 Key Informant 2
344 Group Meeting 10
345 My notes from Group Interview 8
346 My notes from Group Interview 8
347 My notes from Group Meeting 6
348 My notes from Key Informant 4

meant price change. 'With the cooperative we stand strong on the price – our bargaining power has increased. Now middle buyers cannot just come and give any price'.[349]

That prices received by farmers have increased as they shift from selling cocoa to middle buyers towards selling to cooperatives and/or buyers in integrated value chains is further reflected in a comparison of farm-gate prices paid by different buyers during a single cocoa season.

5.1.4   Reported Farm-Gate Prices Paid by Different Buyers

I calculated the average of all farm-gate prices reported by interviewees, to be paid, received or prevailing during the late 2013 cocoa season. Table 5.3 below gives average farm-gate prices by buyer and grade. The table does not represent prices in the entire Liberian cocoa market, only those reported by interviewees – farmers, cooperatives, buyers and external observes. All prices have been converted into Liberian dollars. Whereas interesting patterns are revealed by these figures, I caution against over-interpretation, due not least to the limited number of data points. The uncertainty increases the more the figures are disaggregated, as the data points become fewer. Besides, these averages are based on a mixture of price figures from different localities and counties with different market conditions. Nonetheless, my figures do provide indications of developments and raise questions of interest for further research.

Table 5.3: Average Farm-Gate Prices Late 2013, by Buyer and Grade (LRD/kg)

Grade / Buyer	Wienco (n=9)	LAADCO/ LMI (n=21)	Farmers' Cooperations / Associations (n=15)	Middle Buyers (n=19)	All Buyers (n=64)	Reference Price	All Buyers / Reference Price (%)
Grade 1 (n=34)	116	135	113	99*	121	114	106
Grade 2 (n=12)	-	102	73	99	94	102	92
Subgrade/ Ungraded (n=18)	-	94	77	82	83	88	94
All Grades (n=64)	116	122	95	89			

Source and Notes: Own calculations based on Appendix Tables 5.2a-5.2c; Prices in USD have been converted to LRD = Liberian dollars, at an exchange rate of 82 LRD/USD; n = number of data points; * Includes a price of 125 LRD reported by a middle buyer, but this relatively high price is heavily questioned by a market observer, and in comparison with other figures appears to be an 'outlier', but is nonetheless retained here. If the outlier is excluded the average price declines to 90 LRD/kg.

Three major patterns emerge: 1) middle buyers pay farmers on average less than cooperatives and buyers from integrated value chains, in general as well as for Grade 1 cocoa;

---

349 My notes from Group Interview 8

2) higher grades of cocoa fetch higher prices; and 3) all buyers except middle buyers pay prices at or above the reference price for Grade 1 cocoa. I discuss these patterns in turn.

First, that prices received by farmers increase as they shift from selling to middle buyers towards selling to cooperatives and/or large buyers is suggested when I compare average farm-gate prices from different buyers aggregated over all grades of cocoa, shown on the bottom line of Table 5.3. The table suggests that middle buyers pay on average 89 LRD/kg for cocoa, whereas all other buyers pay more: cooperatives pay 95 LRD/kg, Wienco 116 and LAADCO/LMI pays 122 LRD/kg on average. This pattern also applies to prices for Grade 1 cocoa, for which I have most data points. Middle buyers are reported to pay on average 99 LRD/kg, compared to cooperatives, 113 LRD/kg; Wienco, which buys nothing but Grade 1, and pays 116 LRD/kg; and LAADCO/LMI which gives 135 LRD/kg on average. The middle-buyer average price of 99 LRD/kg includes one 'extreme' price of 125 LRD/kg, reported by a middle buyer but strongly questioned by an external observer well-acquainted with the local cocoa market. If I exclude this extreme price, the average middle-buyer price for Grade 1 cocoa falls to 90 LRD/kg, which reinforces the overall pattern, but also illustrates the sensitivity of the findings to individual 'observations'.

The picture is not as clear when one looks at averages prices for Grade 2 cocoa, where my figures suggest that middle buyers pay more than cooperatives, but these figures are based on limited data and are therefore more uncertain. I will hence not analyse Grade 2 prices in further detail. A similar picture emerges, however, for average prices for sub-grade cocoa/cocoa of unknown or uncertain grade, for which I have more data. These suggest that middle buyers pay more on average than cooperatives, which raises many questions for further inquiry.[350] I cannot, however, draw any conclusions about the relative prices paid for sub-grade cocoa.

The most relevant comparison is perhaps between prices paid by buyers in the emerging integrated value chains (new investors and some cooperatives) for Grade 1 cocoa and prices paid by middle buyers for sub-grade cocoa, because this reflects the choices that farmer increasingly face and the actual changes in selling patterns they are making. This is also where the large price differences are found, shown in Table 5.3, with middle buyers reportedly paying as little as 82 LRD/kg on average for sub-grade or ungraded cocoa. By contrast, the prices farmers may receive if they sell Grade 1 co-

---

350 Could it be because many cooperatives encourage the production of high-grade cocoa, to be sold to buyers such as LAADCO, whereas middle buyers remain somewhat of 'specialists' in Sub-grade cocoa? If so, this may reflect a segmentation of the cocoa market, which is actually consistent with our findings of a more complex cocoa market emerging, containing elements of both spot market and integrated value chains. Another possible explanation is that as the level of competition increases in the domestic cocoa market, middle buyers who want to remain attractive may have to match the price offered by large buyers, and hence pay farmers more, at least in local markets where competition is high. One market actor informed us that middle buyers, in fact, pay the same price as LAADCO for Sub-grade cocoa in one of the counties. (Individual Interviewee 4) A third possible explanation is simply that our few 'observations' of prices paid by cooperatives may give a distorted picture.

coa to cooperatives or Wienco, 113 and 116 LRD/kg on average respectively, is about 40 per cent more. LAADCO/LMI pay even more, reportedly 135 LRD/kg on average for Grade 1.

An obvious and perhaps trivial finding is that farmers who sell Grade 1 cocoa through cooperatives and new investors get better paid than farmers selling poor quality cocoa to middle buyers. However, with more farmers now selling through cooperatives to LAADCO as well as directly to Wienco, these differences in farm-gate prices in 2013 are a further strong indication that farmers have been receiving increased cocoa prices over time, and that this is a result of the structural changes in the cocoa market.

As indicated above, the differences in prices also reflect differences in the quality of cocoa sold. Hence, the second pattern revealed by Table 5.3, is that higher quality cocoa generally fetches higher prices. The average reported farm-gate price for Grade 1 cocoa is 121 LRD/kg, compared to 94 LRD/kg for Grade 2 and as little as 83 LRD/kg for sub-grade or ungraded cocoa. Thus, the average farm-gate price for Grade 1 is 29 per cent higher than that for Grade 2 and 46 per cent higher than the average price for sub-grade/ungraded cocoa. The gradual shift from a spot market to more integrated value chains has meant a dual shift for farmers, a) from selling low quality or un-graded towards higher quality and graded cocoa, and b) from not being rewarded towards being rewarded for higher quality cocoa.

Hence, the price increases enjoyed by Liberian farmers who shift from middle buyers to cooperatives and new large buyers is partly due to increased quality and quality grading of the cocoa sold. Farmers add value to their cocoa and this pays off. This finding is further illustrated by the four farmers quoted earlier, and confirmed by a large market actor. 'The quality of Liberian cocoa is increasing, which leads to increases in the price, which in turn leads to increased demand for cocoa. Hence profits are increasing'.[351] Our findings are supported by farmers in Nimba County interviewed in relation to the planning of a new World Bank project, who reported substantial price increases for cocoa after receiving training and conducting primary processing as early as the 2010/11 cocoa season.[352]

5.1.5 Increased Share of Reference Price and Marketing Margin

According to our data, on average, the farm-gate price from buyers for Grade 1 cocoa in late 2013 was reported to be higher than the reference price, 121 versus 114 LRD/kg, or 6 per cent higher, as shown in the last two columns in Table 5.3 above. More specifically, all buyers except middle buyers were reported to pay prices on average at par with or higher than the reference price for Grade 1 cocoa in late 2013, with LAADCO/LMI paying the most, 135 LRD/kg or 18 per cent above the reference price.[353] (Grade 2 and sub-grade cocoa fetched prices at 92 and 94 per cent of the refe-

---

351 My notes from Individual Interviewee 25
352 World Bank (2012: 72)
353 LAADCO/LMI is reported to pay the highest average farm-gate prices for all grades of cocoa, and to be the only buyer who on average reaches the reference prices for Grade 2 and Sub-grade cocoa.

rence price respectively). This is the third pattern revealed by these data – an important finding, with equally important implications.

First, it suggests that the marketing margin of farmers may have increased over time, which I explore by looking at how the relationship between the farm-gate price and the reference price as well as the world market price has developed. I showed above that the four individual farmers quoted have experienced recent price increases in parity with or well above world market and reference prices. By implication, they have seen their marketing margins increase too. Farmer 1 provides anecdotal evidence of a significant increase in the price received in comparison with the reference price for cocoa. This farmer received 55-60 LRD/kg around December 2009,[354] which amounts to maximum 50 per cent of the reference price for Grade 1 cocoa in the 2009/10 season (cf. Table 5.2 above), whereas the same farmer received 115 LRD/kg or just over 100 per cent of the reference price in late 2013.

My findings in Table 5.3 above show that there is more than anecdotal evidence when they compared with secondary data of farm-gate and reference-price relations in the past. Based on survey data, Gockowski and Wilcox calculated average farm-gate prices in 2006/07, which correspond to 22 LRD/kg when translated from USD to LRD terms at the end-of-year official exchange rates for 2006.[355] These prices can be compared with what apparently is the LPMC-recommended farm-gate cocoa price in 2006, which is equivalent to 38 LRD/kg at the same exchange rate.[356] If there figures are correct, they imply that at the end of 2006, farm-gate cocoa prices were on average 58 per cent of the price recommended by the LPMC (which preceded the reference price). When compared to our overall findings of farm-gate prices equivalent to or above the reference price in 2013 for Grade 1 cocoa (and just under for Grade 2 and sub-grade cocoa) in Table 5.3, the same picture emerges as from the anecdotal evidence. Thus, changes in cocoa prices reported by farmers, combined with data collected on farm-gate cocoa prices in 2013 compared to historical data, suggest that farm-gate prices have almost doubled as a share of the recommended or reference price for cocoa in the last seven years or in an even shorter time.

This may indicate an increase in the marketing margin of cocoa farmers, but for a stronger indication I look at how the share of farm-gate prices to world market prices for cocoa has changed over time. Gockowski and Wilcox also estimated the marketing margins that accrued to Liberian cocoa farmers during the 2006/07 cocoa season, cal-

---

354 Group Interview 8
355 Gockowski and Wilcox (2008), referred to by English (2008: 84 and 99) [partly and probably incorrectly as Gockowski and Wilcox (2007)], calculated average farm-gate prices of 0.365 USD/kg in 2006/07, which correspond to 22 LD/kg (0.365x59.00), at the end-of-year official exchange rate for 2006 (Appendix Table 5.1). [Wilcox (n.d.a: Table 3) similarly calculated average farm-gate prices of 0.511 USD/kg in 2007/08, which correspond to 32 LD/kg (0.511x62.5), at the end-of-year official exchange rate for 2007 (Appendix Table 5.1).]
356 'The farm gate price of cocoa in 2006 was US$0.65 per kg for best grade and US$0.32 per kg for sub-grade quality. LPMC commission is US$0.065 per kg and the transportation cost is US$0.08 per kg. The total delivered cost in Monrovia is US$0.80 per kg for best grade and US$0.47 per kg for sub-grade'. (Republic of Liberia 2007b: 18)

culated as the farm-gate price as a share of the FOB (free on board) price for cocoa.[357] They show that farmers on average received as little as 28 per cent of the FOB price in 2006/07,[358] and on average 32 per cent of the FOB price during the 2007/08 season.[359] Farmers' share of the marketing margin was very low at that time, also in comparison with neighbouring countries. The average price that Liberian farmers received in 2006/07 was as little as 22 per cent of the ICCO price, whereas farmers in Côte d'Ivoire, Cameroon and Nigeria received 43, 76 and 82 per cent respectively.[360] Hence, farmers' marketing margins were markedly low around 2006-2008, when strong buyer market power prevailed at all levels of the cocoa market.

In recent years, when competition and farmers' bargaining power has increased, I expect price signals to be more effectively transmitted and better reflected in farmers' share of the world market price. My data support such a change. First, Table 5.3 above shows that farm-gate prices in late 2013 are about equivalent to or higher than the reference price for Grade 1 cocoa, and I showed earlier that the reference price for late 2013 is about 49 per cent of the world market price for cocoa (cf. Tables 5.1 and 5.2). This suggests that the average farm-gate price for Grade 1 cocoa in late 2013 was roughly 50 per cent of the world market price, more than double the farmers' marketing margin in 2006/07 (22 per cent) – a tremendous increase. Since I don't have data on world market prices for lower grades of cocoa, a similar comparison cannot be made for them.

My findings are supported by secondary data as well as interviewees. According to the LIFE project, changes in farmers' margins and prices have been remarkable. It reports that for the farmers that are sponsored by the project, cocoa prices[361]

> …increased by an average of over 300% from the 2007/08 to 2012/13 seasons and during the same period their percentage of the world market price (all grades) went from about 22% to an average of over 60%.

While this statement is based on project-specific data, which cannot be verified, it is supported by a government observer, who holds that before 2008 Liberian farmers did not get a 'fair share' of the cocoa price. Whereas they used to get 25-40 per cent of the world market price, they now get 60-65 per cent.[362] Yet another observer, independent of the project, refers to Liberian cocoa farmers in general when noting that 'they now

---

357 The FOB price is a measure of the world market price, in this case calculated as the ICCO price less the Liberian-origin discount and less costs for freight and insurance associated with exports to the international market.

358 Gockowski and Wilcox (2008), referred to by English (2008: 84 and 99) [partly and probably incorrectly as Gockowski and Wilcox (2007)].

359 Wilcox (n.d.a: Table 3)

360 Wilcox (n.d.b: 49) A similar conclusion is drawn by the Diagnostic Trade Integration Study conducted in 2007 and 2008, reporting farm-gate prices at 25-35% of the FOB price, compared to 47% in Côte d'Ivoire, 60% in Ghana and 78% in Cameroun (Ministry of Commerce and Industry 2009: 46).

361 ACDI/VOCA (2013)

362 Key Informant 4

receive a "better" …share of the world market price for cocoa than before, in that they receive a better share of the exporters' profit margin'.[363] A third source, a World Bank report, similarly reports that cocoa farmers supported by projects or NGOs receive about 60 per cent of the international cocoa price, 'which is quite standard in the industry'.[364]

The indications that farmers' marketing margin has increased substantially are indeed strong, and reflect a more effective transmission of price signals (from the world market) through the value chain to farmers. This, in turn, is yet another strong indication that the market power of buyers in the domestic Liberian cocoa market has declined and farmers' bargaining power has increased, and lends further support to my conclusion in Chapter 4.

Yet another indication is offered by the reference price. If the picture painted here is correct, farmers have seen the prices they receive for cocoa increase several-fold. When I compare my calculated average farm-gate cocoa prices in Table 5.3 above, ranging between 83 and 121 LRD/kg for different grades, with the average of 22 LRD/kg in 2006/07 calculated by Gockowski and Wilcox, farm-gate prices have increased by between 277 and 450 per cent over the last seven years. Taken together, my findings – that farm-gate prices have increased several-fold during the last four to seven years, that they have more or less doubled as a share of the reference or recommended price during that period, and that all buyers except middle buyers pay farmers the reference price or more for cocoa in late 2013 – have another important implication. They suggest that the introduction of the reference price may actually have played a role by contributing to increased farm-gate prices for cocoa, and thereby partly served as the intended point of reference for price negotiations, strengthening the bargaining power of farmers.

This is further proposed by several key informants. According to a centrally placed public official, the reference price is now disseminated to farmers through the cooperatives, and it helps farmers 'not to be cheated' on the price and to benefit from 'better prices'.[365] The reference price may have helped increase farmers' access to market information, and if so, they are no longer restricted to solely relying on buyers for information about prevailing cocoa prices, which used to be the case in the past.[366] As further noted by English, '[f]or farmers, market information may aid in negotiation of prices or improvement of quality'.[367] This may in turn have contributed to strengthening their bargaining power, as reported by one observer:[368] 'The reference price has come to play an increasingly important role over the years for the farmers and the cooperatives, as witnessed by feedback we have received from them, suggesting that it has been very helpful for their bargaining process'.

---

363 My notes from Key Informant 6
364 World Bank (2012: 72)
365 My notes from Key Informant 7
366 English (2008: 60)
367 English (2008: 56)
368 My notes from Key Informant 6

Hence, by increasing farmers' access to price information and contributing to further strengthening their bargaining power, the reference price may have helped in raising farm-gate prices. According to an additional observer, 'the price of cocoa is published and working to increase the price paid to farmers'.[369] 'Since the reference price was introduced, the cocoa price in Liberia is higher than in Ivory Coast', another one argues, and then continues:[370] 'Now the reference price means that farmers are strong enough to bargain with the buyers. And they are grouping themselves, which gives them a stronger bargaining power and leads to them receiving a higher price compared to before'.

5.1.6 Farm-Gate Prices to Farmers versus Cooperatives – A Qualification

It is important to note that whereas the farm-gate prices for cocoa reported in Table 5.3 above paid by Wienco, cooperatives and middle buyers directly to farmers, those paid by LAADCO are mostly paid to cooperatives, which in their turn pay the farmers. How much of the LAADCO-paid price eventually reaches the farmers depends on how much cooperatives pay their members (and non-members). Cooperatives can be expected to make deductions for their own costs before they pay the farmers. In interviews, leaders and agents of three different farmers' cooperatives report that they pay farmers the same price they receive from their buyers, LAADCO as well as others, for Grade 1 cocoa.[371] A key informant with experience of cooperatives in several counties notes that practices differ, depending on principles and models decided by the cooperatives themselves.[372] According to the informant, one cooperative that reportedly sells Grade 1 cocoa to LAADCO for 1.60-1.65 USD/kg pays 100 LRD/kg cocoa to its member farmers, which is something they have decided and agreed together. At an exchange rate of 82 LRD/USD, this corresponds to a deduction of 24-26 percent. The informant reports that other cooperatives keep 5-10 per cent of the price as commission before paying the farmers. A further, admittedly crude, indication of deductions made by cooperatives can perhaps be provided by Table 5.3 above. My calculations show that the average prices reportedly paid by cooperatives range between 72 and 84 per cent of the average prices reportedly paid by LAADCO. Hence cooperatives may deduct some 16-28 per cent before they pay farmers: 16 per cent for Grade 1, relatively more for lower grades and 22 per cent on average for all grades.

I do not have enough information to draw conclusions about the magnitude of the deductions cooperatives actually make before they pay farmers. The information I have does show, however, that deductions are sometimes made, vary among cooperatives and may be substantial, even up to a quarter of the cooperatives' selling price. A conclusion I can draw is that the prices farmers receive are likely to be lower than those paid by buyers to cooperatives, and hence lower than the reported average farm-gate

369 My notes from Key Informant 3
370 My notes from Key Informant 4
371 Individual Interviewees 13, 25 and 33
372 Key Informant 14

prices paid by LAADCO in Table 5.3 above. All this implies that my findings about increased farm-gate prices and farmers' marketing margins remain valid, but the scale of the increases needs to be adjusted downwards, although I cannot say by how much.

5.1.7   A Discussion of Causes

The reasons for the price increases may be several, as discussed in this section. I have shown that world market cocoa prices have increased considerably in the last eight years. More recently, Liberian border prices have increased also because of the reduced or eliminated Liberian-origin discount, due to the improved quality ratings of Liberian cocoa and Liberian ICCO membership. The depreciation of the Liberian dollar against the US dollar has further implied that the domestic reference price has gradually increased in relation to the world market price in Liberian dollars terms. However, these factors are essentially external to the Liberian cocoa market. I argue that structural changes in the domestic cocoa market likely play a significant – possibly even more important – role in the price increases enjoyed by farmers in recent years. It is not possible to determine the relative importance of the causal factors in quantitative terms, but the data presented here show that several factors are at play, suggest the causal mechanisms through which they operate, and propose that several of them are interlinked.

My findings suggest, first of all, that increased competition among buyers, and from emerging integrated value chains in particular, has created an upward pressure on prices paid to farmers, as buyers' market power has been reduced. The re-entry of cooperatives as cocoa sellers on behalf of farmers has further contributed to counter-vailing buyers' market power. Both these changes have contributed to strengthening farmers' market position and bargaining power, thereby enabling them to negotiate higher prices. Cooperatives have also enabled farmers to bulk and sell cocoa in larger volumes, thus reducing transaction costs for buyers, which is a third factor likely to have contributed to higher farm-gate prices. The emergence of integrated value chains, in particular, has implied several combined changes of potential importance. It has enabled farmers to bypass or shift away from middle buyers, a fourth factor, towards trading directly with large buyers or through cooperatives, who pay better on average according to our data. In addition, these integrated value chains (and cooperatives) have promoted a shift among farmers from selling low quality and ungraded cocoa towards high quality and graded cocoa – a fifth factor – which has been rewarded by higher prices. A final, and sixth, factor is the reference price for cocoa, which may have contributed to raising farm-gate prices by further strengthening the price information available to farmers, and perhaps in particular cooperatives, and hence their bargaining power.

5.2   Implications for Access to Services and Farmers' Investments

As a consequence of the substantial price increases, the incentive for farmers to participate in the cocoa market have been strengthened in recent years. In addition, the structural changes have influenced farmers' opportunities to respond to and benefit from the improved incentives in different ways. In particular, farmers' access to markets and a variety of inputs and services has improved, several of which have been touched upon above and are briefly summarised in the following sub-section, further supported by mainly primary data. In the next sub-section, I look at how farmers actually respond by using these new opportunities to benefit from increased market participation, notably through different productive investments. This sub-section relies largely on my interviews with farmers, as well as other interviewees, complemented by findings from previous chapters and secondary data.

5.2.1   Increased Access and Opportunities to Benefit from Increased Market Participation

Several of the structural changes – increased competition, the emergence of integrated value chains and the re-entry of cooperatives – have contributed to better access to markets, market information and a number of inputs and supporting functions for smallholder farmers.

Firstly, the growing number of market actors buying cocoa and the increased competition between them has meant that farmers' *market access* has increased. The international cocoa market can now be accessed through various channels, not just a single buyer. The emergence of integrated value chains puts farmers in closer contact with demand in the international market, for instance through Wienco, which buys cocoa from farmers and exports directly to overseas buyers. And some cooperatives have managed to export cocoa themselves, thereby coming into direct contact with buyers abroad.

Along with increased competition in the domestic market this has contributed to breaking the isolation of farmers from the world market – and from the world market price. Whereas farmers formerly had no other source of price information than the (single) buyer, with increased competition, buyers cannot retain a monopoly on price information. As buyers compete on price, they reveal price information. Cocoa prices have become more important as signals – carriers of information – about conditions on the world market. Hence, farmers' access to *price and market information* ought to have improved. The new large investors have played a particularly important role, since they offer significantly higher prices than middle buyers. As also discussed above, the reference cocoa prices may have contributed to farmers' – and in particular cooperatives' – increased access to price information. The reference price is set to partly reflect world-market prices, and is disseminated to cooperatives, which in turn are supposed to disseminate this information to farmers.[373] While some farmers I talked to were

---

373 Key Informant 7

aware of the reference price,[374] others were not: 'the reference price is unknown to me, and I am not familiar with the concept'.[375] This suggests that the reference price may 'get stuck' at the level of cooperatives and not play its full informational role for farmers.

Third, the emergence of integrated value chains has contributed substantially to increase farmers' access to *inputs* and various *supporting functions*, which are provided as integrated services by new buyers. Wienco is the only known supplier of *fertiliser and pesticides, fungicides, and herbicides* for cocoa in Liberia. Its establishment in the country in 2011 resulted in cocoa farmers in the areas where it established itself gaining access to these inputs for the first time. The company's business model also allows farmers to buy these inputs on credit, to be repaid with cocoa. They thereby also offer the means by which to purchase the inputs, which represents a real opportunity for cash-constrained farmers. Wienco provides *training* in how to use and apply the fertiliser and chemicals as well as the necessary *equipment* as part of the price for the inputs.[376] In addition, it requires farmers to organise in smaller groups at village level to learn from each other and perform joint labour. Several farmers refer to this means of *accessing scarce labour* for farming as highly useful,[377] as reflected in the notes from my interview with one member of a Wienco farmers' group:[378]

> 'It means a whole lot to me'. We work in groups at each other's farms, and the work gets done faster. 'It brings unity'. 'It brings security among ourselves'. Before we used to work for ourselves, now we help each other. Since I joined the group, 'we feel fine, we feel more relaxed' …We have another kuu for brushing, but our way of doing it is different. Other kuus that you hire only want money, and they don't do it properly. But our kuu group does the brushing properly – we make the cocoa farm 'clean!' We learnt how to do it from Wienco.

It is worth noting that Wienco reportedly charged 25 LRD/kg cocoa (or more) for the inputs and associated services[379] – regardless of the amounts applied – a fifth or more of the cocoa price they pay. One can expect this price to include a certain monopoly rent, since Wienco has a *de facto* monopoly on selling such inputs in Liberia. This means the price is higher than it would be in a more competitive market, and therefore relatively costly for farmers. Indeed, one farmer I interviewed, who enjoyed improved yields on that part of the farm sprayed with Wienco pesticides, nonetheless reported that 'I am happy with the relationship, but once I have paid my debt I will stop the relationship, because it is too expensive'.[380] Thus, even if access to them has increased significantly, fertiliser and chemicals are costly, possibly due to monopoly prising.

---

374 Individual Interviewees 7, 8, 13, 15, 17 and 19
375 Individual Interviewees 14 (quotation from my notes), 5, 11, 12, 21, 29 and 30
376 E.g., Informal Interview 3, Group Interview 3, Individual Interviewees 2, 3 and 35
377 Individual Interviewees 27-29 and 32
378 My notes from Individual Interviewee 29
379 As reported by Individual Interviewee 16, and suggested by Individual Interviewees 14, 26, 28, 30-32
380 My notes with Individual Interviewee 14

The other new buyer, LAADCO, offers varying combinations of integrated services in accordance with contracts of varying length in different parts of the country. It works with and contracts cooperatives, mostly on purely commercial terms, but in certain parts of Lofa it combines its commercial role with its role as implementer of the STCRSP programme. In its commercial role, it provides three kinds of inputs and services to farmers through the cooperatives.[381] First, cocoa *seedlings* are provided free of charge, but accessing them depends upon the previous delivery of cocoa. The seedlings are reportedly high yielding, but the quality of some of them is seriously questioned by some market actors.[382] The seedlings are for farm expansion only, and come with a long-term contract to sell all the cocoa to LAADCO. Second, pre-finance to cooperatives, enabling them to pay farmers cash for cocoa delivered before it is sold to LAADCO, is a *credit service* provided to cooperatives. It is unknown if there is any cost charged for the service. Hence, LAADCO and cooperatives compete with middle buyers not on price only, but also in terms of *cash payment*. Farmers' opportunities to access cash have thus increased: they can get it even if they shift from middle buyers.

Finally, *in-kind loans*, notably in terms of rice, zinc sheets for roofing and cement, are provided through the cooperatives to farmers, who tend to be short of cash before harvesting begins. These loans are to be repaid in cocoa, and are a credit service for *consumer goods* sold to farmers. The prices farmers pay for this service have been reported to be the going market price for the consumer goods in question,[383] but a higher price, not least to cover the capital costs of the company, cannot be ruled out. When interviewees were asked about what farmers pay for consumer goods purchased on credit, I was informed the sums were deducted from the payment received for cocoa, which left the impression that farmers' awareness of prices may have been limited.[384] Together with limited competition among suppliers on consumer goods on credit, this may provide opportunities for monopolistic pricing. Again, access to the embedded service has increased, but it may be expensive because of certain market power of the seller. An external observer warns that the highly opaque conditions under which embedded services of this kind are sold to farmers, particularly in combination with very long-term contracts, run the risk of tying farmers into unfavourable relationships.[385]

In its role as implementer of the STCRSP, LAADCO provides seedlings at subsidised cost, partly on credit, to farmers, as well as pre-finance, *training* in quality control, *transportation* and logistical support for marketing to cooperatives, in exchange for its right to buy cocoa.[386]

The case of LAADCO illustrates the role played by cooperatives as a channel both for integrated services from new buyers and for support from donor-funded projects.

---

381 Unless otherwise stated, the presentation of the LAADCO model is based on Individual Interviewee 1.
382 Individual Interviewee 3
383 Individual Interviewee 4
384 Individual Interviewees 13, 31 and 37, Group Interviews 3 and 7
385 Key Informant 1
386 Individual Interviewee 1

In addition to the inputs and services just discussed, they appear central to increasing farmers' access to *knowledge* and opportunities to learn. Cooperatives provide and channel donor-funded extension services to and training for farmers on improved farming practices, how to produce high-quality cocoa and how to manage farming as a business. The LIFE project reports that comprehensive training has reached 7,500-9,500 farmers.[387] In recent years, cooperatives appear to have played a particularly important role in promoting farmers' processing of cocoa for higher quality by teaching them how to ferment and dry cocoa properly, providing *facilities* for such processing on their own premises, and by grading and controlling the quality the cocoa delivered by farmers.[388] According to one cooperative, its function is 'to teach farmers to ferment and dry so as to get Grade 1 cocoa',[389] and it has been argued that smallholders who belong to cooperatives produce far better quality cocoa than other farmers.[390] Finally, several cooperatives supported by LIFE have developed a warehouse-receipt system, which gives farmers both a *savings opportunity* and increased *payment security* when selling their cocoa to cooperatives.[391]

With increased access to markets, inputs, credit, knowledge and a number of additional supporting functions, the constraints on cocoa farmers are reduced, their opportunities to respond to and take advantage of price incentives are increased and their potential to realise higher returns are considerably enhanced. Whereas increased competition likely implies that farmers can continue to behave more or less as in the past, selling to middle buyers for cash in hand, and still get a higher price for their cocoa, it is the integrated value chains and cooperatives that seem to offer the greatest opportunities for farmers to increase returns.

First, simply by applying the basic processing procedures for fermentation and drying of cocoa, based on learning how to take care of the cocoa after harvest, farmers may increase the *quality* of the cocoa they are already producing. They thereby *add value* to their cocoa to an extent that is reflected in the price differentials between e.g., Grade 1 and sub-grade cocoa. Cocoa farmers' value addition may thus increase substantially, by on average 46 per cent, as suggested by Table 5.3 above.

Second, farmers can increase the *productivity and output* of existing farms in several ways. By using fertiliser and 'chemicals' – in particular to deal with severe black-pod disease – bought on credit, combined with instructions on how to apply them, farmers can increase returns from existing cocoa trees, even those that are ageing. By applying what they have learned about improved crop husbandry, for instance more frequent under-brushing and working with fellow farmers in local labour groups, farmers can increase the productivity of their trees and the total cocoa output of their farms. Farmers can rejuvenate their farms by replacing some old trees with new seedlings, either from seeds collected from their existing trees or improved varieties from the integrated

387 ACDI/VOCA (2013)
388 E.g., Group Interview 3; Key Informant 2
389 My notes from Individual Interviewee 33
390 Key Informant 1
391 E.g., Key Informant 1

value chain and/or cooperative. These behavioural changes to increase returns entail some costs, in terms of effort, time and labour as well as payment for fertiliser, chemicals, seedlings and farm labour. Some inputs may come at high cost, but with higher cocoa prices farmers may be more willing to pay those costs, whereas in the past investing human and financial resources in cocoa farming was simply not profitable. Besides, several of the inputs and services were simply not available in the past. With increased opportunities to raise yields from farms and add value to the cocoa produced, combined with higher cocoa prices, incentives as well as opportunities for profitable smallholder participation in the cocoa market have certainly increased.

When better access to markets and support functions is combined with new buyers' willingness to invest in lasting contractual relationships with farmers and cooperatives to ensure future purchases of high-quality cocoa at competitive prices, smallholders' incentives as well as opportunities to make long-term investments in cocoa production and marketing by *expanding their farms* into new land are also, and thirdly, reinforced.

5.2.2   *Farmers Respond to New Opportunities by Investing in their Farms*

Increased cocoa prices combined with better access to markets and a variety of support functions have reinforced farmers' incentives and opportunities to raise productivity, output and value addition and hence their potential returns from cocoa-market participation. That Liberian cocoa farmers do respond to improved price incentives in the market and take advantage of the opportunities provided is illustrated by their shorter and longer-term investments in their farms. Appendix Table 5.3 summarises my findings, based on individual interviews with farmers.

A major finding is that of 26 farmers individually interviewed, every one of them informed us of their increased activity on their farms, in terms of short and long-term investment, in various ways and to varying extents. First, 21 of 22 farmers – I was not able to get information about all aspects from all farmers – or 95 per cent – report that they are processing and/or have learnt or are able to *process high quality* cocoa. This finding is further supported by the previously reported finding that farmers interviewed have achieved price increases partly by processing and selling higher quality cocoa. Cooperative members and leaders in a group interview confirm this finding, by recounting that farmers were taught how to prepare quality cocoa and that this helped them achieve a higher price.[392] Another cooperative also produces Grade 1 cocoa, according to its leaders,[393] and a large-buyer interviewee reports that the quality of Liberian cocoa is increasing.[394] By increasingly processing and marketing quality cocoa, smallholders are *adding value* to their cocoa, which is now bought by buyers from integrated value chains and promoted by cooperatives. In the past, such processing was not worthwhile, as middle buyers mixed qualities and paid for all cocoa as low-quality cocoa, just as cocoa exported from Liberia was treated and paid for as low-quality cocoa on the world market.

---

392 Group Interview 6
393 Individual Interviewee 25
394 Individual Interviewee 35

According to Appendix Table 5.3, more than half the farmers interviewed (11-15 of 19) report learning/having learnt and applying *improved farming practices* (crop husbandry), particularly by under-brushing their farms more often. About half of them (9-10 of 19) also report working jointly in farmers' groups/kuus, hence benefiting from shared knowledge about crop husbandry and shared farm labour. However, only seven of 22 farmers have applied fertiliser and/or chemicals for e.g., pest control, of which five are in partnership with Wienco, one with LCC, and one is independent. As further shown in the table, two additional farmers told us they were hoping or willing to use such inputs. An external observer confirms the limited use fertiliser, fungicides and pesticides to date, which means that black-pod may continue to have severe effects on the farms.[395] A leader of a Wienco farmers' group illustrates these experiences by relating how farmers were taught to use fertiliser and chemicals and how they apply them to their farms jointly in the group – chemicals are sprayed every three month. The group is much appreciated by the farmers, who are easily motivated to work jointly since all of them benefit, and women can be included. Farmers, whose yields have increased somewhat, have also learned how to ferment and dry cocoa to produce Grade 1.[396] Any use of fertiliser and chemicals by 'Wienco farmers' represents an increase since 2011 when the company was established in Liberia, since the general picture is that the 'use of chemical inputs such as fertilizers and pesticides is negligible in the cocoa sector'.[397] Wienco reportedly works with some 1,400 farmers, of whom some 400 in Lofa County.[398]

Of the 26 farmers interviewed, only one has refrained from planting new cocoa trees either as replacements or to expand the farm, and thus refrained from making longer-term farm investments. About half the farmers (11 of 21 farmers) report *replanting new cocoa trees* on their existing farms, and thus further rehabilitating their (not seldom) old farms. However, perhaps the most important and surprising sign of farmers' response to improved price incentives and increased opportunities is our finding that farmers are investing in *expanding their farms* by planting cocoa trees on entirely new land. As a matter of fact, most of the farmers individually interviewed have expanded their cocoa farms – 17 or 18 of the 21 farmers who gave information on this. Of these 21 farmers, only two reported difficulties in accessing land to expand their farms, which shows that for these farmers access to land is not an immediate constraint on expansion. During a group interview, farmers and leaders of a cooperative reported that their small farms have been expanded and continue to expand as farmers plant more seedlings.[399] A group interview with external observers confirms the picture of cocoa farmers being more engaged and increasing their farm sizes in recent years, for example in Bong County.[400] Another external observer reports cocoa planting

---

395 Key Informant 2
396 Individual Interviewee 28
397 Republic of Liberia (2014: 42)
398 Individual Interviewees 2 and 35
399 Group Interview 6
400 Group Interview 3

and expansion in Nimba,[401] while yet another paints a slightly different picture: cocoa replanting is taking place, and as a result the total acreage of cocoa farms has increased, but this is a limited and recent trend.[402] Investments to increase the land used for cocoa production are further supported by official figures on the total area under cocoa cultivation, which is estimated to have increased from 10,000 ha to 45,260 ha between 2007 and 2011.[403] Certainly, not all the investments have been made by smallholders, since the LCC plantation was established in 2011 and other large farms may have been established.

Finally, Appendix Table 5.3 shows that when planting new cocoa trees, two-thirds of farmers interviewed (14 of 21) use seeds and/or seedlings from old trees, whereas about one-third (8 of 21) use *higher-yielding/improved varieties* (or supposedly so), which are in short supply, as reported earlier. Some farmers use a combination of both, while others expressed a wish to obtain improved and higher yielding varieties. Combined with my finding in Chapter 3 that the supply of improved cocoa seeds/seedlings appears to have increased in recent years, this suggests that farmers are increasingly using improved varieties.

5.3 Implications for Farmers' Choices and Livelihood Strategies

Increased access to support functions and opportunities for beneficial market participation illustrates how the structural changes in the Liberian cocoa market have increased the choices available to farmers. Smallholders now have more alternatives to choose between in considering how to engage and with whom to interact in the cocoa market. They can select various combinations of prices, services, conditions and lengths of collaboration, by choosing to sell to different kinds of buyers. This enhanced freedom of choice increases their opportunities to manage and adapt the livelihood strategies of their farming households, since Liberian smallholders are not only producers but also household consumers.

The more diversified structure of the Liberian cocoa market, with emerging integrated value chains co-existing with remaining elements of spot markets, offers new alternatives for smallholder farmer engagement. Farmers can choose between selling cocoa to middle buyers in the spot market, as well as between different middle buyers, or selling to farmers' organisations and thereby, at least in certain cases, to new large investors such as LAADCO, or engage directly with Wienco. In some instances, they can enter an out-grower scheme with the LCC. While not all alternatives are available in all locations, all but one of the 28 farmers I encountered had at least two alternatives

---

401 Key Informant 13
402 Key Informant 2
403 Republic of Liberia (2014: 9), referring to FAOSTAT data

to choose from.[404] Smallholder farmers' have greater freedom in choosing marketing channels.

Different marketing channels represent different packages of services, effort and financial returns, which serve different farmers more or less well, depending on their situation. Selling to a middle buyer on the spot market may be attractive to a farmer in urgent need of cash, e.g., to pay for children's school fees or for medical services, or with limited knowledge and ability to process cocoa into a higher quality. Several farmers still resort to this practice[405] – some because they were unable to attend to their farm for one reason or another.[406] Other farmers report being already indebted to middle buyers, e.g., for food purchases towards the end of the rainy season, and that they sell their cocoa to them as a means to repay their debt.[407] For a farmer in no immediate need of cash, selling to a cooperative – where payment is delayed and verified through a warehouse receipt – may be an attractive option in order to receive a higher price, even though it requires more time, effort and cost to produce high quality cocoa and payment is delayed.

Similarly, with the reactivation of cooperatives and the creation of Wienco-related farmers' groups, farmers can choose to remain independent or to organise themselves, and they can choose between different forms of self-organisation. I found that, regardless of higher prices offered and services provided by cooperatives, some farmers actively chose to remain independent.[408] One cooperative member expressed a wish to self-manage without inputs from LAADCO or Wienco,[409] and others have left the cooperative because they were dissatisfied with it.[410] Hence, the availability of alternatives has allowed farmers to test what works for them. Some farmers tried the Wienco model, for example, but have decided to leave it once the current contract is discharged.[411]

The integrated services available to farmers include financial services, which offer alternative forms of credit and savings, such as credit for farm inputs and certain consumer goods, and savings in terms of cooperative warehouse receipts. Similarly, pre-payment by LAADCO to cooperatives provides farmers with an alternative to selling to middle buyers, if they want to get cash for cocoa sold. More choice of financial services should increase farmers' opportunities to smooth their income and expenditure streams, and facilitate year-round livelihood strategies. Related to this is reduced uncertainty about the future, in particular by means of long-term contracts. These

---

404 One female farmer could not afford to pay the membership fee to the cooperatives, and have not sole any cocoa in recent years (Individual Interviewee 9). Another woman farmer refers to her husband being in charge of selling, but gives the impression that he sells where alternatives may be available (Individual Interviewee 20).

405 E.g., Individual Interviewees 10, and as reported by e.g., by Individual Interviewee 33

406 E.g., Individual Interviewee 30

407 Individual Interviewees 10, 12 and 14

408 For instance Individual Interviewees 15, 21 and 30

409 Individual Interviewee 11

410 Individual Interviewees 15, 21 and 30

411 Individual Interviewees 14 and 32. The fact that other farmers are leaving Wienco for a cooperative is reported by Individual Interviewee 31.

make it easier for farmers to adopt a longer-term perspective and plan for the future, and ought to facilitate farmers' long-term investments and farm expansions.

Moreover, farmers do not have to choose one or other alternative. The diversity of the market has allowed farmers to benefit from different services and returns from different marketing channels by participating in both the spot market and the integrated value chains. By diversifying their market outlets, farmers' spread and reduce their risks. There are several indications that farmers combine options, and in a group interview with external observers a former cocoa trader reported on this practice:[412]

> Farmers tend to underreport yield, e.g., to the cooperatives, so that they can continue to sell some produce to middlemen in order to get some cash in hand, while selling some cocoa to the cooperative, so as to be part of the benefits that membership entails, for instance in terms of protection, support and services via the cooperative, e.g., as donor handouts, and better price. They strategise to use the two sources of buyers to combine cash inputs with other services/high price... And they strategise very consciously.

Farmers' so-called side-selling to middlemen, associated with the underreporting of yields, is reflected in our interviews with cooperatives, some of which recount how they struggle to access all the cocoa marketed by farmers.[413] Side-selling was also reported by large buyers and cooperatives, as shown in Sub-Sections 4.2.3 and 4.3.2 above.[414] Although many farmers use both marketing channels, most of those interviewed report having shifted away from the spot market.[415] Only one farmer in late 2013 indicated that he was selling on both the spot market and through an integrated value chain.[416]

5.4 Smallholder Cocoa Farmers' Returns and Benefits

This section looks at how increased cocoa prices, access and opportunities, as well as farmers' behavioural responses are reflected in their financial and physical returns and

---

412 Notes for Group Interview 10

413 Individual Interviewees 13 and 33

414 Note that although the prevalence of side-selling is here seen to reflect farmers' alternative marketing channels and their ability to make strategic choices – an improvement compared to fewer alternatives and choices in the past – side selling *per se* is not necessarily a beneficial phenomenon. It partly seems to reflect the circumstance that smallholder farmers are cash constrained – a real problem to many of them – and may also have negative consequences. Both cooperatives and large buyers of integrated value chains find side-selling problematic to their own cocoa marketing activities and it could even threaten the development and sustainability of both kinds of organisations with negative consequences also for smallholder farmers in the longer term. The problem of side selling has been studied, for example, in the case of coffee cooperatives in Rwanda by Muyawamariya (2013) and more broadly in African cotton value chains by Poulton et al. (2004).

415 Cf. the last column of Appendix Table 5.4, where individually interviewed farmers report their marketing channels.

416 Individual Interviewee 10

perceived benefits of cocoa-market participation – as well as their future potential. While quantifying these developments is beyond the scope of this research, our data suggest certain patterns and tendencies. The section draws heavily on my interviews with farmers, complemented by official data and my earlier findings. Appendix Table 5.4 lists my findings, as reported by farmers individually interviewed.

When it comes to the returns to farmers from cocoa-market participation, I have already shown in Section 5.1 that there are strong indications that farmers obtain higher prices, partly as a result of processing their cocoa into higher quality. In Sub-Section 5.2.2, I also show that farmers add value to their cocoa. These are positive signs and suggest that farmers may see their incomes and profits grow with cocoa-market participation.

As regards smallholder farmers' *profitability* or profits earned from cocoa-market participation, there are no data available, and possibly none exist. Farmers do not seem used to seeing their farms as business entities or to keeping records of profits and losses, as indicated e.g., by the provision of farming-as-a-business training by certain NGOs reported earlier. Among the farmers interviewed, I came across only four who made some reference to profit or accounts, as shown by Appendix Table 5.4. One farmer claims to keep accounts and make profit calculations.[417] Another reportedly kept no records in 2011, but by implication did so in 2012 and 2013.[418] A third finds it difficult to achieve profitability, because labour costs exceed income.[419] And finally, a farmer with both an old farm with declining cocoa yields and a new one that is just about beginning to produce, finds that the cost of managing the old farm is increasing more than the yields from the new, which suggests declining profitability.[420]

Whereas data about profitability are non-existent, most farmers (20 of 26 individually interviewed) provided some information about their *incomes* from cocoa, which is directly observable for them and easier to report. As shown by Appendix Table 5.4, the results are mixed, particularly as regards changes in income from cocoa over time. Three farmers reported receiving no income, and of the 17 who reported income from cocoa, six (the largest group) saw increases over the last few years, four saw declines, two saw no change and another two reported that their incomes varied from year to year. Of the six reporting growing incomes, one farmer had experienced a large change in the preceding five years.[421] The rather limited number of farmers seeing their incomes grow appears somewhat surprising, given the high price increases reported earlier. Besides, this contrasts with the incomes of farmers participating in the LIFE project, which reportedly had 'an average 400 per cent increase from cocoa income alone between 2008 and 2012'.[422] The experiences of the other farmers reveals important information may help to explain the moderate incomes.

---

417 Individual Interviewee 13
418 Individual Interviewee 19
419 Individual Interviewee 14
420 Individual Interviewee 18
421 Individual Interviewee 19
422 Key Informant 1

First, one of the three farmers reporting no income has not sold any cocoa in recent years, because the old trees are dying and produce virtually no cocoa, whereas the trees newly planted are not expected to yield until after four years.[423] The other two farmers have also only recently planted trees and expect no income for some years.[424] One of the two farmers who saw no major change in recent years noted that his income has remained almost stable. This is because earlier, when cocoa production was high, prices were low, whereas now, prices are high but the trees are not producing as before and some are dying.[425] Similarly, the four farmers experiencing declining incomes reported old and dying trees, black pod, declining yields and falling total production. The low productivity of Liberian cocoa trees due to their age is a generally recognised problem in the sector.[426]

Indeed, many farmers report low and/or declining yields from the trees and/or output from their farms, hence *productivity and production*, precisely for these reasons, as shown by Appendix Table 5.4.[427] This partly reflects the circumstance that many farms are old, but as shown earlier, most farmers interviewed are rejuvenating and extending their farms. Hence, several farmers also report good and increasing yields and/or output from trees treated with chemicals, rehabilitated farms and/or new plantings.[428] One farmer tells of cocoa yields increasing considerably and a several-fold increase in total production in only two years, but also of declining productivity on the old farm with dying trees.[429] Altogether, only eight farmers individually interviewed reported a clear increase in cocoa production over the preceding few years.[430] However, farmers in group interviews with two different cooperatives report that improved farming practices have resulted in higher cocoa yields,[431] and leaders from a third cooperative note that farmers get better returns from their cocoa farms.[432] Nonetheless, also with regard to physical returns from cocoa farming, the picture appears mixed.

My interpretation is that our data reflect a smallholder cocoa sector in transition. The structural changes I observed in the cocoa market, and the improved incentives and opportunities for smallholder farmers to participate beneficially have only occurred in recent years, and the farmers' response is equally or even more recent. Hence, returns from farmers' investments in their farms can only be expected to become evident over time. Gradually, both physical returns, in terms of productivity and output, and financial returns, in terms of income and profit, can be expected to increase. Two additional sources lend support to this interpretation. First, the Government Cocoa Export Strategy reports that in spite of increased cocoa production, overall yields declined

---

423 Individual Interviewee 9
424 Individual Interviewees 24 and 38
425 Individual Interviewee 29
426 Recently reported for instance by Republic of Liberia (2014)
427 This applies, for instance, to Individual Interviewees 9, 26, 29, 30, 31 and 32.
428 For example Individual Interviewees 8, 13, 14 and 18
429 Individual Interviewee 13
430 Individual Interviewees 6, 8, 11, 13, 15, 17, 19 and 27
431 Group Interviews 8-9
432 Individual Interviewees II 33

from 2005 to 2011, which reflects the increased area brought under cultivation[433] and the time needed for new trees/farms to reach full productivity. Second, a key informant reports that farmers have begun replanting only recently, and the new trees have not started to yield, so that while total acreage has increased, this has not yet influenced cocoa production.[434]

Despite the mixed picture of cocoa output among the farmers interviewed, official figures show that *total cocoa production* displays a clear upward trend and considerable increases too, although their accuracy remains uncertain. As shown in Table 3.1 above, production estimates by the Central Bank suggest that cocoa production increased by some 650 per cent between 2006 and 2013, albeit more slowly, by some 17 per cent, between 2010 and 2013. These data may be consistent with my findings and interpretation, for example if the initial increase in total production reflects an increasing number of farmers reactivating their cocoa farms, and if the slower production growth more recently reflects the ageing tree stock and its partial replacement by new trees that have yet to yield.

The fact that farmers have made productive investments in their cocoa farms improves their chances of increasing physical and financial returns in the future. Their long-term investments in new trees also suggest that farmers believe in the future of the cocoa market, a belief explicitly expressed by most of the farmers interviewed. Twenty of the 26 farmers individually interviewed told of their *expectations* of their future as cocoa farmers. All but four of them expressed belief in exclusively positive developments for them as cocoa farmers, which they articulate as increased yields/returns or production,[435] demand and number of buyers,[436] cocoa prices,[437] income,[438] security[439] and benefits.[440] One farmer expects to have money in the future,[441] another expects good things,[442] two believe the future will be better,[443] another that it will be bright.[444] According to the last-mentioned farmer, cocoa is for the future and is long-lasting; it will provide income year after year and bring security for the future.[445] A few farmers worry about the future, however, because, for example, trees are not bearing and income is small.[446]

Many of our farmers also report *perceived benefits* that they are already experiencing by participating in the cocoa market. These essentially relate to how incomes from

433 Republic of Liberia (2014: 9), referring to FAOSTAT data
434 Key Informant 2
435 Individual Interviewees 5, 9, 10, 12, 17, 18, 24, 29 and 31
436 Individual Interviewee 8
437 Individual Interviewees 8, 14, 18, 20, 29, 32, 37 and 38
438 Individual Interviewees 27 and 37
439 Individual Interviewee 37
440 Individual Interviewee 6
441 Individual Interviewee 18
442 Individual Interviewee 10
443 Individual Interviewees 12 and 27
444 Individual Interviewee 37
445 Individual Interviewee 37
446 Individual Interviewee 26

cocoa farming facilitate their meeting their own livelihood needs and those of their families. Twenty farmers informed us about what cocoa means to their livelihoods. For several, cocoa is an important source of income,[447] the major one,[448] or even the only source of income/cash.[449] The income from cocoa is reported to help a lot[450] and to bring much benefit.[451] One farmer sheds light on another important implication: he does not have to borrow money, but can be independent.[452] The money earned from cocoa sales enables farmers to buy, build or improve their houses,[453] to pay children's school fees and thus to send children to school or even to good schools,[454] to pay for medication,[455] and to buy food, rice, oil, zinc and other materials.[456] Indeed, several farmers relate how incomes from cocoa help them support their children and families, resolve domestic problems and meet family obligations – in short, to manage family life.[457]

5.5   Conclusion: Increasingly Inclusive Cocoa Market

This chapter has examined the implications for smallholder cocoa farmers of the structural changes that have taken place in the Liberian cocoa market in recent years, in terms of their possibly more beneficial participation in the market. It has reviewed changes in the incentives available to farmers, the opportunities for their beneficial market participation, farmers' responses and their returns. This section summarises the findings, and draws conclusions about what they mean for the inclusive nature of recent cocoa-market developments.

5.5.1   Summary

The chapter began by looking at how the structural changes and resulting strengthened bargaining power of farmers has translated into the prices that farmers receive and in their marketing margin – their share of the world market price – by collecting various price data from primary sources and comparing them with price references from secondary sources. A major finding is that the combined data strongly indicate that Liberian farmers have experienced *significant increases in the prices received for cocoa in recent years,* particularly high-grade cocoa. This is suggested by price increases re-

---

447 Individual Interviewees 7, 12 and 20
448 Individual Interviewees 17, 31, 32 and 37
449 Individual Interviewees 13, 18, 30 and 27
450 Individual Interviewee 17
451 Individual Interviewee 30
452 Individual Interviewee 29
453 Individual Interviewees 7, 11, 12, 15, 18 and 20
454 Individual Interviewees 7, 11, 14, 17, 19, 20, 30, 32 and 38
455 Individual Interviewee 18
456 Individual Interviewees 10, 27, 30, 32 and 37
457 Individual Interviewees 11, 17, 20, 29, 30 and 38

ported by a majority of interviewees, combined with individual farmer's experience of considerable increases. Second, it is suggested by data collected on farm-gate prices from different buyers in late 2013 in comparison with secondary data on reference prices and historical prices. In absolute terms, my data suggest that *farm-gate prices have increased several-fold – three to four times – in the last seven years for Grade 1 cocoa.* In relative terms, *farm-gate prices have almost doubled as a share of the recommended or reference price for cocoa in the last 4-7 years.* By late 2013, the average reported farm-gate price for Grade 1 cocoa is above the reference price for the highest quality cocoa. While there are several external explanations for these price increases, my findings suggest that structural changes in the domestic cocoa market and related factors are likely to play a significant – possibly dominant – role and interact to reinforce one another: increased competition and the re-entry of cooperatives, strengthening the bargaining power of smallholder farmers and reducing transaction costs; the emergence of integrated value chains, which together with cooperatives pay higher prices, grade cocoa and reward high-quality cocoa. Together with increased competition, the reference price may have increased price information and thus further strengthened farmers' bargaining power.

A second major finding is that that there are equally strong indications that *the marketing margin of Liberian cocoa farmers has increased substantially in the last seven years.* My analysis of the combined data suggests that the average farm-gate price for Grade 1 cocoa in late 2013 is roughly half – 50 per cent – of the world market price, which is more than double the farmers' marketing margin of 22 per cent in 2006/07. This is a remarkable increase. Some qualification is needed, however, in that the numerical levels of the reported increases in farmers' cocoa prices and marketing margins may be overstated, because some individually reported farm-gate prices in my primary data set are prices paid to cooperatives, not farmers. However, the overall findings nevertheless hold true. The doubling or so of farmers' marketing margins means that smallholder farmers' share of the world market price for cocoa has increased in relation to – and at the expense of – buying agents and buyers in the domestic value chain. This, in turn, is yet another strong indication that the market power of buyers in the domestic Liberian cocoa market has declined and farmers' bargaining power has increased, and lends further support to our conclusion in Chapter 4. Furthermore, this section has shown that additional changes in factors beyond those discussed in Chapter 4, such as the reference price and the grading and production of quality cocoa, may also have strengthened the farmers' position. Since these changes are largely related to farmers' selling cocoa to cooperatives and new buyers in integrated value chains, this helps us in understanding the role played by these new market actors.

A consequence of the considerable and rather rapid price increases is that *smallholder farmers' incentives to participate in the cocoa market have certainly been strengthened in recent years.* I then considered how the structural changes in the cocoa market have influenced farmers' opportunities to respond to and benefit from the improved price incentives in different ways, and thereafter looked at how farmers have actually responded. An important finding is that recent changes in the cocoa market have together contributed to *increasing farmers' access to output markets,* through various market channels, *and to a host of inputs and supporting functions,* essentially in the form of integrated services. These include market information, through increased competition and the reference price, inputs such as improved cocoa seeds/seedlings, fertiliser, pesticides and other chemicals, extension services and training, farm labour, and a series of financial services: credit for inputs and consumer goods, savings opportunities, payment security and cash payment. These increasingly beneficial conditions have created new opportunities for smallholder farmers to participate in the cocoa market. However, some of these integrated functions come at high, or unknown, cost, related to the monopolistic or strong selling power of input providers in the new integrated value chains. An additional finding is that the *smallholder cocoa farmers interviewed are very responsive to the new market opportunities created, and increasingly so,* as further supported by some of my previous findings and complementary secondary data. Farmers increasingly make productive investments in their cocoa business in a number of ways. They add value to the cocoa produced by processing high quality; adopt improved farming practices; apply fertiliser and chemicals; replant trees on old farms; and plant on new land to expand their farms. In these regards, smallholder farmers *participate more actively* in the Liberian cocoa market.

Thereafter I discussed the choices available to farmers. A central finding is that as a consequence of the structural changes in the Liberian cocoa market, *smallholder farmers' freedom of choice has increased,* in terms of how to participate in the cocoa market. Farmers have more alternatives, and can choose between or combine different ways to participate, such as through the spot market and/or an integrated value chain, and select the most beneficial option available. *This has in turn created opportunities for and facilitated the management of the livelihood strategies of their farming households,* and there are signs of farmers responding to the new opportunities by making both active and strategic choices.

I finally looked at what cocoa farmers' behavioural responses to strengthened incentives and new opportunities for market participation have meant for their financial and physical returns, perceived benefits, and expectations of and potential for the future, based primarily on interviews with farmers, complemented by other data. My overall finding is that *farmers' returns from cocoa-market participation display a somewhat mixed picture,* in terms of incomes and physical output so far. As expected, data about smallholder cocoa farmers' profitability is non-existent. Data about changes in their incomes from cocoa reveal mixed results – some farmers see increases, others not – which seems to be at odds with high income growth reported by the most influential donor-funded project in the cocoa sector. The findings may be partly due to the fact that some farmers started to grow cocoa only recently and have not yet realised incomes; and that production is based on old and dying cocoa trees with poor and declining yields, whereas the new trees planted have not yet started yielding. Indeed, many farmers report low and/or declining productivity and production for these reasons. Others report good and increasing yields and/or output – again a mixed result, when compared with official data showing several-fold increases in total cocoa production in the post-war period.

My interpretation is that the data reflect a smallholder cocoa sector in transition. Whereas the cocoa <u>market</u> has undergone substantial change in recent years, smallholder cocoa <u>farming</u> has only begun to adapt to these changes, and finds itself in a process of transition from stagnation and decline towards increased productivity and output in the future. Once this process gains momentum, farmers may see their physical and financial returns grow more consistently. Whereas many farmers already experience benefits from participating in the cocoa market, I recognise that not all farmers participate and benefit to same extent. However, most cocoa farmers interviewed express belief in the future, and their long-term investments in their cocoa farms have certainly increased their chances of higher returns over time.

5.5.2   Conclusions

Based on my findings about the implications of recent changes in the Liberian cocoa market for smallholder farmers, in terms of their increased benefit and increased participation, *the overall conclusion of this chapter is that the Liberian post-war cocoa market has become more inclusive.* This more inclusive nature does not mean that the market by late 2013 was characterised by inclusiveness, but the process of change in recent years means it has become increasingly inclusive over time. The data presented in this chapter, combined with findings in previous chapters, almost consistently point in one direction – more active participation by smallholder farmers in the cocoa market in ways that are increasingly beneficial to them.

Smallholder farmers' benefit from participating in the cocoa market has increased markedly in recent years, and in several ways. The most important economic benefit is the substantial price increases farmers selling cocoa have experienced, and a comprehensive increase in their marketing margins. Farmers' share of the world-market price has more or less doubled in recent years and the economic incentives to participate in the cocoa market have consequently been strengthened. In terms of financial returns, there are no data on profitability, and of farmers' income from cocoa, the results are mixed so far, although some data point to high income growth. However, conditions for increased returns in the future are being created by farmers' investments in their cocoa businesses, in particular their productive investments.

The conditions for smallholder farmer participation in the cocoa market have also become more beneficial. Farmers' increased marketing margins, in particular, reflect their stronger position in the cocoa market and their correspondingly increased bargaining power – a major improvement in conditions for farmers' interactions with cocoa buyers compared the past. Cocoa farmers and their organisations are on a more balanced – if not necessarily equal – footing than before when negotiating and trading cocoa and associated services and conditions, although probably less so when it comes to inputs. Cocoa farmers' conditions have also improved greatly in terms of access to output markets through a variety of channels, not least cooperatives; to market information, e.g., through increased competition; and to various inputs and supporting functions, not least financial services, in particular through integrated value chains. Whereas some integrated functions come at high cost, they are more widely available and opportunities for farmers to engage in longer-term contractual relationships with buyers have increased. Smallholder farmers' freedom of choice for how and with whom to interact in the cocoa market has increased, with more alternative buyers and combinations of services and conditions to choose between. Although all options are not available to all farmers everywhere and at all times, and farmers' choices are certainly constrained, their opportunities for beneficial participation in the cocoa market as well as for managing their livelihood strategies have nonetheless increased.

In response to stronger incentives and opportunities, smallholder farmers participate more actively in the Liberian cocoa market in several ways. Farmers are investing resources for the short- and long-term development of their cocoa business, hence making productive investments. Many farmers increasingly add value to the cocoa produced by processing it into higher quality, which fetches a higher price. Farmers also seek to enhance the productivity and output of existing farms by increasingly adopting improved farming practices, fertiliser and chemicals, replacing old trees with new, often improved, seedlings, and expanding their farms on to new land to further increase cocoa output and marketed supply. This means that farmers are more actively using and spending resources on inputs and supporting functions, such as credit and extension, now increasingly available to them – not primarily in the markets, though, which remain poorly developed, but through cooperatives and integrated value chains.

Farmers' engagement in such cooperatives and value chains is another strong indication of their increasing participation in the output market for cocoa. And they are making strategic choices between the marketing channels available to them, or fashioning their own combinations of such channels. They have also become more active in the market through their organisations, which conclude contractual relationships, even long-term ones, with large buyers in integrated value chains, bulk and sell cocoa in volume, export directly to overseas buyers, and serve as channels for inputs and support functions from buyers and donor projects. The supply of cocoa through farmers' organisations has increased. In addition, the mixed record of recent changes in the production and supply of cocoa among the farmers interviewed is not inconsistent with the conclusion that Liberian farmers produce and supply more cocoa. This is suggested by official data on total cocoa production, which display a clear upward trend and considerable increases during the post-war period. Given that Liberian cocoa is only produced for the market, this is also an indication of the increased total marketed supply of cocoa, which is further supported by figures on total official exports, which increased several-fold during the post-war period, as shown in Chapter 3 (Table 3.1). While data on changes in the number of cocoa farmers are not available, the combination of my primary data on mixed output-cum-supply with official data on large increases in total production-cum-official exports suggest that the number of active cocoa farmers has increased. I interpret these findings as additional indication of increased smallholder farmer participation in the cocoa market, while the farmers' long-term investments in old and new cocoa farms hold out the promise of increased participation in the future.

My conclusion that the Liberian cocoa market has become more inclusive is based on the criteria established in Chapter 2, namely that smallholder farmers' participation has grown and on increasingly beneficial terms. As shown, I argue that their benefit has increased in both economic terms, notably marketing margin, and in the conditions under which they participate in the market. I also suggest their participation has increased in the sense that farmers now engage in the market in more – and new – ways and in larger numbers.

Having identified major structural changes in the post-war Liberian cocoa market in the previous chapter, examined their implications for smallholder cocoa farmers and concluded that they mean the cocoa market has become more inclusive in this chapter, I next seek to identify the institutional changes that may underlie these developments.

6 Major Institutional Changes – Contributing Explanations

This chapter identifies major institutional changes in the Liberian cocoa market in the recent post-war period that, I suggest, have made a particular contribution to the inclusive developments observed in the market. Identification, and, in particular, the significance of these underlying institutional changes has essentially been traced backwards from my preceding analysis of recent developments in the Liberian cocoa market and their implications for smallholder farmers. The chapter discusses how the institutional changes have influenced behavioural constraints and opportunities for different market actors, and hence incentives for behaviour, thus offering institutional explanations for altered and new behavioural patterns, interactions and outcomes observed in the cocoa market.

I only seek to identify institutions that have been changed, and only changes making the cocoa market more or less inclusive. As already noted Chapter 2, this is not a complete or detailed analysis of all institutional changes or of the entire institutional set-up relevant to the Liberian cocoa market. With one exception – land rights – unchanging institutions are not discussed, notably those informal ones associated with socio-political patron-client relationships.

Changes have occurred in the broader institutional environment of the cocoa market as well as in specific arrangements within it: some changes have been intended and formalised, others have emerged organically as an unintended consequence of other changes. Using the concepts defined in Sub-Section 2.1.2, I distinguish three groups of institutional change, which are examined sequentially. The first section reviews intentional changes in the formal rules of the cocoa market's institutional environment – government reform measures – influencing overall conditions for who may enter and operate in the market, as well as rules for cocoa grading and pricing. Thereafter, Section 6.2 discusses several unplanned changes in informal rules of interaction between actors in the cocoa market that have emerged spontaneously in response to initial reform measures and the resulting entry of new market actors. A final set of rule changes, intentional changes in formal institutional arrangements for interaction between specific actors within the market, are discussed in Section 6.3. A final section contains concluding remarks.

6.1 Intentional Change in the Environment of the Cocoa Market

This section presents three major changes in formal rules that have been undertaken by the Government of Liberia. These have entailed changes in the overall institutional environment of the cocoa market. It also discusses what they have meant for market actors. In addition, comment is made about land rights, which are expected to be important but do not appear to have been changed.

Historically, as noted in Chapter 3, trade in Liberian cocoa was largely controlled by the Liberian Produce Marketing Corporation (LPMC), but during the conflict years it was unable to perform its duties, so that the market was informally deregulated and private traders filled the void. Our analysis suggests that during the early post-war years the Liberian cocoa market was characterised by strong market power exercised by private traders in both the domestic and export markets. As English notes, around 2007 'the LPMC had nominal authority to register exporters, establish grades, and provide access to export facilities',[458] but in practice it appears to have remained weak in providing regulatory and support functions. The institutional environment generally provided weak incentives for, and imposed constraints on, production, trade and investment in the cocoa sector, in particular for smallholder farmers, despite rapidly growing cocoa prices on the world market. This was revealed in an analysis by Wilcox and Pay-Bayee during a cocoa-sector round-table discussion in 2006.[459]

Eventually, institutional reform of the cocoa market was initiated to address some of the problems.[460] The role of the actors involved and the unfolding of this reform process is not entirely clear. Whereas several stakeholders were involved at different stages, our impression is that the driving forces were the donor-funded NGOs active in the sector and the top Liberian executive – the President's office. It was they who initiated the reforms and/or pressured various entities in the government bureaucracy to launch and implement them.[461] Indeed, LPMC, the Ministry of Agriculture and others played central roles. A series of regulatory reforms – referred to as 'Quick Wins' or 'Cocoa Quick Wins', because they did not require legislative approval, only changes in operating procedures and policies – were introduced in the cocoa sub-sector.[462] Most of them appear to have been decided by the President's Economic Management Team (EMT) in 2009; their implementation appears to have been initiated or completed in 2010.[463]

I describe what I assess to be the major measures, together with other institutional changes, underpinning the structural changes observed in the cocoa market.

6.1.1 Deregulation – Facilitating Market Entry and Increasing Competition

Several Quick Wins were introduced to facilitate entry of new market actors and thus promote competition at different levels of the marketing chain, and to reduce discrimination against small exporters. One measure was to reduce the 10,000 USD annual

---

458 English (2008: 30)
459 Wilcox and Pay-Bayee (2006)
460 According to a key public-sector informant, the new government in 2006 wanted to deregulate the sector, eliminate the LPMC monopoly and invite private-sector actors. (Key Informant 15)
461 Based on Key Informants 1, 4, 5 and 6, ACDI/VOCA (2010)
462 ACDI/VOCA (2008, 2010)
463 Key Informants 1 and 6; Economic Management Team (2009)

licensing fees charged by LPMC on all cocoa exporters, and to replace the flat rate – which heavily discriminated and reduced the profitability of small exporters – with a sliding rate linked to average tonnage exported.[464] The high fees had created disincentives to entry for new exporters, particularly smaller ones, and hampered competition in the cocoa market, particularly among exporters. This exporters' licensing fee was totally abolished in 2010.[465] Another Quick Win was the abolition of formally granted regional monopsonies to licensed buying agents (through LPMC's selective issuance of exclusive licenses).[466] This move aimed to encourage competition among buyers 'for the purchasing of cocoa at the farmer level, aggregation of cocoa at the association, clan and district level and transport to exporters in Monrovia'.[467] This too is reported to have been implemented in 2010.[468] These measures were ranked as two of the three most important by a large private market actor.[469]

In addition, a series of 'official and unofficial fees paid by exporters to a variety of government agencies and individuals', amounting to 28 per cent of the export value, were reduced or eliminated in order to encourage exports of more and better quality cocoa as well as returns to farmers. These fees included a 2.5 per cent duty/customs user fee on export value paid to the Ministry of Finance, and a so-called royalty plus various charges paid to LPMC.[470] Reportedly, the LPMC royalty of 50 USD per metric ton was eliminated.[471] Export taxes on cocoa, which amounted to 35 per cent of exporters' income, appear to have been reduced to 25-30 per cent on net income, and now allow exporters to make deductions from gross income for various costs associated with improvements in the quality and handling of cocoa. The apparent purpose was to increase profitability among exporters, help ensure better farm-gate prices and off-set the costs of expanding production and processing high-quality cocoa by smallholders.[472]

Yet another measure, primarily aimed at increasing prices received by farmers and ensuring that all quality cocoa was purchased, is also likely to have contributed to increasing the competition for cocoa, as argued earlier. Farmers, possibly primarily larger farmers, and their organisations have since 2010 been allowed to export directly, just as exporters are allowed to buy cocoa directly from farmers. Farmers may thus by-pass middle buyers, exporters or – as it were – the LPMC, and don't have to pay for their services or contribute to their profit margins.[473] This means that exporters' monopoly has been eliminated. There appears to be no general permission for farmers or cooperatives to export directly, however, but provisional permits seem to be granted.[474] It

---

464 ACDI/VOCA (2008)
465 Key Informant 6
466 Economic Management Team (2009)
467 ACDI/VOCA (2008: 1)
468 Key Informant 6
469 Individual Interviewee 1
470 ACDI/VOCA (2008: 2) (quotation); Economic Management Team (2009)
471 Key Informants 1 and 6
472 ACDI/VOCA (2008, 2010), Key Informants 1 and 6; Economic Management Team (2009)
473 Key Informants 1 and 6
474 ACDI/VOCA (2008: 3)

remains unclear if this imposes constraints on direct exports, or if it is mainly a matter of registration by these exporters.

Finally, while LPMC monopolistic/monopsonistic trading powers had been eliminated in practice, their formal termination also appears to have been officially accepted – even endorsed – by the President.[475] Debate on the future role of the LPMC ensued,[476] but eventually it was concluded that it should no longer 'perform its statutory role of buying, processing and exporting agricultural commodities', but serve as a purely regulatory body.[477] A decision was taken in 2011 and a legal process is under way to transform the LPMC into the Liberia Agriculture Commodity Regulatory Agency (LACRA).[478]

The combination of these deregulatory measures – fee and tax reductions and eliminating formal monopsony and monopoly powers – have altered the rules of the game as to who may enter and participate in the Liberian cocoa market as a buyer and exporter and on what conditions. The rule changes have facilitated market entry and exports and strengthened incentives for traders and exporters to engage in the cocoa market, and can be assumed to have contributed to the increased competition in the domestic and export markets in recent years. Legally eliminating the role of the LPMC as a market actor, restricting it to a regulatory body, ought to have reduced remaining uncertainty among buyers, exporters and investors about its future role in the cocoa market, and thus about the permanency of the deregulatory changes. This, in turn, has helped strengthen incentives for longer-term investments by large buyers-cum-exporters and plantations. I am unable to say whether any one measure has been particularly decisive, but suggest deregulatory measures as a major institutional explanation for two of the structural changes in the cocoa market, increased competition and the entry of a new kind of buyer making productive investments.

6.1.2   Quality Grading System – Increasing Cocoa Prices and Value Addition

Another potentially important institutional change is the introduction of a cocoa-quality grading system compatible with international standards to replace the old FAQ system discussed earlier. The purpose was to prevent international buyers from immediately discounting the price for Liberian cocoa and to promote the processing of high quality cocoa.[479] As mentioned, this system has been gradually implemented, beginning in 2010 at the farm-gate level,[480] where quality control and grading is done by actors in the emerging integrated value chains, such as Wienco and the cooperatives, whereas it is not undertaken by middle buyers. However, by 2011, the system also

---

475 Key Informants 6 and 15
476 See e.g., Wilcox and Pay-Bayee (2006) and Ministry of Commerce and Industry (2009: Annex B).
477 Quotation of a letter from the Minister of Agriculture to the President, including a proposed legal act (Ministry of Agriculture 2012b); Key Informant 4
478 Key Informants 6 and 15; Ministry of Agriculture (2012b)
479 ACDI/VOCA (2008; 2010)
480 Key Informant 1

reportedly operated at the port in Monrovia and thus at export level, which means that LPMC actually graded cocoa according to the new standard and no longer allowed exportation of FAQ-quality cocoa.[481] But since middle buyers don't grade quality and mix qualities, the grading system is not consistently applied or enforced throughout the trading system, as some market actors noted. According to one of them, the new grading system is largely honoured by market actors, but there is no control by government/LPMC, and one key informant appears sceptical about LPMC's ability to perform this task.[482] However, LPMC is reportedly contracting an international company to set-up an institutional structure for comprehensive quality control from the farm-gate throughout the value chain up to exportation.[483]

This measure is ranked important by public and private actors alike as well as external observers, not only for reducing the Liberia-origin discount, but also to the processing of higher-quality cocoa and thus raising the price received by farmers.[484] However, it is the only Quick Win that was initially resisted by LPMC, the President's EMT and certain private actors.[485] It was argued that Liberian cocoa could not yet meet the relevant standards, farmers were not ready to produce high-quality cocoa or enough of it, and that the new system should be introduced only gradually as cocoa quality improved.[486] Some traders lobbied against the new grading system. The system came with indicative farm-gate prices (the reference-price system), and higher quality, hence with higher prices. It is reported that when farmers, as a consequence, started to demand higher prices for higher quality cocoa, some exporters saw short-term profits decline and resisted introduction of the new system. What lobbying exporters in 2010/11 'really wanted was to prevent prices that they had to pay producers from going up'.[487] As discussed earlier, some exporters seem to favour short-term returns, whereas others see longer-term benefits from the new system. One reason buyers continue to purchase ungraded or mixed-grade cocoa at a relatively low price may be that they can process low-quality cocoa into high-quality and thereby benefit from the value addition themselves.[488] As noted by one market actor:[489] 'Some traders even buy wet cocoa, which is to steal from farmers, as they cannot access the value added from fermenting and drying it properly. Processing should take place on the farm, which would enable the farmers to get a better price'.

To judge from the actual decisions about and implementation of the reform measures, lobbying against them by market actors appears to have been moderate, as reported by several national-level public-sector actors – or at least ineffective, beyond a possible slight delay for individual measures. According to one interviewee, the only actors ne-

---

481 Key Informants 1 and 6
482 Individual Interviewee 1; Key Informant 5
483 Key Informants 2 and 6; Group Interview 1
484 Key Informants 1, 3, 4 and 6; Individual Interviewee 1
485 Key Informant 1; Economic Management Team (2009); ACDI/VOCA (2010)
486 Economic Management Team (2009); ACDI/VOCA (2010)
487 Key Informant 1
488 Individual Interviewee 4
489 My notes from Individual Interviewee 35

gatively affected were middle buyers, and they had not approached the government in Monrovia, whereas another noted that there was some, but not much, resistance and it was rather weak, and yet another could not recall any lobbying.[490] The new system changed the standards for the qualities, how they are defined and how they are related to farm-gate prices. My previous analysis of the role of grading in increasing cocoa quality, value addition and prices to farmers suggests that the new grading system has been a significant institutional factor. The increased profitability potential of cocoa exports reinforced incentives for buyers to make productive investments and establish long-term relationships with farmers. Similarly, incentives for farmers to add value to their cocoa by processing high quality, as well as to use the opportunities to invest in their farms offered within the integrated value chains, were strengthened.

6.1.3 Reference-Price System and Information – Increasing Bargaining Power and Prices

An institutional change related to the grading system is the introduction of the reference-price system in 2009, discussed earlier. Grading cocoa required differentiated prices in order to motivate farmers to improve and buyers to promote cocoa quality. However, for reference prices to work, mechanisms for communicating the price needed to be established. Hence one Quick Win was to post/air the reference price to enable farmers to negotiate with buyers and ensure that licensed buying agents and exporters paid acceptable prices for quality cocoa.[491] It has proven difficult to establish a market-information system that effectively disseminates information about reference prices, however, for which both LPMC and the Cooperative Development Agency (CDA) play central roles.[492] One problem is the lack of budget to enable broadcasting of quarterly prices on community radios in local languages. This implies that prices are only announced in newspapers, which are mainly read by citizens in urban areas,[493] in addition to the dissemination by the CDA to cooperatives.[494] At a meeting of the stakeholder forum, the Cocoa Sector Technical Working Group (CSTWG), in late October 2013, discussion ensued about how to disseminate the finally decided LPMC reference prices for October-December 2013. I quote from my notes:[495]

> Information was intended in two newspapers by LPMC, which few people/ farmers read, it was noted, and dissatisfaction was expressed by the other participants. LPMC was urged to ensure speedy sharing of information by several means, including e-mail and text messages also to the group members for further spreading by them to the counties. Concern over the LMPC delay of the whole process was

490 Key Informants 4, 5 and 6
491 ACDI/VOCA (2008; 2010)
492 STCP (2010: 53)
493 Key Informant 6
494 Key Informant 7
495 Group Interview 1

voiced as the harvesting season begins now. A time line for LPMC was proposed, and the demand for monthly price announcements was repeated.

Minutes from a similar meeting in July, referring to the July-September reference prices, reveal similar concerns and complaints.[496] Price information problems notwithstanding, a group of key informants interviewed stated that 'increased market information and information about the reference price, which now reaches out to farmers even in their local vernacular' was one of several major reasons for recent changes in the cocoa market.[497]

My analysis of cocoa prices earlier suggests that the reference price has to an extent served its intended function as a point of reference in price negotiations, improving farmers' and cooperatives' access to market information and thereby strengthening their bargaining power. I also suggest that it has at least partly contributed to higher farm-gate prices. The reference-price system has thus established a rule with an attached value – or norm – for what are perceived to be reasonable farm-gate prices in the Liberian cocoa market, particularly for different quality grades of cocoa (based on a combination of factors such as world market price, transaction costs etc.) prevailing at a certain time. This means that the two institutional set-ups – the reference-price and quality-grading systems – are interrelated and mutually reinforce their impact.

Additional changes in the institutional environment may have influenced developments in the Liberian cocoa market in recent years, but I suggest the ones discussed have been the most influential. Further institutional changes highlighted by interviewees and in documents include: 1) establishment of the first stakeholder coordination forum, the Cocoa Sector Technical Working Group, in 2008[498]; 2) provision of standard weighing scales subject to testing and verification, as a requirement for licensed buying agents[499]; 3) completion of the National Cocoa Development Strategy in 2012[500]; and 4) ICCO membership, which helped to eliminate the discount on exported Liberian cocoa.[501]

6.1.4   A Comment on Land Rights – No Change but Potentially Important

I observed earlier that virtually all cocoa farmers interviewed are investing in their farms – at least half of them in their existing farms, and most of them also in expanding their farms. Indeed, only two of the farmers interviewed reported difficulties in accessing land for expansion. This is a surprising finding and suggests that land tenure – in terms of both securing returns from investments in existing land and accessing new land for long-term investment – may be less of a problem for cocoa farmers than

---

496 CSTWG (2013)
497 My notes from Group Interview 3
498 Key Informants 1, 4 and 6; STCP (2010)
499 ACDI/VOCA (2008; 2010); Key Informant 6; Economic Management Team (2009)
500 Ministry of Agriculture (2012a)
501 Key Informants 1, 4 and 6

expected. My findings do not immediately appear to support the general perception that land rights in Liberia tend to create disincentives for productive investments in land (and discriminate against local communities).[502]

Many of the farmers interviewed have inherited at least part of their farms,[503] which may have facilitated their farm expansion. Accessing land may be more difficult for landless and prospective farmers, such as youths living in the communities. The picture is unclear, however. A key informant identified land availability and tenure as a primary constraint on investment in existing land as well as in farm expansion.[504] That security of tenure may influence Liberian farmers' investment in and generation of re-turns from their cocoa farms is shown by English. She found that during the 2006/07 season farming households with official titles produced on average 30 per cent more cocoa on their land than farmers without legal title.[505] But as noted by Wilcox and Pay-Bayee, '[c]ustomary tenure may or may not provide the necessary safeguards needed to encourage investment in tree stocks'.[506] Land rights are thus a potentially vi-tal issue for smallholder cocoa farming, even if not in the immediate future. This would be in keeping with wider African experience of small-farm commercialisation, where usufruct land rights under collective tenure are found to constitute a constraint, but less than expected.[507] Besides, land rights may be more directly important for produc-tive investments in cocoa farming, and thus, indirectly, for marketing of the produce.

Whereas land rights are a broad area in need of institutional reform and subject to radical proposals in Liberia,[508] so far the overall institutional set-up, with parallel and overlapping statutory and customary land rights, has not undergone major change in the post-war period. Nonetheless, the role of land rights in the inclusive development of Liberian cocoa markets, particularly in the longer term, deserves further examina-tion.

6.2 Institutional Change Emerging Organically in the Cocoa Market

Important institutional changes taking place in the Liberian cocoa market appear to emerge spontaneously as a result of other changes that lead market actors to interact differently with one another, giving rise to new rules of the game in the process. The impetus for such organic change in informal rules has been, for example, the for-mal changes in the institutional environment just discussed, their implications for the structure of the cocoa market and the entry of new kinds of market actors – or several

---

502 World Bank (2008); Cf. Eriksson Skoog (2009: 3-4)
503 At least Individual Interviewees 5-7, 13-14, 16-17, 19, 21, 31 and 37
504 Key Informant 3
505 English (2008: 54)
506 Wilcox and Pay-Bayee (2006)
507 See e.g., a literature review by Wiggins et al. (2011).
508 Land Commission (2012)

of them in combination. In this sub-section I highlight change in such organic institutions that I suggest are significant for the inclusive developments observed. These relate to price formation, competition in output markets, coordination within the value chain and, finally, input markets.

6.2.1 A Changing Price-Formation Mechanism

A first organic change is found in the rules of price formation, to which all the major changes in the institutional environment above appear to have contributed – directly as well as in their impact on market structure. The rules of the game for how prices in the cocoa market are determined – the mechanism for price formation – in particular farm-gate prices, have implications for how inclusive the market is.

First of all, I have argued that increased competition for cocoa – to which deregulation contributed – and the entry of cooperatives have altered the market powers and bargaining positions of market actors, in particular strengthening those of farmers and their organisations. This change can be described as a partial shift away from a buyer's market, wherein conditions for transactions are more or less exclusively determined by buyers, towards at least elements of a seller's market. Sellers now have more say in relation to buyers, as reflected in the circumstance that cocoa prices paid to farmers/cooperatives are at least to some extent negotiated. Sellers do have some bargaining power, which is why negotiation is in any way meaningful. I suggest the rules of the game for how prices are determined in the Liberian cocoa market are changing. The change reflects varying conditions in the international, domestic and local markets. This is a change of particular importance to smallholder farmers, and could also be described as farmers and cooperatives moving from being price takers towards, if not price makers, at least price negotiators. I have argued that the reference-price system has contributed to strengthening farmers' and cooperatives' bargaining power as well as to increasing farm-gate prices, so it too ought to have played a role in the change of price formation.

In addition, the intentional reference-price and quality-grading systems together rule that higher prices are paid for higher quality cocoa. Although these *new pricing rules* are not consistently applied throughout the market, partial institutional change has taken place in this regard, as evidenced by my farm-gate price data. I propose that these changes in price formation and pricing rules have been a central benefit for farmers in terms of the increased prices realised.

6.2.2 New Actors Change Rules for Competition and Cooperation

Recent developments in the Liberian cocoa market have included the entry of new kinds of market actors, a central characteristic of the altered market structure discussed at length above. Large buyers-cum-exporters investing in lasting relationships and cooperatives are novel actors, and play partly new roles in the cocoa market. By their very entry and presence, they change relationships between market actors and thus the rules of the game for interactions between them. Market interaction takes different forms. A distinction is made between *competition*, between buyers at the same node in the cocoa value chain, and *coordination*, between buyers and sellers at different nodes of that chain. I here discuss how the entry of large investors and cooperatives, and the partial withdrawal of NGOs from the seed-and-seedling market, have led to emerging but unintended changes in the rules of the game for competition and collaboration.

Competition in the Output Market

First, rules for competition in the output market have been altered. The entry of new large buyers-cum-exporters has influenced the ways in which competition takes place in the cocoa market and has in turn contributed to changing the rules of the game for competition. Competition between buyers has become increasingly complex. It no longer takes place on the spot market alone, but buyers there compete with buyers in integrated value chains, and integrated value chains compete with each other. In addition, the cocoa price is no longer the only competitive device, but different types of payment conditions, inputs and services, credit and savings schemes, the length of commercial relationships etc. are used as a means to compete. The rules for who competes with whom and in what ways are changing. As competition among buyers for cocoa becomes more complex, the rules adapt, which benefits smallholder farmers, who gain more choices in terms of market channels, prices, payment conditions as well as integrated inputs and services, which they can combine in various ways.

In a similar manner, the re-entry of farmers' cooperatives and associations as market actors has influenced the rules for competition in the cocoa market in two ways. Cooperatives are buyers of cocoa too, from member and non-member farmers. Buyers on the spot market and one of the integrated value chains (Wienco) now also have to compete with cooperatives, as implied earlier. Cooperatives compete on prices and bundles of services that differ from other buyers, although some of them are part of the LAADCO integrated value chain. Secondly, and importantly, the organisation of farmers into cooperatives has strengthened their market position and bargaining power, as discussed earlier. This means that competition among farmers selling cocoa to buyers has declined. Major benefits of these new competition rules for smallholder farmers are, again, stronger bargaining power and more choices in input and output markets.

Coordination in the Output Market

Secondly, rules for collaboration and coordination in the output market are changing. In the part of the cocoa market characterised by a spot market – as well as during the early post-war years when the entire cocoa market was a spot market – coordination of transactions is largely through the price mechanism. The exchange of cocoa between seller and buyer is coordinated on the spot, as itinerant traders offer to buy at a price the farmer is willing to accept then and there. And each transaction is separate, between one farmer and one buyer (cf. the model on different types of value chains in Appendix Figure 2.1.) However, major institutional changes in the coordination of transactions have taken place in recent years.

A major result of the re-entry of cooperatives is a change in the rules of interaction between buyers and sellers of cocoa – hence for collaboration between different nodes in the value chains – most importantly through the cooperative's coordinating function. As discussed in Sub-Section 4.3.3 above, this is a vital function performed by cooperatives, which was essentially missing in the early post-war period and benefits both buyers and farmers. Cooperatives coordinate transactions on behalf of buyers by organising the search for cocoa-supplying farmers, negotiating prices and other conditions and striking deals with them. This means, for example, that since cooperatives organise farmers as members, their membership ledger makes it easy to identify the farmers in surrounding communities willing to sell cocoa, as well as their precise location, and to organise the collection of their cocoa. Buyers, by negotiating farm-gate prices and other conditions and striking a deal with one cooperative instead of hundreds of farmers, save time and other transaction costs. Similarly, cooperatives coordinate transactions on behalf of cocoa farmers, by facilitating farmers' search for and negotiation with buyers. One cooperative identifies, negotiates and strikes a deal with the buyer, instead of hundreds of farmers. Farmer have only to strike a deal with the cooperative, but this is in principle a one-off event, decided collectively and with similar conditions for all farmers. Without cooperatives, many farmers would be unable to be in touch with other than middle buyers. Their transaction costs would be far too high, probably prohibitive. This illustrates how cooperatives economise on transaction costs for both buyers and farmers, and increases the efficiency of the entire value chain, to the benefit of both buyers and farmers, and how new rules emerge in the process. Through their vital coordination function, the re-entry of cooperatives' has introduced new rules for how transactions are organised and coordinated in the Liberian cocoa market and by whom. Explicit coordination of transactions – how to search for, negotiate and strike a deal with a partner – is done by cooperatives.

In a similar manner, the entry of new buyers establishing integrated value chains has contributed yet another complementary set of rules for the coordination of transactions between buyers and sellers. Again, these are rules for explicit coordination of cocoa transactions – stipulating who trades with whom, when and in what manner and on what conditions etc. – in this case codified in and guided by formal contracts. Both cooperatives and integrated value chains have devised formal rules to guide coordination, further discussed in the Section 6.3. It is important to recognise that in both cases, it is not only transactions regarding cocoa output that are coordinated, but also transactions related to integrated inputs and services. Transaction costs are correspondingly reduced for buyers and sellers of both.

Input Market for Seeds and Seedlings

Finally, the rules for interaction in the input market for improved seeds and seedlings appear to be changing. As discussed in Chapter 4, observed changes in the behaviour of NGOs imply that they are largely withdrawing as market actors themselves. By abandoning the practice of providing hand-outs of improved cocoa seeds and seed-

lings, free of charge, NGOs' direct involvement in the market is replaced by a more facilitating role. Some NGOs now promote domestic private nurseries and seed/seedling
providers and thus the development of a domestic market for these inputs. There was
no market for seeds/seedlings serving smallholders in the early post-war years, and it is
not unlikely that NGO handouts have hindered its emergence. This is now changing.

The shift in NGO practice may imply a qualitatively significant change in the rules
for interaction in the potentially emerging input market for improved cocoa seeds and
seedlings. Changing the rules of the game for competition among suppliers has made
it possible and created incentives for domestic private providers to enter the market to
supply these inputs commercially. Hence, and secondly, even if this market remains
poorly developed, the rules for how transactions are conducted between suppliers and
buyers – for coordination – have also been partially altered. Farmers now have to pay
for these inputs, even if at a subsidised price and on credit. The beneficial implication
for farmers is, notwithstanding the cost increase, more access to improved seeds/seed-
lings in the short term and potentially more sustainable access in the longer term.

A second major, and obvious, change in the rules for the potentially emerging
input market for improved cocoa seeds and seedlings is the provision of these as integrated services by large buyers in integrated value chains, notably LAADCO and LCC.
Whereas the LCC nurses its own seedlings, LAADCO buys them, including from one
of the small private nurseries, as discussed in Chapter 4. The provision of these inputs
(as well as others) as integrated services, however, means that their exchange is coordinated not in the market (nor in a hierarchy, as within a firm), but through the hybrid
mechanisms that an integrated value chain entails. In the absence of a well-functioning
market for these inputs, a major benefit for farmers would appear to be their provision
on credit, the consequent increased access to the inputs, the concomitant supply of
extension services and the associated secure output channel.

6.3 Intentional Change in Arrangements within the Cocoa Market

Third, there are the intentional changes in formal institutional arrangements at the
level of the market. New rules for interaction between actors within the cocoa market
have been introduced. This section highlights three sets of rules of particular significance for smallholder participation and benefit: rules for interactions between sellers
and buyers in integrated value chains, between cooperatives and farmers, and between
NGOs and market actors.

6.3.1 Introduction of Contracts within Integrated Value Chains

Integrated value chains are a major novelty in the Liberian cocoa market and have
introduced a number of changes in the rules for exchange of not only cocoa, but in
all related and integrated services. The most important institutional change is the in-

troduction of contracts between buyers and sellers (farmers and cooperatives). These one-season or longer contracts establish relationships between actors and the rules for interaction. They reflect efforts to develop and formalise lasting relationships, and to formalise the rules that guide interactions and to make them apply over an extended period. Certainly, with these contracts come a whole set of more specific rules related to the exchange of cocoa as well as the different combinations of integrated inputs and services, payment and other conditions. The variations in these rules are represented by the two major business models of Wienco and LAADCO, variations in the LAADCO model (fully or semi-commercial), and by the out-grower model of the LCC. Farmers entering the integrated value chains thus step into a whole new set of institutions for interaction, even if some of them are variants of pre-existing ones. The farmers' groups established among Wienco farmers, for instance, appear to build on traditional joint-labour working groups, so-called *kuus*, but with some new rules, including allowing women to be members and participate in joint work. Contractual relationships have had vast consequences for smallholder farmers, as discussed at length, not least by enabling access to integrated services on credit. The beneficial implications were reviewed in Chapter 5.

Through the formal contracts, buyers in integrated value chains seek to ensure enforcement of agreements with farmers and cooperatives that extend into the future, notably in terms of delivery of cocoa in exchange for inputs and services provided in advance on credit. LAADCO, which contracts with cooperatives, seeks to get them to enforce cocoa delivery by farmers,[509] for instance by controlling cocoa delivery by individual farmers to cooperatives. But as already noted, enforcement may be difficult, as at least some farmers choose to side-sell cocoa to other buyers. Eventually, rules for contract enforcement may emerge.

6.3.2   New Economic and Political Institutions of Cooperatives

Also with the re-entry of cooperatives comes a whole set of new formal institutions regulating their commercial interactions with farmers – economic rules – but also political institutions, such as decision making and power distribution within the cooperatives. How well cooperatives function and serve member farmers' interests has implications for cocoa-market participation and benefits. While there are indications of less positive experiences, this research finds that the dominant impact of farmers' organisations has been positive. This suggests that the rules of the game that have become established have been significant for the inclusive development of the Liberian cocoa market.

The *economic institutions* guide commercial interaction between cooperatives and farmers, and include rules on pricing and conditions for exchange of cocoa, other goods and services, credit and payments, etc. Different cooperatives have different rules, for example about how much of the cocoa selling price the cooperative will forward to the

---

509 As reported for instance by Individual Interviewees 4 and 34 and Group Interview 6.

farmers, and how much retain for its own purposes. There are also economic rules for the cooperatives' sharing of profits through the distribution of dividends to members. Farmer benefits obviously depend on the content of the rules and on the extent of adherence to them, and experiences vary. As reported, some farmers perceive that their cooperative leaders have cheated them by not adhering to the rules. Another example of intentional change to economic institutions is the warehouse-receipt system, which has greatly facilitated the bulking and selling of farmers' produce in larger volumes. Additional changes, some of them institutional, highlighted by an external observer as important are warehouse rehabilitation, Farmer Field Schools training in 'farming as a business', village savings clubs and solar-dryer systems.[510] My findings suggest that by and large the cooperatives' economic rules – such as prices paid for cocoa as shown in Sub-Section 5.1, and the warehouse receipt system – have been highly beneficial for farmers.

I did, however, also hear reports from farmers of individual cooperative leaders and agents not adhering to the formal rules, with less beneficial outcomes for farmers. This suggests informal rules have taken precedence over the formal ones. Cooperatives are not only economic units but collectively owned organisations, and their internal management requires *political institutions:* rules for decision making and the distribution of power among members, including cooperative leaders. In the past, before the war, cooperatives controlled by their leaders, managed 'top down', and there were indications of possible 'elite capture' of one cooperative I came across. This suggests some cooperative leaders have assumed political powers beyond those granted by the new formal democratic rules as regards how much to pay farmers or the redistribution of profits to shareholders. This is not the dominant picture arising from my data, but it does recur in relation to one cooperative. Otherwise, most farmers interviewed seemed satisfied with their relationships with cooperatives, although this does not allow me to draw conclusions about the application of democratic political rules within cooperatives. Nonetheless, if at least some of the re-established cooperatives adhere to bottom-up democratic principles whereby farmers can hold their leaders to account, this would seem to represent a significant change in the political rules of the cooperative sector.

6.3.3   New Donor Approaches – Changing Rules for Interaction with NGOs

Although not explicitly studied in this research, my analysis suggests that NGOs have contributed to several of the institutional changes discussed through their implementation of donor-funded projects in the cocoa sector. The new role of NGOs in the cocoa seed/seedling market may have helped change the rules for competition and transactions in that sub-market, and I have also discussed how the LIFE project introduced the warehouse-receipt system to cooperatives. LIFE further reports having trained 32 farmers' organisations in the application of democratic organisational and managerial principles,[511] thus possibly contributing to change in cooperatives' political rules.

---

510 Key Informant 4
511 ACDI/VOCA (2013)

NGOs may have influenced rules for interaction between farmers and cooperatives in several ways. They may also have influenced rules for interaction between cooperatives and buyers, e.g., by linking cooperatives to overseas buyers such as the US-based Transmar, as LIFE did, and to LAADCO, as the STCRSP project did. Moreover, as indicated above, NGOs may have played a significant role as drivers of the Quick-Wins process and intentional change in the overall institutional environment.

I suggest that several of these institutional changes can be linked to two observable and interrelated shifts in donor approaches within agriculture and the cocoa sector in particular during the post-war period in Liberia.[512] Gradual shifts have taken place from emergency to development aid, and from recipient-based to market-based approaches – hence, more sustainable approaches. During the conflict and early post-war years, international aid to Liberia was dominated by emergency relief, with farmers commonly receiving free hand-outs of inputs and tools etc. and a short time perspective. Both LIFE and STCRSP are initiatives with development objectives and longer-term perspectives, which eventually become more common. What further distinguishes these two projects, and some others, is that they seek to promote farmers' and cooperatives' cocoa-market activity as commercially viable businesses. Farmers are seen as agents capable and willing to take action if they have incentives and opportunities to do so, whereas donors and NGOs are seen as facilitators of market-based activity, rather than as providers of inputs and services. As these ideas and values are translated into new NGO/donor practices, they are reflected in the relationship between donors/NGOs and farmers/cooperatives, and in the rules of the game for their interactions – the institutions – which may at least have partly changed over time. However, old donor practices also remain, as forcefully highlighted during a group interview with key informants:[513] 'The big challenge to the development and sustainability of the cocoa sector – that is not addressed or spoken openly about – is that NGOs and donor programmes continue to give hand outs! This is in fact done by all NGOs, even if not all individual programmes'.

Nonetheless, the new approaches have at least introduced new rules of the game, and to the extent that they have also altered the patterns of interaction between donors and farmers, actual institutional change has taken place. They may thus have helped create conditions for more sustainable market development, since hand-outs may contribute to undermining the development of viable input and service markets. There may be reason to look deeper into this issue.

---

512 These two tendencies are somewhat reflected in our data material, but particularly based on GRM International (2010: 6) and the practical experience of the researcher in her earlier position as country manager for Swedish development cooperation in Liberia during 2009-2012, with particular responsibility for the aid portfolio for inclusive economic development, where market development in agriculture was a central component.

513 Group Interview 3

6.4   Summary and Concluding Remarks

The chapter has sought to identify major institutional changes that have contributed to the inclusive developments observed in the Liberian cocoa market in the recent post-war period, based on my preceding analysis of structural change and its implications for smallholder farmers. It has also discussed how the institutional changes have influenced incentives and opportunities for market actors and contributed to overwhelmingly beneficial consequences for farmers. Concluding remarks now follow, and the next chapter ties the various institutional explanations offered here together into a more coherent explanation of the role institutions have played in making the Liberian cocoa market more inclusive.

A first, obvious, conclusion is that *the rules of the game in the Liberian cocoa market are changing.* I have identified changes in a number of institutions of different kinds and at different levels, and how the ways by which they have changed have also varied. This chapter shows that intended and unintended institutional changes have taken place in the overall institutional environment of the cocoa market as well as in specific institutional arrangements for interactions between parties within the market.

The sequencing of the institutional changes has varied – some have developed in parallel, others are clearly interrelated. A second conclusion is that *some of the institutional changes, such as the formal government reform measures, have helped to set off a process of structural change, while others apparently emerged as a consequence of it.* Major government reform measures implied a change in the overall institutional environment of the cocoa market, as a result of deregulation that altered the rules for who may enter and operate as a buyer and exporter in the market, and the introduction of cocoa-quality grading and reference-price systems. There reforms contributed to the entry of new market actors – large buyers of integrated value chains and farmers' organisations such as cooperatives – which has meant a lot for the introduction of new rules at the level of the cocoa market itself. Their very market entry, combined with some initial reform measures, meant that new rules emerged organically for price-formation, competition and for coordination of transactions of cocoa as well as inputs and services. In addition, cooperatives and new buyers established new formal institutional arrangements for interaction between market actors. Within the integrated value chains, contracts were established for complex inter-temporal exchanges between buyers and farmers/cooperatives, and cooperatives developed their own economic and political rules for collaboration with farmers and members. Institutional changes have also taken place in the emerging input market for improved seeds and seedlings, where donors and NGOs have played a role, just as new donor approaches have initiated changes in the rules for interaction between NGOs and farmers.

A third conclusion is, consequently, that *new rules of the game in the Liberian cocoa market have been introduced by the government, the farmers themselves – which may be described as civil society or the private sector – and by the private business sector.* This combination has contributed to the outcomes observed in the cocoa market, and as will be further explained in the next chapter.

However, I do not claim that institutions are changing consistently across the entire Liberian cocoa market. There have been patterns of change in a host of formal rules and in actual practices such as competition and pricing – and hence a process of institutional change has been initiated. Change is likely to be partial, and old rules can be expected to apply selectively, for instance in parts of the spot market in remote areas. All the new rules may not have become established in all localities, or may not always be applied or adhered to by all market – or government or NGO – actors. Indeed, I suggest some old rules may persist or re-establish themselves in certain situations, as reflected in the possible granting of select monopsony power to one large cocoa buyer and the possible re-emergence of elite capture of one of the cooperatives.

This suggests possible resistance to change in the rules of the game, although only limited resistance to formal government reform was reported, as well as of the existence of many institutions that remain unaltered and shape incentives for actors to continue behaving as in the past. There are potentially important economic institutions such as property rights, in particular land tenure institutions relevant to smallholder farmers that do not appear to have changed. The influence of socio-cultural rules of patron-client relationships or Big-Man networks, which apparently remain vital in the social and political structure of Liberian society, may also strongly influence economic institutions relevant to the cocoa market. As discussed, it has not been the task of this research to review the entire institutional set-up of the cocoa market, nor to explain the process of institutional change in detail, including drivers and resistance to change. Such analysis would need to consider the role of prevailing institutions in retarding or facilitating institutional change, and thus the relationship between old and new rules – economic, political as well as socio-cultural – in the process.

While changes in the rules of the game have been introduced by a combination of actors, the central role played by the government is clear.

7   An Institutional Explanation: Causal Mechanisms

The previous chapter identified major institutional changes that I suggest have contributed to making the Liberian cocoa market more inclusive. It also discussed how they have influenced incentives and opportunities for market actors, thus offering several institutional explanations for new behaviour and patterns of interaction in the cocoa market and outcomes in terms of beneficial smallholder participation.

This chapter seeks to tie the different institutional explanations together into a more coherent causal explanation, and thus to synthesise the findings of this research on the role institutions have played for a more inclusive Liberian cocoa market. It does so by proposing four central causal mechanisms through which the institutional changes may have had this influence. The first section presents these mechanisms and how they 'work', the second makes some concluding and other remarks and a final section discusses implications for theory.

7.1   Four Major Causal Mechanisms

This section identifies four major causal mechanisms. It is proposed that they have served to 'channel' the causal impact of the institutional changes on the inclusive nature of the cocoa market. I thus suggest that it is through these mechanisms that the institutional changes have contributed to making the cocoa market more inclusive. The reason for identifying these mechanisms is that several institutions in combination appear to have contributed, precisely by 'working through' or influencing a specific causal mechanism, or several of them. Hence, the causal mechanisms suggested can be seen as intermediate variables – or as functions that several institutions perform.

The institutions and their changes that have played a role are numerous, and will not be discussed in detail again. They have also been categorised in a number of ways: formal and informal rules; the institutional environment and institutional arrangements; intended and unintended/organic changes; introduced or changed by the government, farmers and their organisations, the private business sector, even NGOs. They are here combined into five main groups of new and altered institutions that I argue have played the greatest role in making the Liberian cocoa market more inclusive. These five major institutional changes and the four proposed causal mechanisms are illustrated in Figure 7.1 below.

Figure 7.1: Major Institutional Changes and their Causal Mechanisms

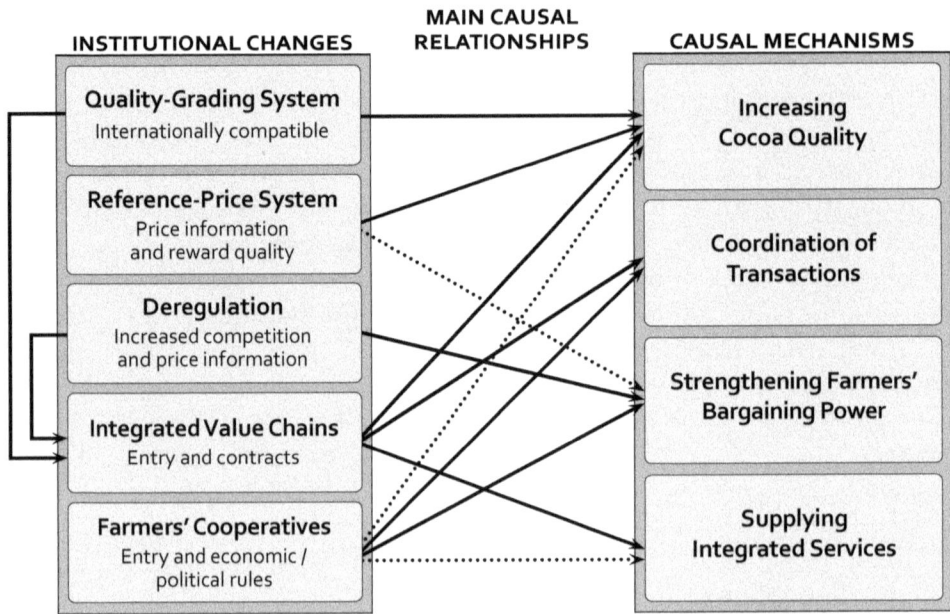

Note: The continuous arrows reflect major or direct causal impacts, the dotted arrows reflect weaker or indirect impacts.

Not all institutions have operated through all four causal mechanisms, but all mechanisms have channelled the causal impact of more than one institutional change – either major/direct or weaker/indirect impact. All institutional changes have had an influential impact in more than one way, some by partly influencing other institutional changes – illustrated by the arrows to the very left in the figure. The first three institutional changes are the three major regulatory reforms initiated by the government. At least two of these (deregulation and quality-grading) created incentives for, and contributed to, the emergence of integrated value chains, which together with the re-entry of cooperatives represent the other two groups of institutional changes. Cooperatives and integrated value chains are not, strictly speaking, institutions in themselves, but as explained earlier, their very market entry as well as the institutional arrangements they introduced changed the rules of the game in the market. The four causal mechanisms proposed as linking institutional change to the more inclusive market are explained in turn.

7.1.1   Increasing Cocoa Quality

In 2009, the government initiated several reforms that were apparently gradually implemented in 2010. Among them was the introduction of a *cocoa quality-grading system* compatible with international standards. This implied that Liberian cocoa was no longer automatically considered inferior and paid for as such on the international market. It could now fetch the full world market price for high-quality cocoa, and increased the profitability potential of exporting Liberian cocoa. This strengthened incentives for buyers to trade in cocoa, but also created incentives to make productive investments to further enhance the profitability potential. Together with the *deregulation measures* also introduced by the government, which facilitated the entry of new buyers and exporters into the Liberian cocoa market, quality-grading contributed to the entry of the new kind of buyers who invested in lasting relationships with farmers and established integrated value chains. A related reform was the introduction of the official *reference-price system,* to which the new buyers subscribe and which establishes a recommended norm that rewards higher-quality cocoa with higher prices, and stipulates recommended farm-gate prices for each quality.

These two complementary reforms also increased the profitability potential for smallholder farmers, and hence the incentive for them to further engage in the cocoa market, in particular to increase cocoa quality, but also to make productive investments – at least when they learnt there were buyers willing to pay well for high-quality cocoa. The new buyers in the *integrated value chains* were among the first to demand high-quality cocoa and reward farmers by paying higher prices for it, and therefore to apply the new formal rules of the combined quality-grading and reference-price systems. I have shown that they reportedly paid farm-gate prices at or above the reference price for Grade 1 cocoa, as did cooperatives. I also showed that higher cocoa quality helps explain the higher prices farmers have received in recent years. The new buyers and cooperatives also increased the opportunities for farmers to process high-quality cocoa by providing relevant services, such as knowledge and access to certain equipment, and developed specific rules for these interactions with farmers. *Cooperatives* have played an important supportive role by actually grading farmers' cocoa, and some cooperatives have made temporary exports of high-quality themselves. One of the new buyers does not buy cocoa from cooperatives, however, but directly from the farmers.

In sum, by *increasing cocoa quality* – the first causal mechanism – the combined quality-grading and reference-price systems, applied by new buyers in integrated value chains and supported by cooperatives, have both enabled and rewarded smallholder farmers' value addition by processing high quality cocoa. This has enabled Liberian cocoa to fetch higher prices on the world market and contributed to increased prices for smallholder farmers.

7.1.2   Coordination of Transactions

The Liberian cocoa market used to be characterised by a spot market, elements of which remain. In the spot market, cocoa transactions are coordinated by the price mechanism, at the price an itinerant trader offers and the farmer is willing to accept on the spot. Each transaction is separate, even where a farmer may be indebted to a local trader and forced to repay by selling cocoa to that trader in the future: in general, though, transactions between farmers and buyers are not organised beyond that.

However, with the entry of cooperatives and integrated value chains, the coordination of transactions in the cocoa market has changed significantly.

First – initiated around 2008, but gaining momentum later – the very *return of cooperatives* as cocoa market actors has established a mechanism for increased and more explicit coordination of transactions between farmers and buyers. Indeed, it introduced new *rules for the coordination* of transactions in the cocoa market regarding the exchange of in particular cocoa (output), but also various inputs and services, between sellers and buyers. A central role of cooperatives has been to collect cocoa from smallholder farmers, to store and sell it in large volumes, with several beneficial consequences for farmers. By coordinating cocoa transactions between many farmers and buyers, cooperatives have made it easier for a large number of smallholder farmers to search for, identify, negotiate and strike deals with buyers, especially larger ones. In particular, they have increased farmers' access to the output market by linking farmers to large and new buyers, and doing so at considerably lower cost than in the past. Without cooperatives, farmers' costs for searching and negotiating deals with large buyers – transaction costs – are probably so high that they effectively prohibit farmers from transacting directly with them. By reducing farmers' transaction costs, and linking farmer's not least to buyers in integrated value chains and the benefits they offer, cooperatives have increased farmers' opportunities for more profitable market participation.

In addition, cooperatives provide various services to farmers. In particular, they serve as a channel for inputs and services from outside – initially from donor-funded NGO projects and eventually from the new buyers in integrated value chains. By coordinating input and service transactions between providers and farmers, the associated costs have likewise been reduced, while farmers' access to various inputs and services has increased. This suggests that farmers' benefit from cooperatives increased even more when the new buyers entered the market in 2011. To perform their coordinating functions, cooperatives established *internal rules* for their own interactions with farmers as regards decision-making and power-sharing (political rules) and economic rules for pricing, payments and services. A *warehouse-receipt system* that facilitates the bulking and selling of large volumes of cocoa appears to have been particularly important.

Cooperatives have similarly facilitated and reduced the costs of transactions for buyers. They now only have to negotiate and organise cocoa deals and input and service delivery with one cooperative (or a few cooperatives) instead of hundreds of farmers. (Hence the re-entry of cooperatives may have further increased incentives for new buyers to make productive investments in cocoa, and to use cooperatives as a channel – which some, but not all, new buyers did.)

Second, the establishment of *integrated value chains* by new buyers has also contributed to increased and more explicit coordination of transactions between buyers and sellers in the cocoa market. They have introduced new rules, notably in terms of *contracts for complex interactions* between farmers/cooperatives and buyers. Contracts have introduced formal rules for exchange of cocoa as well as 'integrated services' on a long-term basis, ranging from one cocoa season up to 20-plus years. By reducing transaction costs for input and output exchanges, cooperatives and integrated value chains have together helped increase economic efficiency within the cocoa value chain. This has generated 'efficiency rents', in terms of increased net returns from cocoa exports, which have accrued to both farmers and buyers. How these returns are shared between market actors within the Liberia cocoa value chain depends on their relative bargaining strength.

To conclude, by increasing *coordination of transactions* for exchanges of cocoa and inputs/services in the market, the establishment of cooperatives and integrated value chains, and the rules they introduced, are proposed to have facilitated and reduced the costs of transactions between smallholder farmers and buyers, benefiting both parties. Economic efficiency within the Liberian cocoa value chain is likely to have increased, and hence also the financial returns to be shared between farmers/cooperatives and buyers/exporters.

7.1.3   Strengthening Farmers' Bargaining Power

A central finding in this research is that structural changes in the Liberian cocoa market since around 2009-2010 have strengthening the bargaining position of smallholder farmers – the third causal mechanism through which institutional changes helped to make the market more inclusive. Two major institutional changes, complemented by a third, have contributed to this.

First, government *deregulation* eliminated the former exclusive buying rights of cocoa buyers in national and local markets as well as restrictions on exporters, which enabled new exporters and buyers to enter the market. The official Liberian export market, once a near monopoly, now involves several large exporters – even some cooperatives export directly – just as the number of large cocoa buyers and middlemen has increased nationally and locally. As a result, *competition* for cocoa produced by smallholders has increased in recent years among exporters as well as buyers at national level and in different parts of the country. An important part of the increased competition is accounted for by the new large buyers establishing integrated value chains. Increased competition for cocoa has reduced the market power of cocoa buyers in relation to cocoa-selling farmers, which has strengthened farmers' bargaining power on the demand side.

Second, the *re-entry of cooperatives* as market actors – cocoa farmers' increased organisation and the increased market activity of cooperatives and associations – has made it possible for farmers to jointly bulk and sell cocoa in larger volumes. This has reduced the number of sellers at the local level and given farmers certain market power, partly countervailing buyer market power. Hence farmers' market position and bargaining power has been strengthened on the supply side too.

These changes in cocoa-market structure have shifted power relationships within it, strengthening smallholder farmers' bargaining power from both the demand and the supply side. With more alternative buyers for farmers to choose between, and fewer buyers for sellers to choose from, a gradual shift has taken place from a buyers' market, where buyers unilaterally dictated prices, towards more negotiated outcomes, with farmers having a stronger say about prices through their organisations. Rules of price formation have thus changed in the process. Besides, increased competition, together with the *reference-price system,* has also meant that price information has become more generally available, and less asymmetrical, at least for cooperatives who are able to use the information in price bargaining. The strengthened bargaining power of small-holder farmers has contributed to the upward pressure on cocoa prices paid to farmers, as reflected in the price increases they have experienced in recent years. The strengthened bargaining power is also reflected in the increased market margin of Liberian farmers, who have seen their share of the world market price increase considerably in recent years, in relation to that of buyers and exporters. This suggests that farmers may have benefited relatively more from the efficiency gains from increased coordination of transactions discussed above.

To sum up, by *strengthening smallholder farmers' bargaining power,* increased competition among buyers resulting from government deregulation, combined with the countervailing market power flowing from farmers' organisation into cooperatives, and reinforced by the reference-price system, have made it possible for smallholders to reap a larger share of returns to cocoa – reflected in considerably higher prices and a larger share of the world market price.

7.1.4   Supplying Integrated Services

The entry of the new kinds of buyer that established *integrated value chains* in the Liberian cocoa market has had far-reaching implications for smallholder farmers' beneficial market participation. Government reforms increased both the incentives for buyers and the opportunities for them to go beyond pure trade in cocoa towards making productive investments: the *quality-grading system* would enable them to fetch higher prices for cocoa on the world market while *deregulation* facilitated their market entry and ought to have reduced uncertainties about the future role of government as an actor in the cocoa market (cf., the arrows to the very left in Figure 7.1 above). To realise current and enhance future profitability of cocoa exports, the new buyers promoted cocoa farmers' value addition and productive investments, seeking to establish lasting relationships with farmers through *formal contracts* for inter-temporal exchange. The contracts enabled them to supply a series of inputs and services on credit, in exchange for secure access to farmers' cocoa after harvest, and they offered high prices for high quality cocoa.

This private supply of inputs and services – notably inputs on credit, coupled with associated extension services, but also learning opportunities and consumer credit – has enabled farmers to access them, in spite of the poorly developed market for inputs and services for smallholder farmers, cocoa farmers in particular. The provision of these supporting functions as integrated services has increased farmers' opportunities to use them and thereby to raise productivity and outputs on their existing farms, as well as to expand their farms. The farmers interviewed in this research have responded strongly to the opportunities provided by investing more time, knowledge, money and physical inputs in their cocoa farms.

Another result of the emergence of integrated value chains that supply integrated services is that the cocoa market has become more diversified, combining traditional spot markets with integrated value chains. The *rules for competition* – who competes with whom, with what and on what conditions – have also changed and become more complex. As a consequence, farmers' alternatives for participating in the cocoa market and with whom have also increased. Farmers' freedom of choice has grown.

Different buyers have introduced different business models, with different kinds of inputs and services provided, contractual periods etc. One of the two major buyers interacts directly with individual farmers whereas the other does so indirectly through the cooperatives. Hence, *cooperatives* play an important role in channeling inputs and services to farmers and coordinating actual transactions in at least one of the integrated value chains. Indeed, the cooperatives also provide various services to farmers, such as extension services and training opportunities, with inputs from donor-funded and NGO projects. And there are signs that farmers make strategic choices among different kinds of buyers.

In conclusion, by *supplying integrated inputs, services and credit* – the fourth causal mechanism – integrated value chains, supported by cooperatives, have increased smallholder farmers' access to cocoa inputs, services and credit, in spite of the virtual absence of markets for these in Liberia. This has increased opportunities for farmers to make productive investments in their cocoa farms, which they reportedly do in several ways, thereby reinforcing the potential for future beneficial returns from cocoa-market participation, as well as increasing their freedom of choice for market participation.

7.2 Concluding and Other Remarks

Through the four causal mechanisms identified here, a combination of five sets of institutional changes is proposed to have contributed to making the Liberian cocoa market more inclusive in recent years. This has several implications. First, *'working through the causal mechanisms' means that the institutional changes have made the cocoa market more conducive for smallholder farmers' participation and benefit by performing a number of functions:* by increasing cocoa quality; coordinating market transactions; strengthening farmers' bargaining power; and by supplying integrated services in the absence of markets for these. In the case of the post-war Liberian cocoa market, performance of these functions has been vital for making the cocoa market more inclusive. A central conclusion is therefore that *the role these institutional changes have played is precisely to perform these particular functions, and it is by performing these functions that the altered rules have made the market more inclusive.*

Second, *the different functions performed by institutional change have been important, not primarily in their own right, but particularly by complementing one another in the process of making the market more inclusive.* In a simplified version, this means that increased cocoa quality has led to higher prices on the world market, which increased incomes within the Liberian value chain, while more explicit coordination within it increased efficiency and reduced transaction costs. Hence, with higher incomes and lower costs, net returns to be shared by market actors increased within the Liberian cocoa market – the cake grew bigger. Since the relative bargaining strength of small-holder farmers also increased in relation to buyers, they received a relatively larger share of the cake – at least in terms of their share of the world market price. With the supply of integrated services and inputs to farmers, their chances to secure and increase returns from cocoa in the future also increased, in spite of the absence of functioning input and service markets. *This suggests that all functions performed have been important for making the market more inclusive, and for opportunities for smallholders' beneficial participation to be sustained.* Without a larger cake, there would not have been enough returns from cocoa exports to share within the value chain, but without a stronger bargaining position for farmers, their share may not have been big enough to motivate their market participation. Similarly, without the supply of integrated services, yields and output from cocoa farms might not increase enough in future to ensure sustained growth and profitability in the market.

Third, *each of the five major institutional changes have contributed significantly to making the market more inclusive by performing more than one function, i.e., by working through more than one causal mechanism.* The entry and rules of the cooperatives, for example, contributed to both increased coordination of market transactions and to strengthening farmers' bargaining power. The same applies to the other institutional changes.

Fourth, *the analysis suggests a strong inter-relatedness of rule changes, not least between rules at different levels.* Cooperatives had begun to re-establish themselves, but did not seem to gain momentum until the government initiated reforms in the overall institu-tional environment of the market, which also stimulated the entry of new buyers from integrated value chains. It may be questioned whether the new buyers would have been willing to make productive investments and establish integrated value chains unless the quality-grading system had been established, for example. As discussed, government regulatory reforms appear to have initiated the process of institutional change, while the entry of cooperatives and integrated value chains both led to the organic emergence of new rules, e.g., for price formation and competition, while also introducing new formal institutional arrangements, such as warehouse-receipt systems and contracts, within the market itself. *I conclude that while changes in the rules of the game in the Liberian cocoa market have been introduced by a combination of actors: the government, the farmers themselves – civil society or micro entrepreneurs, depending on how one chooses to categorise them – and by the private business sector, the central role played by the govern-ment is clear.*

7.2.1   A Note on the Role of Donors and NGOs

Examining the role of donors and NGOs for developments in the Liberian cocoa market has not been an explicit aim of this research, but some observations on their role in institutional change were made in Chapter 6. NGOs appear to have supported and thereby contributed to several of the institutional changes introduced by cooperatives, the new buyers and indeed the government, through donor-funded projects in the cocoa sector. The changes promoted may reflect shifts in donor approaches in post-war Liberia, from emergency to development aid and from recipient-based to more market-based aid, and possibly new practices – and rules – for NGO interaction with market actors, not least with farmers and cooperatives.

This has, for instance, meant partial withdrawal of NGOs as market actors, which may imply a qualitatively significant change in the rules of the game for interactions in the potentially emerging input market for improved cocoa seeds and seedlings. Their reduced hand-outs of free cocoa seeds to farmers appears to have changed the rules of competition among suppliers and made it possible for domestic private providers to enter the market. Even if this market remains poorly developed, the rules for how transactions are made between suppliers and buyers similarly appear to have been partly altered. The suggested beneficial implication for farmers is, despite the circumstance that they now have to pay for inputs they previously obtained for free, increased access to improved seeds/seedlings in the short term, and more sustainable access in the longer term.

7.3   Implications for Theory

This research, based on the case of the post-war Liberian cocoa market, may help to increase our understanding of the broader issue of the role of institutions in the development of inclusive agricultural markets. The institutional explanations may be applicable to other agricultural markets, in particular for export crops, in Liberia, other SSA countries and elsewhere. While this is ultimately an issue of empirical examination, this research claims to complement the existing theoretical literature by offering inputs into an emerging theory on the role of institutions in inclusive agricultural markets. More specifically, it suggests that institutions that promote or perform the following vital functions contribute to inclusive agricultural markets:

- Farmers' value addition (even if only by producing/processing high-quality crops, to maximise returns from the world market)
- Explicit coordination of transactions (along the value chain to increase efficiency and reduce transaction costs)
- Strong bargaining power of farmers (in relation to buyers and other actors in the value chain)
- Provision of integrated services (inputs, credit, and other supporting functions for which markets are non-existent).

It is thus proposes that the role of institutions in the development of inclusive agricultural markets is to perform these functions. Together with the finding that several institutions contribute to performing each function in the Liberian case, this further suggests that it is not one or other particular institution that is important for inclusive markets, but rather the function it performs. Several institutions can perform the same or similar function. The specific form and detail of institutions aimed to promote or ensure competition, for example, can probably be designed in a variety of ways. Similarly, contracts within integrated value chains can take many forms, including various out-grower schemes. The specific institutional design matters, but may differ, as long as the institution performs the basic function of increasing coordination and efficiency within the value chain, which different institutional solutions may do differently well. Besides, this suggests that the precise design of institutions performing 'inclusive functions' can and ought to be adapted to the specific context and the broader institutional environment into which it is to fit, as institutions are inter-related.

The different functions are all important, as they complement one another, but their relative strength and thus importance will depend on the specific contextual circumstances. I particularly want to highlight the complementarity of the coordination function and farmers' bargaining power, and the importance of the institutions that contribute to achieving these. Based on Liberian experience, a *hypothesis* could be that the combination of integrated value chains, cooperatives and rules ensuring competition (deregulation in the Liberian case) promotes inclusive agricultural markets, as reflected in prices received by smallholder farmers. Integrated value chains and cooperatives coordinate transactions (of outputs and inputs/services) on both the supply and the demand side, which increases efficiency, reduces transaction costs and raises net returns (at the given world market price) to be shared within the value chain. Cooperatives and (rules ensuring) competition strengthen farmers' bargaining power from both the supply and the demand side, which increases farmers' share of the returns generated within the value chain. Farmers will see their prices increase due to both efficiency gains and bargaining strength.

I suggest that competition between buyers deserves recognition as a potentially vital 'intermediate function' for farmers' bargaining power – ensured by government enforcement of deregulatory measures or anti-trust legislation – which may be limited if only performed by cooperatives in markets with few and large buyers. Hence, a central role suggested for government in promoting inclusive agricultural markets is to ensure competition among buyers in the output market.

This proposal highlights the importance of strengthening smallholders' market position and bargaining power, and draws attention to the degrees and distribution of market power, in particular the role of competitive markets, in promoting inclusive agricultural markets, which I have not seen explicitly highlighted in the institutional literature. It may seem to at least partly contradict Dorward et al., who argue that policy should not focus on making markets more competitive to support the development of smallholder agriculture in cases where markets are poorly developed.[514] On the other hand, they argue that private provision of integrated services may be a better option in case markets don't work well, which is consistent with my findings on the virtually non-existent input and service markets and the beneficial implications of integrated services for smallholders. Dorward et al. further argue that institutional arrangements are easier to change and may, if they accumulate, eventually change the institutional environment.[515] The findings of this research do not support this suggestion, as change in the institutional environment in the Liberian case preceded and promoted change in the institutional arrangements.

Finally, this research suggests that institutions that perform the four functions identified here can be referred to as inclusive economic institutions in the terminology of Acemoglu and Robinson[516] – inclusive agricultural-market institutions. Hence, I also make a contribution to the theory of inclusive institutions by identifying and specifying institutions within a particular market, and by offering an explanation to what makes them inclusive – the functions they perform.

---

514 Dorward et al. (2005)
515 Dorward et al. (2009)
516 Acemoglu and Robinson (2012)

"Structural changes have contributed to strengthening the market position and bargaining power of smallholder farmers in the Liberian cocoa market.

8   Conclusions

In this research, I have studied post-conflict developments in the Liberian cocoa market to understand if they have made the cocoa market more inclusive or not, and to identify major institutional changes and suggest an explanation as to how they have contributed to the developments observed. Beyond increased knowledge about the Liberian case, the aim has been to enhance our understanding of the role of institutions in the development of inclusive agricultural markets more broadly. To this end, three empirical chapters (Chapters 4-6) examined changes in the structure of and market power within the cocoa market, implications for smallholder farmers' beneficial participation in the market, and major institutional changes that may have influenced the inclusive nature of the market. The analysis in Chapter 7 brought together my findings on the role that institutional changes have played into a coherent institutional causal explanation, and discussed the theoretical contribution that this entails.

This chapter briefly summarises the findings of Chapters 4-7, draws conclusions about my attempt to contribute answers to the research questions, and discusses implications for policy and practice in four subsequent sections. The research seeks to understand general developments and broad issues in the Liberian cocoa market, and the analysis is based on a combination of the comprehensive set of primary data complemented by secondary data, yet with limitations. The findings reveal patterns of change that are almost invariably clear in their direction, which is the main focus of the research. However, the nature of the data does not allow me to determine the extent to which the changes have penetrated the Liberian cocoa market in its entirety. Thus, I do not claim that the changes observed apply generally to the Liberian cocoa market. Nonetheless, the findings based on analysis of the data generated and used offer a well-grounded suggestion of the changes possibly taking place more broadly in the Liberian cocoa market, albeit with local variations. Besides, while the data do not consistently allow me to show changes between specific points in time, I am able to identify a gradual process of change up to late 2013. This means that most of the changes observed refer to the latter part of post-war Liberian history.

8.1   A More Inclusive Liberian Cocoa Market

To identify major changes in the cocoa market relevant to its possible inclusiveness, I started by examining the market structure – market actors within the cocoa value chain, their roles and relationships, and the implications of this for any changes in competition, market and bargaining power, in particular for smallholder farmers. Chapter 4 identified three major patterns of change in the structure of the cocoa market during the latter part of the post-conflict period. A first pattern is that *the number of cocoa buyers has increased* – large and small, at both national and local levels – which has led to increased competition for cocoa from smallholder farmers. Second, *new kinds of buyer have emerged* in the last few years, investing in lasting relationships with cocoa farmers, leading thereby to the emergence of integrated value chains. Consequently, the Liberian cocoa market has become more diversified and complex, combining elements of spot markets with integrated value chains.

These findings do not lend support to concerns that private monopolies may have replaced a state monopoly in the cocoa market. Whereas this seems to have been the case in the early post-war years, recent changes imply that strong, even monopsonistic, market power of private buyers has been reduced, as they now face ever more competition. The direction of change is clear, although certain market power remains, for instance among exporters. There are, however, signs that some buyers in integrated value chains may have a monopsony on buying cocoa in specific localities, which indicates a risk of the emergence of new forms of local market power if the level of competition is not maintained. Besides, input markets for smallholder cocoa farmers remain severely underdeveloped, with market power prevailing. However, input supply has increased within the integrated value chains, and a market for improved cocoa seeds and seedlings may be about to emerge.

The third pattern is that *farmers' organisations have re-entered as market actors* in the cocoa market, with cocoa farmers increasingly organised. Cooperatives and associations bulk and sell farmers' cocoa in larger volumes, thereby coordinating cocoa transactions and countervailing some of the market power of buyers. Despite the overall impression that these organisations strengthen the position of farmers, there are signs that at least some of them may not represent farmers' interests well, which suggests a risk for elite capture.

A major conclusion of this research is that *these structural changes have contributed to strengthening the market position and bargaining power of smallholder farmers* in the Liberian cocoa market, from both the sellers' side, through farmers' organisations, and the buyers' side, through increased competition. Power relationships within the cocoa value chain have shifted in favour of smallholder farmers. The overall changes notwithstanding, a word of caution is needed. If the market power of buyers and input providers and elite capture of farmers' organisations are reinforced, they may partly threaten the overall structural changes in the cocoa market observed so far and hence the bargaining power of smallholder farmers.

To explore the inclusive nature of these structural changes, I examined their implications for smallholder farmer participation in and benefit from the cocoa market in Chapter 5. My data strongly indicate two major findings. In recent years, Liberian cocoa farmers have, first, enjoyed *significant increases in cocoa prices*. Second, they have seen *their marketing margin – their share of world cocoa prices – increase substantially*, in relation to buyers and exporters. The increases are particularly strong for farmers processing high-quality cocoa. My interview-based data suggest that farm-gate prices for Grade 1 cocoa have increased three or four times in seven years, and almost doubled as a share of the official reference price. By late 2013, the average reported price for

Grade 1 cocoa was higher than the reference price. Average prices reported for cocoa increased from 22 per cent of the world market price at the end of 2006, to as much as 49 per cent for Grade 1 cocoa in late 2013 – a remarkable increase. The increased marketing margin, in particular, is yet another indication of farmers' strengthened positions and bargaining power in the domestic cocoa market. An important consequence of growing prices is that the incentives for smallholder farmers to participate in the cocoa market have been reinforced substantially.

A third finding is that structural change has contributed to *increasing farmers' access to output markets – more and new channels for selling cocoa – and to a variety of support functions, not least inputs and credit*, essentially in the form of integrated services. This has created new opportunities for active market participation by farmers, but some of the integrated services come at high cost, which is related to the strong market power of input providers. A related and fourth consequence is that *smallholder farmers' freedom of choice has increased*. With more ways to participate in the cocoa market, farmers' opportunities to manage the livelihood strategies of their households ought to have improved too.

I looked at how smallholder cocoa farmers have responded to stronger price incentives and increased opportunities for market participation, and a fifth finding is that the farmers interviewed are highly responsive. *Smallholder farmers participate more actively in the Liberian cocoa market* by making short and long-term investments to increase returns in a number of ways: adding value by processing high-quality cocoa; increasing productivity and output by adopting improved farming practices; applying fertiliser and chemicals; replanting old trees, partly by using seeds and seedlings of improved varieties; and expanding their farms on to new land. Farmer engagement in cooperatives and integrated value chains is another indication of more active participation, as is increased cooperative activity and cocoa supply. Official data on total cocoa production show considerable increases, and total official exports have increased several-fold over the post-war period.

However, my sixth finding is that *farmers' returns to cocoa-market participation present a somewhat mixed picture when it comes to both incomes and physical output*. Some farmers have seen cocoa incomes rise, others have not. The data suggest that limited income growth may partly be explained by old and dying cocoa trees with poor yields, while newly planted trees have not started yielding yet. Many farmers report low or declining cocoa productivity and production for these reasons, while others report good and growing yields. These findings suggest *the smallholder cocoa sector is in transition*. Whereas the cocoa *market* has undergone substantial change in recent years, smallholder cocoa *farming* has only begun to adapt and finds itself in transformation. Once this process gains momentum, farmers may see more consistent growth in their crop yields and financial returns. As yet, not all farmers participate and benefit to the same extent. However, most express a belief in the future of the cocoa market, and their long-term investments have increased their chances of higher returns over time.

The qualifications notwithstanding, the overall conclusion of my findings – in response to my first research question – is that *recent developments observed in the Li-*

berian post-war cocoa market have certainly made it more inclusive. Smallholder farmers participate more actively in the cocoa market and the benefit for them of market participation has increased markedly in recent years. This does not mean that the Liberian cocoa market is fundamentally inclusive – not all options are available to all farmers everywhere and at all times – but it is more inclusive than before. It may become even more inclusive if the major developments observed are reinforced and the risks I have highlighted – market power of cocoa buyers and input providers and elite capture of cooperatives – are mitigated.

8.2   Institutional Changes that Contributed and How

If these inclusive developments are to be sustained, they must be underpinned by institutions – rules of the game – which enable and promote the new kind of interactions observed in the Liberian cocoa market. Hence institutions ought to have changed and new ones may have emerged. Chapter 6 identified those institutional changes that I suggest have contributed to the developments observed, largely implicitly derived from the findings of preceding chapters. A combination of intended and unintended changes has taken place in the overall institutional environment of the cocoa market and in the more specific institutional arrangements for interaction between parties within the market.

First of all, a *government process of institutional reform* was initiated in 2009, which set off intentional changes in the overall institutional environment, altering formal rules applying to all cocoa-market actors. I identified three major changes as potentially the most important for recent inclusive developments: deregulation of monopsony power of cocoa buyers in markets at national and local level, facilitating market entry and contributing to increased competition and new kinds of buyer making productive investments; the introduction of a cocoa quality-grading system compatible with international standards, contributing to value addition of cocoa and higher prices; and the related reference-price system, increasing and establishing a norm for farm-gate prices, and further strengthening the bargaining power of farmers and cooperatives.

A second set of *institutional changes have emerged organically*, as unintended consequences of the formal reform measures, their implications for the market structure, and the entry of new kinds of market actor. A major change appears to be taking place in the price-formation mechanism, whereby farmers and cooperatives move from being price takers in the cocoa market towards becoming price makers. The rules of the game for competition – who competes with whom and in what ways – also appear to be changing, as a consequence of the entry of new large buyers. The re-entry of cooperatives has led to partly new rules for collaboration between buyers and sellers of cocoa, notably for how transactions are organised and coordinated in the Liberian cocoa market. The partial withdrawal of NGOs as market actors from input markets may have altered the rules for entry and interaction in the potentially emerging cocoa seed and seedling market.

Finally, intentional changes in formal *institutional arrangements between specific actors within the market have also taken place*, and may be of particular significance to smallholder participation and benefit. The most important novelty may be the introduction of written contracts between buyers and sellers (farmers and cooperatives) in the integrated value chains, which with their sub-set of rules for different transactions, integrated services and terms offer opportunities for lasting relationships between buyers and sellers. With the re-entry of cooperatives comes a whole set of new formal institutions affecting their commercial interaction with farmers (economic rules) as well as their internal decision making and power distribution (political rules). Most of these rules benefit farmers, but signs of possible elite capture suggest that new democratic political rules, and by implication the economic rules, may not be adhered to by all leaders. Shifts in NGO approaches to donor-funded projects may have introduced new rules into their interactions with farmers and cooperatives, possibly enabling the more sustainable provision of improved seeds and seedlings.

A first, obvious, conclusion is that *the rules of the game in the Liberian cocoa market are changing*, and these are the major institutional changes I find to have contributed to making the market more inclusive in recent years, by influencing the structural changes observed and the implications for beneficial participation by smallholder farmers. Second, *some institutional changes*, notably the formal government reform measures, *contributed to setting off the process of structural change, whereas others appear to have emerged as a consequence of it*. Third, *the new rules of the game in the Liberian cocoa market have been introduced by a combination of the government, the farmers themselves and by the private business sector*. If the new rules become firmly established throughout the Liberian cocoa market, there may be scope for its inclusive developments to be sustained.

In order to tie the different institutional explanations together into a more coherent causal explanation and synthesise the findings on the role that the institutional changes have played for the more inclusive Liberian cocoa market, Chapter 7 identified four central causal mechanisms. Five major changes of rules or rule clusters – the cocoa-quality grading system, the reference-price system, the deregulation of market entry, the entry and rules of integrated value chains, and the entry and rules of cooperatives – are proposed to have contributed to a more inclusive market through the following major mechanisms:

By enabling and rewarding the *processing of high-quality cocoa*, the combined government quality-grading and reference-price systems, applied by new buyers in integrated value chains and supported by cooperatives, have created incentives and opportunities for value addition by smallholder farmers to cocoa produced, thereby fetching higher prices on the world market and higher prices for farmers.

By *increasing coordination of transactions* of outputs as well as inputs and services, rules introduced by cooperatives and integrated value chains, as well as by their very entry into the market, have facilitated and reduced transaction costs between smallholder farmers and buyers, benefiting both. This has increased economic efficiency within the Liberian cocoa value chain, and hence the financial returns to be shared between farmers/cooperatives and buyers/exporters.

By *strengthening smallholder farmers' bargaining power,* increased competition among cocoa buyers resulting from government deregulation, combined with the counter-vailing market power of cooperatives, selling farmers' cocoa in bulk, and possibly the reference-price system, have made it possible for smallholder farmers to reap a larger share of the returns, in terms of their share of the world market price for cocoa.

By *supplying integrated services, inputs and credit,* integrated value chains – them-selves stimulated by the quality-grading system enabling them to fetch higher prices in the world market – have made it possible for smallholder farmers to make productive investments in their cocoa farms, in spite of the virtual absence of markets for these inputs and services in Liberia.

A major concluding proposition of this research – which concerns the second re-search question on the role of institutions for the inclusive nature of the cocoa market – is that *the institutional changes have contributed to smallholder farmer benefit from and participation in the cocoa market precisely by performing these particular four functions.* Secondly, the different functions *have complemented one another* – the joint perfor-mance of all these functions have been important in making the market more inclu-sive, and for smallholders farmers' chances for continued beneficial participation in the future. In addition, *each of the five major institutional changes has contributed to making the market more inclusive by performing more than one function,* i.e., by working through more than one causal mechanism. Finally, and consequently, the analysis suggests a *strong inter-relatedness of rule changes,* not least at different levels, in performing these functions and thus in making the market more inclusive. However, while changes in the rules of the game have been introduced by a combination of actors, the *central role played by the government* is clear.

8.3   Role of Institutions for Development of Inclusive Agricultural Markets

In addition to increasing our knowledge about the inclusive nature of the Liberian cocoa market and our understanding of the institutional changes that have contributed to this and how, this research aims to make a theoretical contribution to the broader research question on the role of institutions for development of inclusive agricultural markets more generally.

I offer inputs into an emerging theory on the role of institutions for inclusive agricultural markets by suggesting that in order to contribute to inclusive agricultural markets, institutions should perform the following vital functions in combination: a) smallholder farmers' value addition; b) explicit coordination of transactions along the value chain; c) strengthening smallholder farmers' bargaining power; and d) provision of integrated inputs, services and credit for which markets are non-existent or poorly developed.

Given that several institutions can help perform the same functions, it is not ne-cessarily the specific design of a particular institution that is most important. It is the performance of the inclusive function that is vital, and differently designed institutions and different institutions in combination can perform that function. This further suggests that the precise design of institutions performing 'inclusive functions' can and ought to be adapted to the specific context and the broader institutional environment in which it is to fit, as institutions are inter-related.

A central function is to strengthen farmers' bargaining power, and as demonstrated by the Liberian case, farmer organisations contributed to this on the supply side and increased competition among buyers on the demand side. While not identified as one of the central functions to be performed for inclusive markets, I propose that competition between buyers be recognised as a vital 'intermediate function' to be performed in order to ensure farmers' bargaining power, which may otherwise be limited if only performed by cooperatives in markets with few and large buyers. By implication, a central role suggested for government in promoting inclusive agricultural markets is to ensure competition among buyers in the output market.

8.4   Implications for Policy and Practice

These research findings have implications for policy makers and practitioners in Liberia and elsewhere who want to encourage and contribute to the development of inclusive agricultural markets. I make the following recommendations to actors in support of continued inclusive development in the Liberian cocoa market:

1. *Safeguard the achievements to date and continue and expand the process* to ensure institutional and structural change throughout the Liberian cocoa market so as to include and benefit all smallholder farmers, including in remote areas. *Immediately mitigate the risks* regarding the market power of cocoa buyers and elite capture of farmer organisations, which may threaten the progress made.

2. *Promote local and national competition between cocoa buyers* throughout the country, in particular between integrated value chains, which are also input suppliers. It is the government's role to ensure this by eliminating formal rules or informal practices that enable monopsony buying power, and by facilitating entry of new buyers. Donors can encourage the government in this and must ensure they do not hamper competition through the projects they fund – with civil society as a watchdog.

3. *Encourage smallholder farmers to organise* into effective cocoa-trading cooperatives, and the democratic development of cooperatives, with leaders held to account by members. The main responsibility rests with farmers and cooperative leaders. Donor-funded projects and local and international NGOs can support these initiatives and serve as watchdogs – with the government as a guardian.

4. Create conditions for the development of *markets for inputs and services for smallholders*, such as improved cocoa seeds/seedlings and financial services. This responsibility rests with government, but donors and NGOs can facilitate the process and should avoid crowding out emerging private initiatives through unsustainable hand-outs.

5. Promote further *coordination within the cocoa value chain* throughout the cocoa-producing counties by facilitating the entry of new investors, not least domestic ones; alternative business models for integrated value chains; outgrower schemes for larger farms; relationships with input-providers and farmers' organisations; and by seeking ways to motivate and include middlemen and traditional buyers. Government is responsible for creating an enabling environment, while innovative donor-funded projects and cocoa-sector stakeholder groups can play an important role as facilitators and brokers.

6. Ensure that all Liberian cocoa is *processed into high-quality cocoa*, and that cocoa is graded and rewarded accordingly throughout the value chain and by all buyers. This requires collaboration among market actors, perhaps through cocoa-sector stakeholder groups and business organisations, and government is central in enforcing the standard.

To the extent that the conclusions based on the case of the Liberian cocoa market are applicable to other agricultural markets – perhaps in particular for export crops in Liberia, other SSA countries and elsewhere – which is an issue for empirical examination, the following general recommendations may be useful:

1. Undertake institutional changes that encourage farmers' *value addition*, increase *coordination and efficiency* within the agricultural value chain, strengthen *smallholder bargaining power* and ensure the supply of *inputs and services*, not least credit.

2. Promote coordination of transactions through *farmer cooperatives*, while ensuring that cooperatives are not captured by the elite and developing *integrated value chains*.

3. Strengthen farmers' bargaining power by ensuring *competition* in the output market, as well as in input and service markets, and by encouraging their *organisation*.

4. Encourage *integrated value chains* based on contractual relationships, while preventing monopsony and monopoly power, to increase farmer access to output markets and to inputs and services in the absence of functioning markets for these.

Saclepea, Nimba County, Eastern Liberia, May 2015. A community garden for cocoa and other crops, where an NGO is helping women smallholders to improve their farming. Photo by author Gun Eriksson Skoog from one of her field trips.

References

Acemoglu D (2012): 'Success and Failure of Nations: Institutional Bottlenecks', Zeuthen Lectures, MIT, MA

Acemoglu, D and Robinson, JA (2012): Why Nations Fail: The Origins of Power, Prosperity and Poverty, Crown Business, New York

ADCI/VOCA (2008): 'Rehabilitation of the Cocoa Value Chain/Sector in Liberia: Suggestions for "Quick Wins" to the Ministry of Agriculture', mimeo, Monrovia

ACDI/VOCA (2010): '"Cocoa Quick Wins" Summary and Implementation Chronology', Presentation to ACC, January 28, mimeo, Monrovia

ACDI/VOCA (2012a): 'November 2012 LIFE Project Farmers' Association Membership Update', list, Monrovia

ACDI/VOCA (2012b): 'Prodeedings of the Liberia Cocoa Certification Workshop', March 12-14, Monrovia

ACDI/VOCA (2013): 'Liberia Livelihood Improvement for Farming Enterprises (LIFE) Project', July, mimeo, Monrovia

ACDI/VOCA (n.d.): 'Commercial Cocoa Nursery Initiative in Liberia, Mimeo, Monrovia

Adam Smith International (2013): 'Sector Scoping and Prioritisation: Overview and Conclusions', DOAM-Liberia

African Union (2014): Common African Position (CAP) on the Post-2015 Development Agenda, Addis Ababa

Beach, D and Brun Pedersen, R (2013): Process-Tracing Methods: Foundations and Guidelines, University of Michigan Press

Bennett, A & Checkel, J (2012): 'Process Tracing: From Philosophical Roots to Best Practices', Ch 1 in Bennett, A & Checkel, J (eds): Process Tracing in the Social Sciences: From Metaphor to Analytic Tool, Georgetown University, Washington DC, & Simon Fraser University, Vancouver BC

Booth, D and Therkildsen, O (2012): 'The Political Economy of Development in Africa: A Joint Statement from Five Research Programmes, on behalf of: Africa Power and Politics Programme; Development Leadership Programme; Elites, Production and Poverty: A Comparative Analysis; Political Economy of Agricultural Policy in Africa; Tracking Development', Political Economy of Development in Africa Conference, Copenhagen, Vol. 30

Central Bank of Liberia (2003-2013): Annual Report, various years, Monrovia

Clower, R. W.; Dalton, G.; Harwitz, M.; Walters, A. A. et al. (1966): Growth Without Development: An Economic Survey of Liberia, Northwestern University Press

Coase, Ronald (1937): 'The Nature of the Firm', Economica, Volume 4, Issue 16, pp. 386-405

CSTWG (2013): 'Cocoa Sector Technical Working Group (CSTWG) Monthly Meeting Minutes, July 18, 2013', mimeo, Monrovia

Dahlman, Carl J. (1979): 'The Problem of Externality', Journal of Law and Economics, 22 (1): 141–162

Davis LE & North DC (1971): Institutional Change and American Economic Growth, Cambridge University Press

del Castillo, G. (2012): 'Aid, Employment and Inclusive Growth in Conflict-Affected Countries: Policy Recommendations for Liberia', Working Paper 47, UNU-WIDER

Dorward, A. R.; Kydd, J.; Morrison, J. & Poulton, C. (2005): 'Institutions, Markets and Economic Co-ordination: Linking Development Policy to Theory and Praxis', Development and Change 36(1): 1-25

Dorward, A. R.; Kirsten, J. F.; Omamo, S. W.; Poulton, C. & Vink, N. (2009): 'Institutions and the Agricultural Development Challenge in Africa', Ch. 1:3-34 in Kirsten et al. (2009)

Economic Management Team (2009): 'Rehabilitation of the Cocoa Sub-Sector: "Quick Wins for Improvement of the Sector" – Proposed ACDI/VOCA Changes and Recommended Actions by the Economic Management Team', mimeo, July 7, Office of the President, Monrovia

English, A (2008): 'Determinants of Liberian Farmgate Cocoa Prices', A Masters Thesis, University of Tennessee, Knoxville TS

Eriksson Skoog, G. (2000): The Soft Budget Constraint – The Emergence, Persistence and Logic of an Institution, Kluwer Academic Publishers, Dordrecht

Eriksson Skoog, G. (2009): 'Internal Concept Paper: Economic Development – Towards a Strategic Focus', Memo for Team Liberia's Thematic Discussion, Swedish International Development Cooperation Agency, Monrovia

Evers, B; Opondo, M; Barrientos, S; Krishnan, A; Amoding, F & Ndlovu, L (2014): 'Global and Regional Supermarkets: Implications for Producers and Workers in Kenyan and Ugandan horticulture, Capturing the Gains Working Paper 39

Fafchamps, Marcel (2004): Market Institutions in Sub-Saharan Africa: Theory and Evidence, The MIT Press, Cambridge M.A. and London

Gabre-Madhin, E. Z. (2006): 'Building Institutions for Markets: The Challenge in the Age of Globalization', mimeo, IFPRI

Gabre-Madhin, EZ (2009): A Market for All Farmers: Market Institutions and Smallholder Participation, Agriculture for Development, Centre for Effective Global Action, UC, Berkeley

George, A & Bennett, A (2005): Case Studies and Theory Development in the Social Studies, MIT Press, Cambridge & London

Gerdes, Felix (2013): Civil War and State Formation: The Political Economy of War and Peace in Liberia, Campus Verlag

Gereffi, G; Humphrey, J & Sturgeon, T (2005): 'The Governance of Global Value Chains', Review of International Political Economy, 12:1

Gereffi, G & Korzeniewicz, M (1994): Commodity Chains and Global Capitalism, Greenwood publishing Group, Westport

Gockowski, J.J. & Wilcox, M.D. (2008): 'Liberia Agricultural Policy Brief – Reforming Cocoa and Coffee Markets in Liberia', mimeo

GRM International (2010): Support for Agriculture and Forestry in Liberia: A Review and Proposal, An Independent Study Conducted for Sida

GRM International (2012): 'Support to the Development of Markets and Value Chains in Agriculture in Liberia', Ref. 2011-001004, Tender, July, in consortium with Swisscontact & Agribusiness Systems International

Grow (2015): 'Cocoa Technical Report', Final report of the Sida-funded Grow programme in Liberia, September, Monrovia

Henderson, J; Dicken P; Hess, M; Coe, N & Wai-Chung Yeung, H (2002): 'Global Production Networks and the Analysis of Economic Development', Review of International Political Economy, 9:3

Hughes, D; Muir, K; Nelson E & Rogers, B (1989): 'Liberia Agricultural Marketing Study', Undertaken for USAID/Liberia by Robert R Nathan Assoc. Inc.

Ianchovichina, E & Lundstrom, S (2009): 'Inclusive Growth Analytics: Framework and Application', Policy Research Working Paper 4851, the World Bank, Washington DC

IFAD (2011): 'The Republic of Liberia Smallholder Tree Crop Revitalization Support Project (STCRSP) Project Design Report', 11 October, West and Central Africa Division, Programme Management Department

Kaplinsky, R (2000): 'Globalisation and Unequalisation: What Can be Learned from Value Chain Analysis?', Journal of Development Studies, 37:2 117-46

Kaplinsky, R & Morris, M (2001): A Handbook for Value Chain Research, Vol. 113, International Development Research Center, Canada

Kirsten, J. F.; Dorward, A. R.; Poulton, C. & Vink, N. (eds.) (2009): Institutional Economics Perspectives on African Agricultural Development, IFPRI

Land Commission (2012): Land Rights Policy Statement, Approved by the Land Commission, Republic of Liberia, draft, dated 9.7.12

Langlois, R N (ed.) (1986): Economics as a Process: Essays in the New Institutional Economics, Cambridge University Press, Cambridge and New York

Liebenow, J. G. (1987): Liberia: The Quest for Democracy, Indiana University Press

LPMC (2006): 'Cocoa Price Circular', facsimile in Republic of Liberia (2007), Volume 2.2, p. 191

LPMC (2011): '201112 Local Cocoa Exporters of Liberia', list, Monrovia

LPMC (2012a): 'Annual Cocoa Export (Tons) from January 1 – December 31, 2011', table, Monrovia

LPMC (2012b): 'Cocoa Indicative Farmgate Prices and Quality Standards', October – December 2012, circular, Monrovia

LPMC (2012c): 'Declared Local Cocoa Exporter Listing 2012-13', list, Monrovia

LPMC (2012d): 'The Liberian Produce Marketing Corporation Cocoa Indicative Farmgate Prices and Quality Standards', July 1 – September 30, 2012, circular, Monrovia

LPMC (2012/13): 'Cocoa Reference Price', January – March 2013, circular, Monrovia

LPMC (2013a): 'Annual Cocoa Export (Tons) from January 1 – December 31, 2012', table, Monrovia

LPMC (2013b): 'Cocoa Reference Price', April – June 2013, circular, Monrovia

LPMC (2013c): 'Cocoa Reference Price', October – December 2013, circular, Monrovia

LPMC (2013d): 'Exporter Registered Update', compiled July, list, Monrovia

LPMC (2014): 'Annual Cocoa Export Statistics (January 1 – December 31, 2013', table, Monrovia

Menger, C (1963): Problems of Economics and Sociology, University of Illinois Press, Urbana, First Published 1883

Ministry of Agriculture (2012a): National Cocoa Development Strategy: The Case for Optimizing Farmer Income from Cocoa Production in Liberia, Republic of Liberia

Ministry of Agriculture (2012b): No Title, Letter from the Minister of Agriculture to the President of the Republic of Liberia, dated April 3, Reference RL/MOA/FAC/M-307/'12, with Attachment: Copy of Proposed Act: 'Executive Law: Chapter_. Liberia Agriculture Commodity Regulatory Agency (LACRA)', Monrovia

Ministry of Commerce & Industry (2009): Liberia Tapping Nature's Bounty for the Benefit of All: Diagnostic Trade Integration Study (DTIS), The Integrated Framework National Implementation Unit, Monrovia

Muyawamariya, G; D'Haese, M & Speelman, S (2013): 'Exploring Double Side-Selling in Cooperatives, Case Study of Four Coffee Cooperatives in Rwanda', Food Policy, 39 (April): 72-83

North, Douglass C. (1990): Institutions, Institutional Change and Economic Performance, Cambridge University Press, Cambridge and New York

Ostrom, E. (2005): Understanding Institutional Diversity, Princeton University Press

Ostrom, Elinor; Gibson, Clark; Shivakumar, Sujai and Andersson, Christer (2002): Aid, Incentives, and Sustainability: An Institutional Analysis of Development Cooperation, Main Report, Sida Studies in Evaluation 02/01, Sida, Stockholm

Poliski, M and Ostrom, E (1999): 'An Institutional Framework for Policy Analysis and Design', W98-27, Mimeo, Department of Political Science, Indiana University, Bloomington

Ponte, S (2008): 'Developing a "Vertical" Dimension to Chronic Poverty Research: Some Lessons from Global Value Chain Analysis', Working Paper 111, Chronic Poverty Research Centre

Poulton, C; Gibbon, P; Hanyani-Mlambo, B; Kydd, J; Maro, W; Nylandsted Larsen, M;

Osorio, A; Tschirley, D & Zulu, B (2004): 'Competition and Coordination in Liberalized African Cotton Market Systems', World Development, 32 (3): 519-536

Prah, Cynthia (2010): 'Year Four Annual Report October 2009 – September 20010, Narrative', The Sustainable Tree Crops Program (STCP) Phase II, Version: 19 October

Radelet, Steve (2007): 'Reviving Economic Growth in Liberia', Working Paper 133, Center for Global Development

Republic of Liberia (1961): 'Liberian Produce Marketing Corporation', Chapter 57, Executive Law in Liberian Codes Revised, Vol. III, pp. 440-445, Monrovia

Republic of Liberia (1962): 'Articles of Incorporation of the Liberian Produce Marketing Corporation', in Notary Certificate, Notary Public, Montserrado County

Republic of Liberia (2007a): Comprehensive Assessment of the Agriculture Sector in Liberia (CAAS-Lib), Ministry of Agriculture, Monrovia

Republic of Liberia (2007b): Liberia Market Review (LMR), Conducted December 2006 – February 2007, Ministry of Agriculture, Monrovia

Republic of Liberia (2009): 'New Price Structure for Cocoa', press release by the Ministry of Agriculture, 9 December, http://www.moa.gov.lr/press.php?news_id=118

Republic of Liberia (2012): Liberia National Export Strategy 2012-2017, Monrovia

Republic of Liberia (2013a): Agenda for Transformation: Steps toward Liberia RISING 2030, Monrovia

Republic of Liberia (2013b): Liberia RISING 2030, Monrovia (to be replaced by 2010 or 2012 Draft Versions)

Republic of Liberia (2014): National Export Strategy: Cocoa Sector Export Strategy 2014-2018, Monrovia

Robinson J (n.d.): 'Why Regions Fail: The Mexican Case', mimeo, Harvard University, MA

Schotter, A (1986): 'The Evolution of Rules', in Langlois (1986), 117-133

Springfield Centre (2008): A Synthesis of the Making Markets Work for the Poor (M4P) Approach, Swiss Agency for Development and Cooperation

STCP (2010): 'The Sustainable Tree Crops Program (STCP) Phase II, Year Four Annual Report, October 2009 – September 2010, Narrative', Version 19 October

STCRSP (2013): 'Overview of the Smallholder Tree Crop Revitalization Support Project (STCRSP) – Lofa County', International Fund for Agricultural Development (IFAD) and Government of Liberia Funded, Power-Point Presentation to the Technical Cocoa Sector Working Group (CSTWG) 21 November, Monrovia

UNECA (2013): Economic Report of Africa 2013, United Nations Economic Commission for Africa, Addis Abeba

USAID (2011): 'Evaluation of the Liberia Sustainable Tree Crops Program (STCP)', April, submitted by Social Impact Inc.

Utas, M (2012) (ed): African Conflicts and Informal Power: Big Men and Networks, Zed

Books

van der Veen, R (2004): What Went Wrong With Africa – A Contemporary History, KIT Publishers, Amsterdam

Wiggins, Steve; Argwings-Kodhek, Gem; Leavy, Jennifer and Poulton, Colin (2011): 'Small Farm Commercialisation in Africa: Reviewing the Issues', Research Paper 23, Future Agricultures Consortium

Wilcox, M (2007): 'Tree Crop Sub-Sector', Republic of Liberia (2007), Volume 2.1, pp 68-139

Wilcox, Michael D. (n.d.a): 'Reforming Cocoa and Coffee Marketing in Liberia', power-point presentation

Wilcox, Michael D. (n.d.b): 'Tree Crops to Ensure Income Generation and Sustainable Livelihoods in Liberia: Unlocking the Potential of the Cocoa Sub-Sector: R5. Market and Information Systems Report', submitted to STCP Regional Program Manager, International Institute of Tropical Agriculture in Accra

Wilcox, Michael D. & Abbott, Philip C. (2004): 'Market Power and Structural Adjustment: The Case of West African Cocoa Market Liberalization', Presented at the American Agricultural Economics Association Annual Meeting, Denver

Wilcox, M & Abbott, P (2006): 'Can Cocoa Farmer Organizations Countervail Buyer Market Power?', Presented at the American Agricultural Economics Association Annual Meeting, Long Beach

Wilcox, Michael D. & Pay-Bayee, MacArthur M. (2006): 'Outcomes from the Liberian Cocoa Sector Roundtable, held on May 26, 2006, in Monrovia, Liberia', submitted to the Ministry of Agriculture, Republic of Liberia

Williamson, Oliver E. (1975): Markets and Hierarchies: Analysis and Antitrust Implications, The Free Press, New York

Williamson, Oliver E. (1979): 'Transaction-Cost Economics: The Governance of Contractual Relations', Journal of Law and Economics, Volume 22, Number 2, pp. 233-261

World Bank (2008): Liberia: Insecurity of Land Tenure, Land Law and Land Registration in Liberia, Report No. 46134-LR

World Bank (2012): 'Project Appraisal Document on a Proposed Credit in the Amount of SDR 9.7 Million (US$15.0 Million Equivalent) to the Republic Liberia for a Smallholder Tree Crop Revitalization Support Project', Report No: 68524-LR, May 9

Yin, R (2014): Case Study Research: Design and Methods, Fifth Edition, SAGE, Los Angeles and London

Appendix

Appendix Figure 2.1: Five Global Value Chain Types

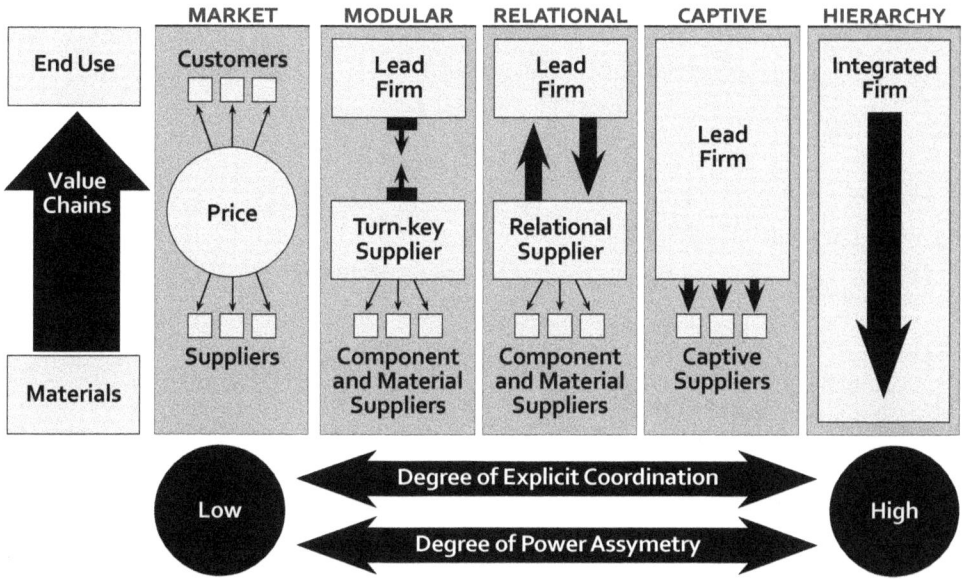

Note & Source: Thin arrows illustrate coordination by price, thick arrows illustrate coordination by flows of information and control. Adapted from Gereffi et al. (2005: 89: Figure 1)

Appendix Figure 4.1: Overall Cocoa Value Chain in Liberia with a Smallholder Focus

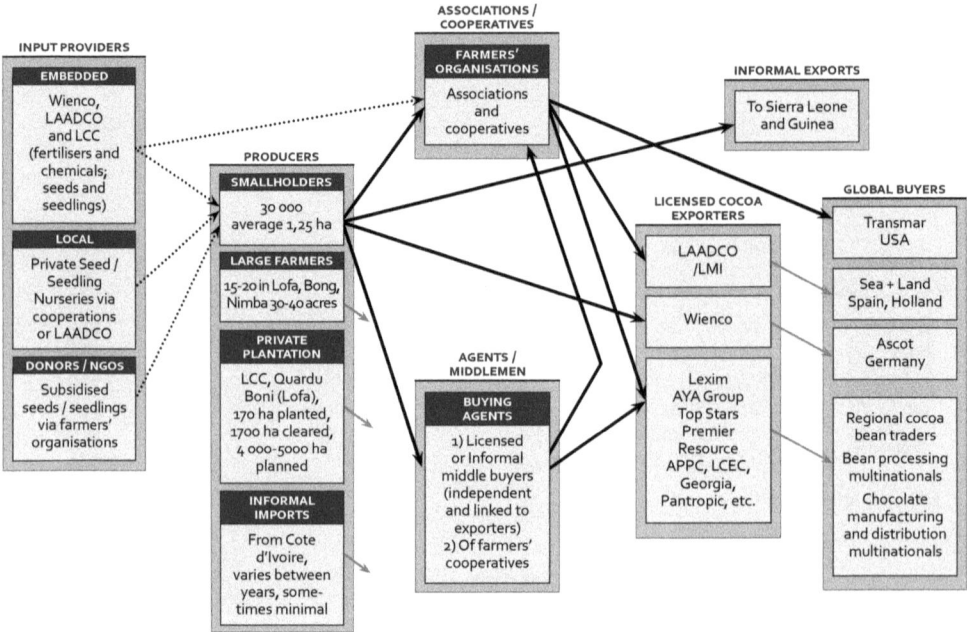

Based on field research October/November 2013 and various written sources

Appendix Table 5.1: Exchange Rate of Liberian to US Dollar 2001-2013 (LRD/USD)

Year	2001	2002	2003	2004	2005	2006	2007	2008	2009	2010	2011	2012	2013
End of Period	49.50	65.00	50.50	54.50	56.50	59.00	62.50	64.00	70.50	71.50	72.50	72.50	82.50
Annual Average	46.04	56.76	46.64	52.28	54.72	58.00	60.77	63.29	67.81	70.19	71.93	72.50	81.88

Source: Central Bank of Liberia, Annual Reports 2003, 2006, 2008, 2011 & 2013

Appendix Table 5.2a: Reported Farm-Gate Cocoa Prices for Grade 1 Paid by Different Buyers Late 2013

Middle Buyer	Wienco	LAADCO/LMI		Farmers' Coop/Ass	Farmer	Farmers' Coop/ Ass	Buyer	External Obser- ver	COMMENTS
	125 LRD						II 2		
	125 LRD						II 35		
	125 LRD							KI 12	
	125 LRD				II 29				
	125 LRD				II 31				
	120 LRD				II 27				
	100 LRD				II 14				
	100 LRD				II 28				
	100 LRD				II 32				
	Average accord. to farmers: 112 LRD								111.67 LRD
		1.90 USD	156 LRD					II 36	
		1.65-1.77 USD	135-145 LRD					II 1	
		1.75 USD	144 LRD					II 4	
		1.70 USD	139 LRD					II 34	Reported to be 60% of ICCO price (2.824 USD/kg)
		Average acc. to buyers: 145 LRD							144.75 LRD
		1.65 USD	135 LRD					KI 12	
		1.65 USD	135 LRD					KI 13	
		1.65 USD	135 LRD					G 3	
		1.60-1.65 USD	131-135 LRD					KI 14	
		1.26 USD	103 LRD					GI 3	Remote area
		Average acc. to observers: 128 LRD							128.20 LRD
		1.65-1.75 USD	134-144 LRD			GI 9			
		1.65 USD	135 LRD			II25			Paid to both coop & farmers
		1.65 USD	135 LRD			II 23			Reported 165 LRD in my notes, inter-preted to mean 1.65 USD, given price repor- ted by II 25
		1.60 USD	131 LRD			GI 7			
		Average acc. to farm's coop/ass: 135 LRD							135.00 LRD
				110 LRD		GI 8			
				100 LRD				KI 14	
				130 LRD	II 38				Interpreted as Grade 1, given price reported by II 25
				115 LRD	II 18				
				115 LRD	II 13				Paid by coop/coop agent to farmer, same as from buyer to coop
				110-115 LRD	II 14				
				110 LRD	II 19				
				110 LRD	II 17				
				Average acc. to farmers: 115 LRD					115.42 LRD
125 LRD							Inform. I, Middle Buyer		Questioned by External Observer, II 12 – possible outlier
80-90 LRD								II 12	Contrasted with possible outlier
70-110 LRD						II 33			Paid to coop & farmers
90-100 LRD						GI 8			
Average: 99 LRD									98.75 LRD; Average without the possible outlier: 90.00 LRD

Note: Reference price for grade 1: 1.39 USD=114 LRD/kg. USD/kg prices converted to LRD/kg prices at exchange rate of 82 LRD/USD

Appendix Table 5.2b: Reported Farm-Gate Cocoa Prices for Grade 2 Paid by Different Buyers Late 2013

PRICE PAID BY BUYER (per kg)				SOURCE				COMMENTS
Middle Buyer	Wienco	LAADCO/LMI	Farmers' Coop/Ass	Farmer	Farmers' Coop/Ass	Buyer	External Observer	
		1.50 USD / 123 LRD				II 4		
		0.75 USD / 62 LRD					GI 3	
		1.20 USD / 98 LRD			GI 7			
		110 LRD		II 16		II 16		Sold to LAADCO agent, Assumed Grade 2, Could be Grade 1, Farmer-cum-middle buyer
		115-120 LRD		II 16		II 16		Current price from LAADCO agent, Assumed Grade 2, Could be Grade 1, Farmer-cum-middle buyer
		Average acc. to buyers: 117 LRD						116.83 LRD
		Average acc. to farmers: 114 LRD						113.75 LRD
			80 LRD	II 18				
			70 LRD	II 17				
			65-70 LRD	II 11				Grade 1 mixed, became Grade 2
			Average acc. to farmers: 73 LRD					72.50 LRD
110-115 LRD						Inform.I, Middle Buyer		Questioned by External Observer II 12 – possible outlier
80-90 LRD							II 12	Contrasted with possible outlier
105 LRD				II 16		II 16		Bought from farmers, Assumed Grade 2, Could be Grade 1, Farmer-cum-middle buyer
80-110 LRD				II 16		II 16		Willing to pay farmers, Assumed Grade 2, Could be Grade 1, Farmer-cum-middle buyer
Average acc. to buyers: 104 LRD								104.17 LRD
Average acc. to farmers: 100 LRD								100.00 LRD

Note: Reference price for grade 2: 1.24 USD=102 LRD/kg. USD/kg prices converted to LRD/kg prices at exchange rate of 82 LRD/USD

Appendix Table 5.2c: Reported Farm-Gate Cocoa Prices for Sub-Grade Paid by Different Buyers Late 2013

PRICE PAID BY BUYER (per kg)					SOURCE				COMMENTS
Middle Buyer	Wienco	LAADCO/ LMI		Farmers' Coop/Ass	Farmer	Farmers' Coop/Ass	Buyer	External Observer	
		1.10-1.25 USD	90-103 LRD				II 4		Claims LAADCO and middle-buyer price the same
		90 LRD						GI 3	Remote area
		90-100 LRD				GI 7			Reported USD in my notes, inter-preted to mean LRD
				100 LRD	II 6				
				1.14 USD = 94 LRD	II 37				80 USD/1 bag, bag assumed to be 'big bag' of approx. 70 kg (II 11)
				85 LRD	II 13				Paid by coop/coop agent to farmer, same as from buyer to coop
				25-30 LRD	II 17				
				Average acc. to farmers: 77 LRD					76.60 LRD
1.10-1.25 USD = 90-103 LRD							II 4		Claims LAADCO and middle buyer price the same
80-90 LRD							II 31		Wet cocoa
80 LRD							Inform. I, Middle Buyer		
Average acc. to buyers: 87 LRD									87.20 LRD
80-90 LRD							II 12		
50 LRD							KI 14		
< 50 LRD								GI 3	
Average acc. to observers: 62 LRD									61.67 LRD
110 LRD					II 21				Could be higher quality, but sold at local market to 'any' buyer
100-115 LRD					II 15				Oct-Nov, Grade 1 but not paid for
90 LRD					II 33				
85 LRD					II 12				
50-70 LRD					II 30				
40-50 LRD					II 15				June, Grade 1 but not paid for – not included in average
Average except June price acc. to farmers: 91 LRD									90.50 LRD; Average if June price included: 82.92 LRD

Note: Reference price for sub-grade (and mixed and unknown): 1.07 USD=88 LRD/kg. USD/kg prices converted to LRD/kg prices at exchange rate of 82 LRD/USD

Appendix Table 5.3: Farmers' Investments to Expand Cocoa Quality, Output and Farm

Source	Processing Cocoa for High Quality = Value Addition	Enhancing Productivity & Output on Existing Farm			Expansion of / New Farm (Land)	Farmer's Affiliation		
		Crop Husbandry / Farming Practices	Fertiliser / Chemicals	Planting Seedlings		Coope-rative	Wienco & LCC	Indepen-dent
II 5	Knows how to, Solar dryer	Buys labour	n.a.	Replants	n.a.	X		
II 6	Varying quality	Under brushes, Cuts canopy, Learning	-	Replants, Impro-ved seedlings	n.a.	X		
II 7	Grade 1	Under brushes, No labour	n.a.	Replants, Impro-ved seedlings	New farm on land available	X		
II 8	Expects training for certification	Rehabilitation	n.a.	Improved seedlings	Expansion	X		
II 9	n.a.	- No labour	-	Improved & own seedlings	Expansion			X
II 10	-	- No labour	-	Replants, Own seeds	- No land	X		
II 11	Grade 1	Brushes more often, Uses kuu, Manages farm better, Training	-	Replants, Own seeds	New farm	X		
II 12	Well dried, Quality unknown	Brushes more often, Uses kuu	-	Own seeds	Expansion			X
II 13, makes profit calculations	Grade 1 & Sub-grade	Training, Brushes more often, Uses kuu, Increa-sed maintenance	-	Own seeds, some improved	Expansion	X		
II 14	Grade 1, Improved quality, Training	Gets help with brushing	Pesticides, Exten-sion, Training	Improved & own seedlings	Expansion	X	W	
II 15	Grade 'A'	Brushes more often, Uses kuu	- Hopes to fertilise on own	Replants	Expansion	Former left		X
II 16	Good quality, Learning	n.a.	-	n.a.	Expansion			X
II 17	All grades, Uses solar dryer	n.a.	-	n.a.	Expansion	X		
II 18	All grades	Under brushes, Learns farm management	- Willing	Replants, Own seeds, Wants new varieties	Expansion	X		
II 19	Grade 1 & lower quality, Learning	n.a.	-	High yielding & own seedlings	Expansion, constrained, Lacks forest land	X		
II 20	n.a.	Under brushes, Uses kuu	-	Own seeds	Expansion			X
II 21	Grade 1 implicit	-	n.a.	n.a.	Expansion	Former		X
II 24	n.a.	n.a.	Fertiliser & spraying by LCC	Improved seedlings	New farm		LCC	
II 26	Grade 1 implicit	Under brushes more often, Difficult	Fertiliser, Some pesticides, Equipment	n.a.	-		W	
II 27	Grade 1 implicit	Brushes, Group labour, Discusses problems & learns	Chemicals, Wants to use fertiliser	Replants	-		W	
II 29	Grade 1, Lear-ning, Wants solar dryer	Joint work in group, Kuu for brushing, Learning	Fertiliser, Chemicals	Own seeds, Learned nursery, Wants improved	Expansion		W	
II 30	Grade 1 & mixed, Learnt to ferment & dry	Brushes twice a year, Joint work in group, Learning	Fertiliser, Spray-ing, Training	Replants, Own seeds	n.a.	Former Left	Former Left	X
II 31	Grade 1 implicitly	n.a.	-	Puts seeds in nursery	n.a.			X
II 32	Grade 1 implicitly	Brushes, Joint work in group	Fertiliser, Medicine	Replants, Own seeds	n.a.		W	
II 37	Built dryer to improve quality	n.a.	-	n.a.	Expansion	X		
II 38	n.a.	n.a.	-	Replants, Own seeds	Possibly new farm			X
# Responses of 26 farmers	22	19	22	21	21	12, 3 former	5 W, 1 for-mer,1 LCC	9
Total Number Positive	21	11-15 improvement, 9-10 joint labour	7, 2 willing or hoping	11 plant, 8 im-proved, 14 own	17-18			
Share Positive (%)	95	58-79, 47-53	32	52, 38, 67	81-86			

Appendix Table 5.4: Reported Cocoa Farm & Farmer Returns & Perceived Benefits

Source	Yields / Productivity	Output / Volume	Income	Profit / Profitability	Belief in Future	Livelihood Benefits	Combines Spot & VC
II 5	-	None yet – new plantation	Last year from cut-down old trees	-	Trees will deliver after 3 years	n.a.	Cooperative
II 6	Productivity of trees increasing	2012 600 kg, 2013 expects more, 800 kg	Increase, 4,800 LD 2012, expects 8,000 LD 2013	n.a.	Benefit may increase	n.a.	No, only coop
II 7	n.a.	2011 50 kg 2012 47 kg	No increase in last 5 years	n.a.	n.a.	Important for money, to improve house & send children to school	Cooperative, but wants other buyer
II 9	Low & declining, old & dying trees	Little production 2012, none 2013	Not sold any in recent years	n.a.	Expects returns of new trees after 4 years	n.a.	-
II 10	n.a.	Before unknown, 2012 4 bags, 2013 2 bags	Varying, some years increase, some years decline	n.a.	Expects to produce more next year, good things, Plans to replant all trees	Benefitted a lot, pays for oil, other family materials	Middle buyer/ other farmer to whom is indebted & coop agent
II 11	Increased yields 2013 due to more brushing, but poor yields discouraging	300 kg annually 2005-2012, Expects increase 2013	n.a.	n.a.	Has to remain patient, continue to expand the farm	Enables pay school fees, build house & manage family life	2006-2007 middle buyers, Now, only to coop, but looks for good alternative buyer
II 12	n.a.	Varying, 2011 less than 2012, 2012 1.5 big bag, 2013 a little less, 2014 expects more again	2012 13,000 LD, 2013 3,200 LD so far but will be less	n.a.	Will be better, as new farm is coming on, Expects prod. to increase 2014, Will extend farm more	To get money, built a house from 2012 savings	2012 coop agent, 2013 middle buyers to get cash for school fees, Can choose among many buyers
II 13	Increasing much, but also declining productivity of old farm with dying trees	2011 150 kg, 2012 425 kg/3 ha, 2013 already 526 kg	Increase last year, poor income from old farm	Makes profit calculations & keeps records	n.a.	Gets all income from cocoa	Cooperative/ LAADCO, Some farmers side-sell, but very little
II 14	Increased yields on sprayed areas	2011 does not remember, 2012 300 kg, 2013 295 kg so far, problem with dying trees	Income declined 2013, as old trees died	Difficult get profitability as labour cost exceeds income	Prices will increase, will expand farm every year	Pay children's school fees of 6,200 LD	2011 middle buyers to whom indebted, 2013 Wienco, & coop?
II 15	n.a.	2011 6 bags, 2012 5 bags, 2013 expects 7.5 bags	n.a.	n.a.	n.a.	Built house from cocoa savings, Can live well on cocoa if good income	Any buyer
II 16	n.a.	2013 60 kg already, expects 45-50 kg more	n.a.	n.a.	n.a.	n.a.	Yes, anybody, coop & LAADCO agents

Table continues on next page

Appendix Table 5.4: *Continued from previous page*

Source	Yields / Pro-ductivity	Output / Volume	Income	Profit / Profi-tability	Belief in Future	Livelihood Benefits	Combines Spot & VC
II 17	n.a.	2011 only 2 bags due to black pod, 2012 2.5 bags, 2013 1.5 bags so far, expects totally 3 bags	2011 sold small volumes to middle buyers, 2012 10,000 LD	n.a.	Expects new farm to start yielding a litt-le next year	Major income source, Helps so much, with school fees, local constra-ints & family matters	2011 middle buyers, since then only coop
II 18	Poor produc-tivity of old farm/trees, Not bearing as much as in the past, New farms is bea-ring already	2011 2.5 bags, but only 1 bag 2012 & 2013, as replacing old trees	Experienced more income increase, Some increase last 5 years, not so much, but now going upwards	Expenditure for managing old farm is in-creasing more the yields from new farm	Production will increase a lot when new trees come on, Will have mo-ney in future, Prices will go up in coming years	Especially for medication, Bought a three-room house, De-pends only on cocoa	Before any buyer, 2012 Transmar, now coop
II 19	n.a.	2011 10-30 kg, 2012 only 90 kg, 2013 50 kg so far, expects 40-60 kg more	Increased – a large change in last 5 years	Kept no re-cords in 2011	n.a.	Enables pay children's school fees	2011 middle buyers, 2012 & 2013 coop
II 20	Not so good yields, due to black pod	2012 does not know, 2013 1 bag so far	n.a.	n.a.	Prices are going up	Important in-come source, Solved most domestic problems, build houses, good schools fees, various family obliga-tions	n.a.
II 21	n.a.	2012 4 big bags	n.a.	n.a.	n.a.	n.a.	Before middle buyer, 2012 Transmar (via coop?), 2013 any buyer
II 24	-	Not yet	-	-	Expects yields in 2-3 years	-	-
II 26	Small increase 2012, as some benefit of inputs, decline 2013 (implicit), Now trees not bearing enough	Large production before, 2011 not around, 2012 1.5 bag, 2013 expects 1 bag, half was black, leaves go dry	2012 Jan-May 1,050 LD, more in Oct & Dec, Small income last 5 years is worrying	n.a.	Worried as trees not be-aring & small income	Some small money	2013 Wienco
II 27	Little returns before due to black pod, Started bearing due to chemicals	Increasing, 2012 no production as applied chemicals, 2013 35 kg	Only small income before	n.a.	Expects in-come to in-crease, Hopes next harvest better & afford fertiliser, Future will be better	Happy when it bears, worries when not, Can buy food/rice and eat, Only source of cash	2013 Wienco
II 29	Trees are not producing, some are dying	Declining, 2011 3 big bags, 2012 only 2.5 big bags due to weather, 2013 only 2 bags	Almost stable in past years, as earlier prod. high but prices low, now prices high but production gone down	n.a.	Expects good yields & prices, so to earn more money, But worries about paying debt	If good yields, helps children & family, does not have to borrow money but can be independent	n.a.

Table continues on next page

Appendix Table 5.4: *Continued from previous page*

Source	Yields / Productivity	Output / Volume	Income	Profit / Profitability	Belief in Future	Livelihood Benefits	Combines Spot & VC
II 30	2012 trees not bearing as before, despite spraying, some rotting, black pods & dying, Declining	Before, used to be more, 2011 7 bags, 2012 only 10 bags, 2013 only 3 bags	Income varies, because both quantity and prices go up and down	n.a.	Worrying does not help, only prays to God price will go up	Very much benefit, Depends on to support family/children, school feels, buy zink	2012 middle buyer, due to low quality, & Wienco, 2013 middle buyers
II 31	No increase in yields, Problem with black pod	2011? only 3 bags, 2012 6 bags, 2013 only 2 bags	Declined last years, as prices fluctuated & production varies too	n.a.	Plans to set up business as trader & sell to large exporters in Monrovia, Expects new trees to give better yields	Most important source of income	Any local buyer & Wienco, 2012 local buyers, 2013 Wienco
II 32	No improvement in spite of inputs, Trees don't bear 2013, Some are dying	2011 4 bags, 2012 5 bags, 2013 only 3 bags	Used to earn more before, but income has declined due to low yields	n.a.	Price will increase	Only benefits from cocoa, school fees & rice, Most important source of income	2012 local buyer, 2013? to Wienco & kuu members
II 37	Bears good	2011 3 bags, 2012 4 bags, 2013 only 2 bags due to black pod, Producing more than before	Now receives some money, Before not much	n.a.	C is for future & long lasting, Will provide income year after year, brings security, Future is bright & price will go up	No future in rice so will buy it for cocoa money, Most important source of income	Middle buyer 2011, cooperative 2013
II 38	-	-	-	-	Price will increase	Investment will enable send children to school & support family	-

Administrative map of Liberia and its 15 counties, retrieved from the UN Cartographic Section, 16 November 2013. Public Domain.

www.ingramcontent.com/pod-product-compliance
Lightning Source LLC
Chambersburg PA
CBHW041431270326
41935CB00021B/1843